Middle School 3-2

기말고사 완벽대비

적중 100

영어 기출 문제집

중3

시사 | 송미정

Best Collection

구성과 특징

교과서의 주요 학습 내용을 중심으로 학습 영역별 특성에 맞춰 단계별로 다양한 학습 기회를 제공하여
단원별 학습능력 평가는 물론 중간 및 기말고사 시험 등에 완벽하게 대비할 수 있도록 내용을 구성

Words & Expressions

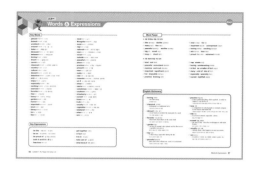

Step1 Key Words 단원별 핵심 단어 설명 및 풀이
Key Expression 단원별 핵심 숙어 및 관용어 설명
Word Power 반대 또는 비슷한 뜻 단어 배우기
English Dictionary 영어로 배우는 영어 단어

Step2 실력평가 단원별 수시평가 대비 주관식, 객관식 문제풀이

Step3 서술형 대비 학업성취도 및 수행능력평가 대비 서술형 문제풀이

Conversation

Step1 핵심 의사소통 소통에 필요한 주요 표현 방법 요약
핵심 Check 기본적인 표현 방법 및 활용능력 확인

Step2 대화문 익히기 교과서 대화문 심층 분석 및 확인

Step3 교과서 확인학습 빈칸 채우기를 통한 문장 완성 능력 확인

Step4 기본평가 시험대비 기초 학습 능력 평가

Step5 실력평가 단원별 수시평가 대비 주관식, 객관식 문제풀이

Step6 서술형 대비 학업성취도 및 수행능력평가 대비 서술형 문제풀이

Grammar

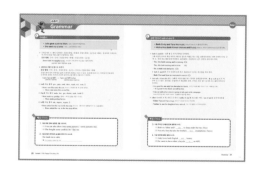

Step1 주요 문법 단원별 주요 문법 사항과 예문을 알기 쉽게 설명
핵심 Check 기본 문법사항에 대한 이해 여부 확인

Step2 기본평가 시험대비 기초 학습 능력 평가

Step3 실력평가 단원별 수시평가 대비 주관식, 객관식 문제풀이

Step4 서술형 대비 학업성취도 및 수행능력평가 대비 서술형 문제풀이

Reading

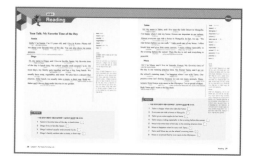

Step1 구문 분석 단원별로 제시된 문장에 대한 구문별 분석과 내용 설명
확인문제 문장에 대한 기본적인 이해와 인지능력 확인

Step2 확인학습A 빈칸 채우기를 통한 문장 완성 능력 확인

Step3 확인학습B 제시된 우리말을 영어로 완성하여 작문 능력 키우기

Step4 실력평가 단원별 수시평가 대비 주관식, 객관식 문제풀이

Step5 서술형 대비 학업성취도 및 수행능력평가 대비 서술형 문제풀이
교과서 구석구석 교과서에 나오는 기타 문장까지 완벽 학습

Composition

|영역별 핵심문제|

단어 및 어휘, 대화문, 문법, 독해 등 각 영역별 기출문제의 출제 유형을 분석하여 실전에 대비하고 연습할 수 있도록 문제를 배열

|단원별 예상문제|

기출문제를 분석한 후 새로운 시험 출제 경향을 더하여 새롭게 출제될 수 있는 문제를 포함하여 시험에 완벽하게 대비할 수 있도록 준비

|서술형 실전 및 창의사고력 문제|

학교 시험에서 점차 늘어나는 서술형 시험에 집중 대비하고 고득점을 취득하는데 만전을 기하기 위한 학습 코너

|단원별 모의고사|

영역별, 단계별 학습을 모두 마친 후 실전 연습을 위한 모의고사

교과서 파헤치기

- **단어Test1~3** 영어 단어 우리말 쓰기, 우리말을 영어 단어로 쓰기, 영영풀이에 해당하는 단어와 우리말 쓰기
- **대화문Test1~2** 대화문 빈칸 완성 및 전체 대화문 쓰기
- **본문Test1~5** 빈칸 완성, 우리말 쓰기, 문장 배열연습, 영어 작문하기 복습 등 단계별 반복 학습을 통해 교과서 지문에 대한 완벽한 습득
- **구석구석지문Test1~2** 지문 빈칸 완성 및 전문 영어로 쓰기

Lesson 7

Small Ideas, Big Differences

🗣 의사소통 기능

- 궁금증 표현하기
  A: I wonder who those men are.
  B: They're the Wright brothers.

- 생각할 시간 요청하기
  A: What can we do with these VR glasses?
  B: Let me see.... Maybe we can play soccer.

🗣 언어 형식

- 가정법 과거
  The water inside **would** quickly **boil** over **if** the lid **did not have** that hole.

- so that 주어 can 동사원형
  The hole also prevents the window from fogging up **so that** you **can** enjoy that fantastic view.

Words & Expressions

Key Words

- **amount** [əmáunt] 몡 양, 총계
- **balance** [bǽləns] 몡 균형 동 균형을 잡다
- **boil** [bɔil] 몡 끓기 동 끓이다
- **breathing** [bríːðiŋ] 몡 호흡, 숨
- **careful** [kέərfəl] 휑 주의 깊은, 조심스러운, 세심한
- **carefully** [kέərfəli] 튄 주의 깊게, 조심스럽게
- **cause** [kɔːz] 동 ~을 야기하다 몡 원인
- **company** [kʌ́mpəni] 몡 회사, 동료
- **cook** [kuk] 동 요리하다
- **couch** [kautʃ] 몡 소파, 긴 의자
- **cracker** [krǽkər] 몡 크래커
- **crispy** [kríspi] 휑 바삭한
- **death** [deθ] 몡 죽음
- **emergency** [imə́ːrdʒənsi] 몡 비상사태
- **especially** [ispéʃəli] 튄 특히
- **fantastic** [fæntǽstik] 휑 환상적인
- **fog** [fɔːg] 몡 안개 동 수증기가 서리다
- **helpful** [hélpfəl] 휑 유용한, 도움이 되는
- **hide** [haid] 동 숨기다, 숨다
- **hidden** [hídn] 휑 숨겨져 있는
- **hill** [hil] 몡 언덕
- **lid** [lid] 몡 뚜껑

- **mirror** [mírə] 몡 거울
- **necessary** [nésəsèri] 휑 필수적인
- **north** [nɔːrθ] 휑 북쪽의, 북부의
- **notice** [nóutis] 동 알아채다, 의식하다
- **pane** [pein] 몡 판유리
- **perhaps** [pərhǽps] 튄 아마, 어쩌면
- **pressure** [préʃər] 몡 압력
- **prevent** [privént] 동 막다
- **product** [prádʌkt] 몡 생산물, 상품
- **quickly** [kwíkli] 튄 빨리
- **recently** [ríːsntli] 튄 최근에
- **repair** [ripέər] 동 수리하다
- **result** [rizʌ́lt] 몡 결과
- **roof** [ruːf] 몡 지붕
- **rope** [roup] 몡 밧줄
- **shaped** [ʃeipt] 휑 ~ 모양의
- **sometimes** [sʌ́mtàimz] 튄 때로, 때때로
- **steam** [stiːm] 몡 수증기, 김
- **stick** [stik] 몡 막대 모양의 물건
- **surprisingly** [sərpráiziŋli] 튄 놀랍게도
- **swallow** [swálou] 동 삼키다
- **twist** [twist] 동 비틀다, 돌리다

Key Expressions

- **be made up of** ~로 구성되다
- **be on an airplane** 비행기를 타다
- **boil over** 끓어 넘치다
- **build up** 점점 커지다
- **cause death** 죽음을 야기하다
- **come out** 나오다
- **fog up** 안개로 흐려지다, 김이 서리다
- **in an emergency** 비상 상황에서
- **in the future** 미래에
- **keep A from -ing** A가 ~하는 것을 막다

- **let A B**(동사원형) A가 B하게 하다
- **let out** 내보내다
- **look around** 주위를 둘러보다
- **look at** ~을 보다
- **look out** 밖을 내다보다
- **pass through** 거쳐 지나가다, 통과하다
- **play a helpful role** 도움을 주는 역할을 하다
- **prevent A from -ing** A가 ~하는 것을 방지하다
- **the result of ~** ~의 결과
- **think about** ~에 대해 생각하다

Word Power

※ 서로 비슷한 뜻을 가진 어휘

□ **careful** 주의 깊은, 조심스러운 – **cautious** 조심성 있는
□ **cause** ~을 야기하다 – **bring about** 야기하다
□ **hide** 숨기다, 숨다 – **conceal** 숨기다, 감추다
□ **perhaps** 아마, 어쩌면 – **probably** 아마도

□ **carefully** 주의 깊게, 조심스럽게 – **cautiously** 신중하게
□ **helpful** 유용한, 도움이 되는 – **useful** 도움이 되는
□ **necessary** 필수적인 – **essential** 필수적인, 가장 중요한
□ **repair** 수리하다 – **mend** 수선하다, 고치다

※ 서로 반대의 뜻을 가진 어휘

□ **careful** 주의 깊은, 조심스러운, 세심한 ↔ **careless** 부주의한, 조심성 없는
□ **cause** 원인 ↔ **result** 결과
□ **helpful** 유용한, 도움이 되는 ↔ **unhelpful** 도움이 되지 않는

□ **carefully** 주의 깊게, 조심스럽게 ↔ **carelessly** 부주의하게
□ **death** 죽음 ↔ **birth** 탄생
□ **necessary** 필수적인 ↔ **unnecessary** 불필요한, 쓸데없는

※ 과거분사 ❶ 동사원형 +-ed

□ **advertise** 광고하다 → **advertised**
□ **cry** 울다 → **cried**
□ **damage** 피해를 입다 → **damaged**
□ **prevent** 막다, 예방하다 → **prevented**
□ **stop** 막다 → **stopped**

□ **balance** 균형을 잡다 → **balanced**
□ **clean** 청소하다 → **cleaned**
□ **plan** 계획하다 → **planned**
□ **provide** 제공하다 → **provided**
□ **study** 공부하다, 연구하다 → **studied**

※ 과거분사 ❷ 불규칙 변화형

□ **am/is/are** 이다/있다 → **been**
□ **begin** 시작하다 → **begun**
□ **cost** (비용, 대가가) 들다 → **cost**
□ **draw** 그리다 → **drawn**

□ **fly** 날다, 비행하다 → **flown**
□ **lead** 이끌다 → **led**
□ **lie** 눕다, 놓여 있다 → **lain**
□ **light** 불을 비추다 → **lit**

□ **take** 가져가다, 차지하다 → **taken**
□ **seek** 찾다, 구하다 → **sought**
□ **understand** 이해하다 → **understood**
□ **wear** 입다 → **worn**

English Dictionary

□ **amount** 양, 총계
→ the degree to which something is a lot or a little; how much something is
어떤 것이 많은가 적은가의 정도; 어떤 것이 얼마나 있는지의 정도

□ **balanc** 균형을 잡다
→ to be in a position where you will stand without falling to either side, or to put something in this position
어느 쪽으로도 치우치지 않는 위치에 있거나 혹은 어떤 것을 이 위치에 놓다

□ **breathing** 호흡, 숨
→ the process to take air into the lungs and let it out again
공기를 폐 속으로 들여마시고 내뱉는 과정

□ **emergency** 비상사태
→ an unexpected and dangerous situation
예상치 못한 위험한 상황

□ **especially** 특히, 특별히
→ very much; more than usual or more than other people or things
매우 많이; 다른 사람이나 사물 이상으로, 흔히 있는 것 이상으로

□ **helpful** 유용한, 도움이 되는
→ willing to help, or useful
기꺼이 도와주려고 하는; 유용한

□ **necessary** 필수적인
→ needed in order to achieve a particular result
어떤 특정한 결과를 얻기 위해 필요한

□ **notice** 알아채다, 의식하다
→ to become aware of 알게 되다

□ **normally** 보통, 보통 때는
→ in the usual or expected way 보통의 혹은 예상되는 방식으로

□ **prevent** 막다
→ to stop something from happening or someone from doing something
어떤 것이 일어나는 것을 막거나 혹은 어떤 사람이 어떤 것을 하는 것을 막다

□ **product** 생산물, 상품
→ something that is made to be sold, usually something that is produced by an industrial process
팔기 위해 만든 어떤 것, 보통 산업적 과정을 통해 만들어진 어떤 것

□ **recently** 최근에
→ not long ago 오래 전이 아닌

□ **repair** 수리하다
→ to put something damaged back into good condition
어떤 망가진 것을 다시 좋은 상태로 만들다

□ **swallow** 삼키다
→ to make food go down the throat
음식을 목 안으로 내려가게 하다

서답형

01 다음 짝지어진 단어의 관계가 같도록 빈칸에 알맞은 말을 쓰시오.

> careful : cautious = helpful : _____

02 다음 영영풀이가 가리키는 것을 고르시오.

> to stop something from happening or someone from doing something

① advise   ② help
③ provide   ④ prevent
⑤ discourage

중요

03 다음 중 밑줄 친 부분의 뜻풀이가 바르지 <u>않은</u> 것은?

① The hotel is currently under <u>repair</u>. (수리하다)
② The <u>result</u> is entirely unpredictable. (결과)
③ My hobby is to collect round-<u>shaped</u> piece of stone. (형태의)
④ Who's going to <u>cook</u> supper? (요리하다)
⑤ He struggled to <u>hide</u> his disappointment. (숨기다)

04 다음 주어진 문장의 빈칸에 공통으로 들어갈 말로 가장 적절한 것은?

> • Employees should be fully aware of _____ procedures.
> • The pilot was forced to make a/an _____ landing.

① breathing   ② fantastic
③ necessary   ④ dangerous
⑤ emergency

서답형

05 다음 문장의 빈칸에 들어갈 말을 〈보기〉에서 골라 쓰시오.

> ┤ 보기 ├
> be made up of / cause death / look around / think about / pass through

(1) The typhoon is expected to _____ _____ the East Sea between Sunday and Monday.
(2) In some places like Africa, diarrhea can _____ _____ due to dehydration and lack of medicine. *diarrhea: 설사
(3) Some theorists _____ _____ culture and cultural diversity in different ways.

중요

06 다음 문장의 (A)와 (B)에 각각 공통으로 들어갈 말이 바르게 짝지어진 것은?

> • Can you look ___(A)___ the window and see whether she is coming?
> • Everyone let ___(A)___ a sigh of relief.
> • All the pressure built ___(B)___ and he was off work for weeks.
> • Dokdo is made ___(B)___ of 89 islets and reefs. *islet: 작은 섬

① out – out   ② out – up
③ at – out   ④ at – up
⑤ around – up

01 다음 짝지어진 단어의 관계가 같도록 빈칸에 알맞은 말을 쓰시오.

> death : birth = necessary : _____

02 다음 주어진 영영풀이에 맞는 단어를 쓰시오.

> to become aware of

➡ _____

03 다음 문장의 빈칸에 들어갈 말을 〈보기〉에서 골라 쓰시오.

> ┌─ 보기 ─┐
> twist / rope / pane / lid / hill

(1) The thief broke the _____ in order to unlock the door.
(2) We climbed to the very top of the _____.
(3) I saw her _____ the ring on her finger.

04 다음 우리말에 맞게 빈칸에 알맞은 말을 쓰시오.

(1) 놀랍게도 그것은 한국에서보다 외국에서 훨씬 더 저렴하다.
➡ _____ it's much cheaper abroad than in Korea.

(2) 그 남자 아이돌 그룹은 최근에 재결성되었다.
➡ The boy-band has _____ been re-formed.

(3) Paul은 그의 차를 조심스럽게 차고에 주차했다.
➡ Paul parked his car _____ into the garage.

05 다음 우리말에 맞게 주어진 단어를 사용하여 영작하시오.

(1) 잘 마무리된 지붕은 수년 간 비바람에 잘 견뎌야 한다. (weatherproof, the well-finished, roof, years)
➡ _____

(2) 얼마나 빨리 서류를 준비할 수 있으신가요? (quickly, paperwork)
➡ _____

(3) 그는 막대기로 모래 위에 동그라미 하나를 그렸다. (stick, circle)
➡ _____

06 다음 우리말과 일치하도록 주어진 어구를 바르게 나열하시오.

(1) 그의 얼굴이 거울에 비쳤다.
(his / reflected / was / in the mirror / face)
➡ _____

(2) 나는 목이 아파서 삼키기 힘들었다.
(hurt / had / swallow / a sore throat / it / and / to / I)
➡ _____

(3) 수증기에 다치지 않도록 조심하렴.
(the steam / be / to / hurt / careful / yourself / with / not)
➡ _____

Conversation

1 궁금증 표현하기

> **A** I wonder who those men are. 저 남자들이 누군지 궁금해.
> **B** They're the Wright brothers. 그들은 라이트 형제들이야.

■ 대화 상대방에게 궁금한 점을 물을 때 "I wonder ~." 또는 "I am wondering ~.", "I was wondering ~." 등과 같은 표현을 쓸 수 있다.

■ 이때 wonder와 함께 의문사(what/when/where/why/how)를 이용한 간접의문문을 사용하거나 혹은 if 절을 사용하기도 한다.

- I wonder why I get tired so much. 난 내가 왜 이리 피곤한지 모르겠어.
- If I ate less, I wonder how much weight I would lose. 내가 적게 먹으면 얼마나 살이 빠질지 궁금해.
- I wonder if I should wear a coat or not. 코트를 입어야 할지 말지 모르겠어.
- I wonder if you are going to attend the meeting at 2 p.m. 2시에 회의에 참석하실 건지 궁금합니다.

■ "I wonder if you ~."라는 표현은 상대방에게 부탁할 경우에도 쓰일 수 있다.

- I wonder if you could tell me the right direction to the subway station.
  제게 지하철역에 가는 정확한 방향을 가르쳐 주실 수 있나요?
- I wonder if you could give me a discount a little bit. 할인을 조금 해주실 수 있나요?

핵심 Check

1. 다음 대화의 밑줄 친 우리말에 맞게 주어진 단어를 바르게 배열하시오.
   A: 난 최초의 비행기가 어떻게 생겼는지 궁금해.
       (looked / I / plane / what / like / wonder / the / first).
   B: Look! There is a model. It looked like a big bird.

   ➡ _____

2 생각할 시간 요청하기

A What can we do with these VR glasses? 이 VR 안경으로 뭘 할 수 있을까?

B Let me see.... Maybe we can play soccer. 어디 보자… 아마 우리 축구할 수 있을 거야.

■ "Let me see."는 '잠깐만.', '어디 보자.'의 뜻으로 어떤 것을 기억해 내거나 잠시 생각을 정리할 시간이 필요할 때 사용하는 표현이다. 같은 표현인 "Let me think." 또는 "Just a moment." 등을 사용하여 생각할 시간을 요청할 수 있다.

생각할 시간 요청하기

• Let me see. 어디 보자.

• Let me think. 생각 좀 해보자.

• Just a moment. 잠깐만.

• Just a second. 잠깐만.

• Wait a moment. 잠깐만.

■ let은 동사원형을 목적격보어로 취하는 점에 유의한다.

• Let me think about it. (○)

• Let me thinking about it. (✕)

• Let me to think about it. (✕)

핵심 Check

2. 다음 대화의 빈칸에 들어갈 말로 적절하지 <u>않은</u> 것은?

A: What can we do with this VR glasses?

B: _____ .... We can play soccer.

① Let me see
② Let me think
③ Just a moment
④ Just a second
⑤ Let me see what I can do

Real-Life Zone

G: I like these crackers. They're really good.

B: Yeah, me, too. ❶I wonder why crackers have these little holes in them.

G: I don't know. ❷Let me think…. Um … well … maybe it's because the holes ❸make the crackers look tastier.

B: That's ❹possible, but there must be some other reasons.

G: Let's ❺look up crackers on the Internet and see what it says.

B: Okay. Oh, look at this.

G: It says during baking, steam ❻comes out through the holes and that makes the crackers thin.

B: It also says that the holes make the crackers crispy.

G: Wow! So ❼that's why they have holes!

G: 난 이 크래커가 좋아. 정말 맛있어.

B: 응, 나도 좋아해. 나는 크래커에 왜 이 작은 구멍들이 있는지 궁금해.

G: 잘 모르겠어. 생각해 보자…. 음… 아마 그 구멍들이 크래커를 더욱 맛있게 보이도록 해 주기 때문이 아닐까.

B: 그럴 수도 있겠네. 하지만 다른 이유들이 있을 거야.

G: 크래커에 관해 인터넷에 찾아보고 뭐라고 하는지 알아보자.

B: 좋아. 오, 이것 봐.

G: 굽는 동안, 그 구멍들을 통해 수증기가 빠져나와서 크래커를 얇게 만드는 거래.

B: 또한 구멍들은 크래커를 바삭하게 만드는 거래.

G: 와! 크래커에 구멍들이 있는 거구나!

❶ 'I wonder ~.'는 궁금증을 나타내는 표현으로, "I am wondering ~.", 'I was wondering ~."과 같은 표현으로 대체할 수 있다. ❷ '잠깐만.', '어디 보자.'의 뜻으로 어떤 것을 기억해 내거나 잠시 생각을 정리할 시간이 필요할 때 사용하는 표현이다. ❸ make+목적어+목적보어(동사원형): 목적어를 목적보어하게 만들다 ❹ possible: 가능성 있는, 있을 수 있는 ❺ look up: (정보를) 찾아 보다 ❻ come out: 나오다 ❼ 'that is the reason why they have holes!'의 줄임말이다.

Check(√) True or False

(1) Both G and B did not know why crackers have little holes in them.　T ☐ F ☐

(2) According to the Internet, the little holes in crackers make them thin and crispy.　T ☐ F ☐

Wrap Up 1-2

B: Hi, Kate. Today's Saturday, so ❶what about going to the Einstein Science Park today?

G: ❷That sounds like a good idea. I heard that they have special programs on Saturdays. ❸I wonder what they are.

B: ❹Let me see…. I saw an advertisement in the newspaper. ❺Here it is.

G: What does it say?

B: It says that today they have two shows: the Smart Design Show and the International Drone Show in Einstein Hall 101.

G: ❻They both sound fantastic.

B: I'll call them and ask what time they start.

B: 안녕, 케이트. 오늘은 토요일이야. 그래서 말인데, 오늘 아인슈타인 과학 공원에 가는 건 어때?

G: 좋은 생각이야. 나는 토요일마다 특별한 프로그램들이 있다고 들었어. 나는 그것들이 무엇인지 궁금해.

B: 어디 보자…. 내가 신문에서 광고를 봤어. 여기 있어.

G: 뭐라고 쓰여 있니?

B: 여기에 따르면 오늘 두 가지 공연이 있대. 아이슈타인 홀 101호에서 있는 스마트 디자인 쇼와 국제 드론 쇼야.

G: 둘 다 환상적일 것 같아.

B: 내가 전화해서 그것들이 몇 시에 시작하는지 물어볼게.

❶ 상대방에게 무언가를 제안하는 표현으로, 'How about ~?'으로 바꿔 쓸 수 있다. ❷ 상대방의 제안을 승낙하는 표현으로, 'That sounds good.'으로 바꿔 쓸 수 있다. ❸ wonder와 함께 의문사(what/when/where/why/how)를 이용한 간접의문문을 사용하기도 한다. ❹ '잠깐만.', '어디 보자.'의 뜻으로 어떤 것을 기억해 내거나 잠시 생각을 정리할 시간이 필요할 때 사용하는 표현이다. ❺ '여기 있습니다.'라는 표현으로 단어나 어구가 정해진 위치를 벗어난 도치 문장이다. ❻ 이때 They는 앞서 언급된 'two shows'를 가리킨다.

Check(√) True or False

(3) There are going to be more than two shows on weekdays.　T ☐ F ☐

(4) Both G and B are going to visit the Einstein Science Park today.　T ☐ F ☐

Listen & Speak 1 Listen

1. G: Look at this picture. I wonder who ❶ those men are.
   B: They're the Wright brothers. They ❷ invented the airplane.
2. G: I wonder why they are standing ❸in front of the bicycle shop.
   B: They had a bicycle shop. They sold and repaired bicycles.
3. G: I wonder ❹what the first plane looked like.
   B: Look! There is a model. It looked like a big bird.
4. G: I wonder ❺where they first tried to fly their airplane.
   B: They tested their airplane on a hill in North Carolina.

❶ that의 복수형으로 지시형용사로 쓰였다.
❷ invent : 발명하다
❸ in front of ~: ~의 앞에
❹ 의문사 what을 사용한 간접의문문으로, '최초의 비행기가 어떻게 생겼는지'라고 해석한다.
❺ 의문사 where가 사용된 간접의문문으로, '그들이 어디서 최초로 비행을 시도했는지'라고 해석한다.

Listen & Speak 1 A-1

B: Look at this invention. It can ❶help us cook without electricity.
G: Is that possible? ❷I wonder how it works.
B: It uses sunlight to cook food.
G: Wow. ❸That would be really helpful when you go camping.

❶ help는 목적보어로 동사원형이나 to부정사를 취한다.
❷ 'I wonder ~.'는 목적어로 의문사를 이용한 간접의문문을 취하기도 한다.
❸ That은 음식을 요리하기 위해 햇빛을 이용하는 것(using sunlight to cook food)을 가리킨다.

Listen & Speak 1 A-2

B: Hi, class. ❶Have you ever heard about the Moai? They are tall, human-shaped stones in Chile. ❷Most of the stones are four meters tall, but the tallest one is 20 meters tall. I was wondering ❸how people moved them long ago. So I searched the Internet and learned that they used ropes. Isn't ❹that amazing?

❶ 'Have you ever ~?'는 상대방에게 어떤 일을 해 본 적이 있냐고 묻는 표현이다.
❷ Most of ~: ~의 대부분
❸ 의문사 how가 쓰인 간접의문문으로, '어떻게 사람들이 그것을 오래 전에 옮겼는지'라고 해석한다.
❹ 이때 that은 돌을 옮기기 위해 밧줄을 사용한 것(using ropes to move the stones)을 가리킨다.

Listen & Speak 1 B-1

A: I wonder ❶who those men are.
B: They're the Wright brothers. ❷They invented the airplane.

❶ 의문사 who가 쓰인 간접의문문으로, '그 남자들이 누군지'라고 해석한다.
❷ 이때 they는 앞서 언급한 the Wright brothers를 가리킨다.

Listen & Speak 1 B-2

A: I wonder ❶what the first plane looked like.
B: Look! There is a model. ❷It looked like a big bird.

❶ 의문사 what이 쓰인 간접의문문으로, '최초의 비행기는 어떻게 생겼는지'라고 해석한다.
❷ 이때 It은 'the first plane'을 가리킨다.

Listen & Speak 1 B-3

A: I wonder ❶what country they're from.
B: They're from the U.S.

❶ 의문사 what이 쓰인 간접의문문으로, '그들이 어느 나라에서 왔는지'라고 해석한다.

Listen & Speak 2 Listen

1. G: ❶What can we do with these VR glasses?
   B: Let me see.... ❷Maybe we can play soccer.
2. B: How does the ball float in the air?
   G: Let me see.... I think air ❸pushes the ball up.
3. G: How does this train start to move?
   B: ❹Let me see.... I think you can move it with a smartphone app.
4. G: What can we do with this drone?
   B: Well, let me see.... Maybe we can ❺take pictures from the sky.

❶ 의문사 what이 쓰인 직접의문문으로, 'VR 안경으로 뭘 할 수 있지?'라고 해석한다.
❷ maybe: 아마도 (= probably)
❸ push up: ~을 밀어 올리다
❹ '잠깐만.', '어디 보자.'의 뜻으로 어떤 것을 기억해 내거나 잠시 생각을 정리할 시간이 필요할 때 사용하는 표현으로 "Let me think." 또는 "Just a moment." 등으로 대체할 수 있다.
❺ take a picture of ~: ~의 사진을 찍다 (= take a photo of ~)

Listen & Speak 2 A-1

G: Look at the number. It's ❶going up quickly.

B: When people ❷pass by, the number increases.

G: Oh, you're right. ❸What does the number mean?

B: Let me see.... Oh, when people ❹step on the floor, energy is made. It shows ❺the amount of energy that is made.

G: Wow, that's amazing!

❶ go up: 올라가다, 증가하다
❷ pass by: 지나가다
❸ 의문사 what이 쓰인 의문문으로, '그 숫자들이 뭘 의미하지?'라고 해석한다.
❹ step on: ~을 밟다
❺ the amount of ~: ~의 양

Listen & Speak 2 A-2

G: ❶We're going on a field trip tomorrow to the Invention Museum.

B: I've heard that ❷it has a lot of creative inventions.

G: ❸That's why I'm so excited. ❹How about planning the tour before we go?

B: Good idea. Let me see.... I have the school letter and a map of the museum.

G: Perfect. ❺Let's get started.

❶ 현재진행형 문장이지만 의미는 미래에 무엇을 할 것이라고 해석한다.
❷ 대명사 it은 'the Invention Museum'을 가리킨다.
❸ 'That's the reason why I'm so excited.'의 줄임말이다.
❹ 상대방에게 무언가를 제안할 때 쓸 수 있는 표현으로, 'What about ~?'으로 대체할 수 있다.
❺ '시작하자'라고 해석한다.

Listen & Speak 2 B-1

A: What can we do with this VR glasses?

B: ❶Let me see… We can play soccer.

❶ 이와 같은 표현인 "Let me think." 또는 "Just a moment." 등을 사용하여 생각할 시간을 요청할 수 있다.

Listen & Speak 2 B-2

A: What can we do with this drone?

B: Let me see… ❶We can take pictures from the sky.

❶ take pictures from the sky: 하늘에서 사진을 찍다

Listen & Speak 2 B-3

A: What can we do with the smart watch?

B: Let me see… We can ❶send text messages.

❶ send: ~을 보내다

Wrap Up 3~4

G: John, look. The school ❶is having an invention competition.

B: Really? ❷That sounds interesting.

G: Yeah. ❸You should enter that. You always have great ideas.

B: Does it say ❹when the competition is?

G: Let me see…. It says it's November 11. That's two weeks from today.

B: I wonder what I have to do to enter the competition.

G: It says here you should talk to Mr. Harrison, the science teacher.

❶ 현재진행형 문장이지만 의미는 미래에 무엇을 할 것이라고 해석한다.
❷ 대명사 That은 'an invention competition'을 가리킨다.
❸ 이때 should는 강한 강요의 의미가 아니라 부드럽게 권유하는 의미로 해석한다.
❹ 의문사 when이 사용된 간접의문문으로, '언제 그 대회가 시작하는지'라고 해석한다.

● 다음 우리말과 일치하도록 빈칸에 알맞은 말을 쓰시오.

Listen & Speak 1 Listen

1. G: Look at this _____. I wonder who _____ men are.
   B: They're the Wright brothers. They _____ the airplane.

2. G: I wonder _____ they are standing in _____ of the bicycle shop.
   B: They had a bicycle shop. They sold and _____ bicycles.

3. G: I wonder _____ the first plane _____ like.
   B: Look! There is a model. It looked _____ a big bird.

4. G: I _____ where they first _____ to fly their airplane.
   B: They _____ their airplane on a hill in North Carolina.

Listen & Speak 1 A-1

B: Look at this _____. It can help us _____ without _____.
G: Is that _____? I wonder how it _____.
B: It uses _____ to cook food.
G: Wow. That would be really _____ when you go camping.

Listen & Speak 1 A-2

B: Hi, class. Have you ever _____ about the Moai? They are tall, human-_____ stones in Chile. _____ of the stones are four meters _____, but the tallest one is 20 meters tall. I was _____ how people _____ them long ago. So I _____ the Internet and _____ that they used _____. Isn't that _____?

Listen & Speak 1 B-1

A: I wonder _____ those men are.
B: They're the Wright brothers. They _____ the airplane.

Listen & Speak 1 B-2

A: I wonder what the first plane _____ like.
B: Look! There is a _____. It looked _____ a big bird.

Listen & Speak 1 B-3

A: I _____ what _____ they're from.
B: They're _____ the U.S.

해석

1. G: 이 사진을 봐. 나는 그 남자들이 누구인지 궁금해.
   B: 그들은 라이트 형제야. 그들은 비행기를 발명했어.
2. G: 나는 그들이 왜 자전거 가게 앞에 서 있는지 궁금해.
   B: 그들은 자전거 가게를 가지고 있었어. 그들은 자전거를 팔고 수리했어.
3. G: 나는 최초의 비행기가 어떻게 생겼는지 궁금해.
   B: 봐! 저기 모형이 있어. 그것은 큰 새처럼 생겼었네.
4. G: 나는 그들이 어디에서 처음으로 비행을 시도했는지 궁금해.
   B: 그들은 노스캐롤라이나주의 한 언덕에서 그들의 비행기를 시험했어.

B: 이 발명품들을 봐. 이것은 우리가 전기 없이도 요리할 수 있도록 도와줘.
G: 그게 가능해? 나는 그것이 어떻게 작용하는지 궁금해.
B: 이것은 음식을 조리하기 위해 태양광을 사용해.
G: 와. 그것은 캠핑을 갈 때 정말 유용할 것 같아.

B: 안녕하세요, 여러분. 여러분은 모아이에 대해 들어 본 적이 있나요? 그것들은 칠레에 있는 크고 사람 모양을 한 돌입니다. 대부분의 돌들은 높이가 4미터이지만, 가장 큰 것은 높이가 20미터입니다. 저는 오래 전에 사람들이 어떻게 그것들을 옮겼는지 궁금했습니다. 그래서 저는 인터넷을 검색했고 그들이 밧줄을 이용했다는 것을 알게 되었습니다. 그 사실이 놀랍지 않나요?

A: 나는 그 남자들의 누구인지 궁금해.
B: 그들은 라이트 형제야. 그들은 비행기를 발명했어.

A: 나는 최조의 비행기가 어떻게 생겼는지 궁금해.
B: 봐! 저기 모형이 있어. 그것은 큰 새처럼 생겼었네.

A: 나는 그들이 어느 나라 출신인지 궁금해.
B: 그들은 미국 출신이야.

해석

Listen & Speak 2 Listen

1. **G:** _____ can we do with these VR glasses?
   B: _____ me see.... _____ we can play soccer.
2. **B:** _____ does the ball _____ in the air?
   G: Let me see.... I think air _____ the ball up.
3. **G:** How does this train start to _____?
   B: Let me _____.... I think you can move it _____ a smartphone app.
4. **G:** What can we do with this drone?
   B: Well, let me see.... Maybe we can take _____ from the sky.

1. G: 우리가 이 VR 안경으로 무엇을 할 수 있을까?
   B: 어디 보자.... 아마 우리는 축구를 할 수 있을 거야.
2. B: 어떻게 그 공이 공중에 뜰까?
   G: 어디 보자.... 내 생각에는 공기가 공을 위로 밀어 올리는 것 같아.
3. G: 이 기차는 어떻게 움직이기 시작 할까?
   B: 어디 보자.... 내 생각에는 네가 스 마트폰 앱으로 그것을 움직일 수 있을 것 같아.
4. G: 우리가 이 드론으로 무엇을 할 수 있을까?
   B: 음, 어디 보자.... 아마 우리는 하늘 에서 사진을 찍을 수 있을 거야.

Listen & Speak 2 A-1

G: _____ at the number. It's going up _____.
B: When people _____ by, the number _____.
G: Oh, you're right. What does the number mean?
B: _____ me see.... Oh, when people _____ on the floor, energy is _____. It shows the amount of energy that is made.
G: Wow, that's _____!

G: 저 숫자를 봐. 빠르게 올라가고 있어.
B: 사람들이 지나갈 때, 그 숫자가 증가해.
G: 오, 네 말이 맞아. 그 숫자는 무엇을 의미 할까?
B: 어디 보자.... 오, 사람들이 바닥을 밟 을 때 에너지가 만들어져. 그것은 만 들어지는 에너지의 양을 보여 줘.
G: 와, 놀라워!

Listen & Speak 2 A- 2

G: We're going on a _____ trip tomorrow to the _____ Museum.
B: I've heard that it has a lot of _____ inventions.
G: That's why I'm so _____. How about _____ the tour before we go?
B: _____ idea. Let me see.... I have the school letter and a map of the _____.
G: Perfect. Let's get _____.

G: 우리는 내일 '발명 박물관'으로 현장 학습을 가.
B: 나는 그곳에 창의적인 발명품들이 많 이 있다고 들었어.
G: 그것이 내가 들뜬 이유야. 우리 가기 전에 관람 계획을 짜는 것은 어때?
B: 좋은 생각이야. 어디 보자.... 나는 학 교에서 받은 안내서와 박물관 지도가 있어.
G: 완벽해. 시작하자.

Listen & Speak 2 B-1

A: _____ can we do with this VR glasses?
B: Let me see... We can _____ soccer.

A: 우리가 이 VR 안경으로 무엇을 할 수 있을까?
B: 어디 보자.... 우리는 축구를 할 수 있어.

Listen & Speak 2 B-2

A: What can we do _____ this drone?
B: Let me _____... We can take pictures _____ the sky.

A: 우리가 이 드론으로 무엇을 할 수 있 을까?
B: 어디 보자.... 우리는 하늘에서 사진을 찍을 수 있어.

Listen & Speak 2 B-3

A: _____ can we do with the smart watch?

B: Let me see… We can _____ text messages.

A: 우리가 이 스마트워치로 무엇을 할 수 있을까?

B: 어디 보자…. 우리는 문자 메시지를 보낼 수 있어.

Real-Life Zone

G: I like _____ crackers. They're really good.

B: Yeah, me, too. I wonder _____ crackers have these little _____ in them.

G: I don't know. Let me _____…. Um … well … _____ it's because the holes make the crackers _____ tastier.

B: That's _____, but there _____ be some other _____.

G: Let's _____ up crackers on the Internet and see _____ it says.

B: Okay. Oh, look at this.

G: It _____ _____ baking, steam comes out _____ the holes and that makes the crackers _____.

B: It also says that the holes make the crackers _____.

G: Wow! So that's _____ they have holes!

G: 난 이 크래커가 좋아. 정말 맛있어.

B: 응, 나도 좋아해. 나는 크래커에 왜 이 작은 구멍들이 있는지 궁금해.

G: 잘 모르겠어. 생각해 보자…. 음… 아마 그 구멍들이 크래커를 더욱 맛있게 보이도록 해 주기 때문이 아닐까.

B: 그럴 수도 있겠네. 하지만 다른 이유들이 있을 거야.

G: 크래커에 관해 인터넷에 찾아보고 뭐라고 하는지 알아보자.

B: 좋아. 오, 이것 봐.

G: 굽는 동안, 그 구멍들을 통해 수증기가 빠져나와서 크래커를 얇게 만드는 거래.

B: 또한 구멍들은 크래커를 바삭하게 만드는 거래.

G: 와! 크래커에 구멍들이 있는 거구나!

Wrap Up 1-2

B: Hi, Kate. Today's Saturday, so _____ about _____ to the Einstein Science Park today?

G: That _____ like a good idea. I heard _____ they have special programs on _____. I wonder _____ they are.

B: Let me see…. I saw an _____ in the newspaper. _____ it is.

G: What does it _____?

B: It _____ that today they have two shows: the Smart Design Show and the International Drone Show in Einstein Hall 101.

G: They _____ sound _____.

B: I'll call them and ask _____ time they start.

B: 안녕, 케이트. 오늘은 토요일이야. 그래서 말인데, 오늘 아인슈타인 과학 공원에 가는 건 어때?

G: 좋은 생각이야. 나는 토요일마다 특별한 프로그램들이 있다고 들었어. 나는 그것들이 무엇인지 궁금해.

B: 어디 보자…. 내가 신문에서 광고를 봤어. 여기 있어.

G: 뭐라고 쓰여 있니?

B: 여기에 따르면 오늘 두 가지 공연이 있대. 아인슈타인 홀 101호에서 있는 스마트 디자인 쇼와 국제 드론 쇼야.

G: 둘 다 환상적일 것 같아.

B: 내가 전화해서 그것들이 몇 시에 시작하는지 물어볼게.

Wrap Up 3~4

G: John, look. The school is having an invention _____.

B: Really? That _____ interesting.

G: Yeah. You should _____ that. You always have great _____.

B: Does it say _____ the competition is?

G: Let me see…. It says it's November 11. That's two weeks _____ today.

B: I _____ what I _____ to do to enter the competition.

G: It says here you should _____ to Mr. Harrison, the _____ teacher.

G: 존, 봐. 학교에서 발명대회가 열린대.

B: 정말? 흥미로울 것 같아.

G: 응. 너는 참가해야 해. 너는 항상 아이디어가 훌륭하잖아.

B: 대회가 언제인지 나와 있니?

G: 어디 보자…. 11월 11일이래. 오늘로부터 2주 뒤야.

B: 대회에 참가하기 위해 내가 무엇을 해야 하는지 궁금해.

G: 여기에 따르면 너는 과학 선생님이신 해리슨 선생님께 말씀드려야 해.

[01~02] 다음 대화를 읽고 물음에 답하시오.

> B: Look at this invention. It can help us cook without electricity.
> G: Is that possible? (A)<u>난 그게 어떻게 작동하는지 궁금해.</u>
> B: (B)<u>It</u> uses sunlight to cook food.
> G: Wow. That would be really helpful when you go camping.

01 위 대화의 밑줄 친 (A)의 우리말을 바르게 영작하시오. (5 words)

➡ _____

02 위 대화의 밑줄 친 (B)가 가리키는 것을 찾아 쓰시오. (2 words)

➡ _____

[03~04] 다음 대화를 읽고 물음에 답하시오.

> G: Look at the number. It's going up quickly.
> B: When people pass by, the number increases.
> G: Oh, you're right. What does the number mean?
> B: (A)<u>Let me see</u>…. Oh, when people step on the floor, energy is made. It shows the amount of energy that is made.
> G: Wow, that's amazing!

03 위 대화의 밑줄 친 (A)와 바꿔 쓸 수 있는 것은?

① Let me see what I can do
② Let me see if it's right
③ Let me think what the number is
④ Let me think why people pass by
⑤ Let me think

04 How is the energy made? Answer in English with 9 words.

➡ _____

[01~03] 다음 대화를 읽고 물음에 답하시오.

G: I like these crackers. They're really good.

B: Yeah, me, too. I wonder why crackers ⓐ have these little holes in them.

G: I don't know. Let me ⓑthinking.... Um ... well ... maybe it's because the holes make the crackers look tastier.

B: That's possible, but there ⓒmust be some other reasons.

G: Let's look up crackers on the Internet and see ___(A)___ it says.

B: Okay. Oh, look at this.

G: It says during ⓓbaking, steam comes out through the holes and that makes the crackers thin.

B: It also ⓔsays that the holes make the crackers crispy.

G: Wow! So that's ___(B)___ they have holes!

서답형

01 위 대화의 밑줄 친 ⓐ~ⓔ 중 어색한 것을 찾아 바르게 고치시오.

_____ ➡ _____

02 위 대화의 빈칸 (A)와 (B)에 들어갈 말이 바르게 짝지어진 것은?

① what – why ② what – how
③ how – what ④ how – why
⑤ when – why

서답형

03 위 대화에서 주어진 영영풀이가 가리키는 단어를 찾아 쓰시오.

the hot gas that is produced when water boils

➡ _____

[04~06] 다음 대화를 읽고 물음에 답하시오.

B: Hi, Kate. Today's Saturday, so what about going to the Einstein Science Park today?

G: That sounds like a good idea. ① I heard that they have special programs on Saturdays. (A)난 그 프로그램들이 뭔지 궁금해.

B: Let me see.... I saw an advertisement in the newspaper. ②

G: What does it say? ③

B: It says that today they have two shows: the Smart Design Show and the International Drone Show in Einstein Hall 101. ④

G: They both sound fantastic.

B: ⑤ I'll call them and ask what time they start.

04 위 대화의 ①~⑤ 중 주어진 문장이 들어가기에 가장 적절한 곳은?

Here it is.

①　　　②　　　③　　　④　　　⑤

서답형

05 위 대화의 밑줄 친 (A)의 우리말을 바르게 영작하시오.
(5 words)

➡ _____

06 위 대화를 읽고 대답할 수 <u>없는</u> 것은?

① When are Kate and her friend going to the park?

② What kind of programs do the park have?

③ How many times do the programs take place on Saturdays?

④ Where are the programs taking place?

⑤ Who will call the park for the information?

[07~08] 다음 글을 읽고 물음에 답하시오.

B: Hi, class. Have you ever (A)[hear / heard] about the Moai? They are tall, human-shaped stones in Chile. (B)[Most / Most of] the stones are four meters tall, but the (C)[taller/tallest] one is 20 meters tall. I was wondering how people moved them long ago. So I searched the Internet and learned that they used ropes. Isn't that amazing?

07 위 글의 괄호 (A)~(C)에서 알맞은 것을 바르게 짝지은 것을 고르시오.

　　(A)　　(B)　　(C)
① hear – Most – tallest
② hear – Most of – taller
③ heard – Most of – tallest
④ heard – Most of – taller
⑤ heard – Most – tallest

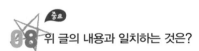

08 위 글의 내용과 일치하는 것은?

① The Moai is the tallest stone in Chile.
② The tallest Moai is twenty meters tall.
③ The Moai is made up of stones only from Chile.
④ The average Moai is less than four meters tall.
⑤ It is not scientifically proved whether people used ropes.

09 다음 중 짝지어진 대화가 <u>어색한</u> 것을 고르시오.

① A: Look at this invention. It can help us cook without electricity.
　 B: Sounds amazing! I wonder how it works.

② A: I wonder what the first train looked like.
　 B: Look! There is a miniature model over there.
③ A: I wonder why they are standing in front of the bicycle shop.
　 B: They had a bicycle shop. They sold and repaired bicycles.
④ A: I wonder what country they're from.
　 B: They're from France.
⑤ A: I wonder where they first tried to fly their airplane.
　 B: They tested their airplane 100 years ago.

[10~11] 다음 대화를 읽고 물음에 답하시오.

G: We're going on a field trip tomorrow to the Invention Museum.
B: I've heard that it has a lot of creative inventions.
G: That's why I'm so excited. How about planning the tour before we go?
B: Good idea. (A)Let me see... I have the school letter and a map of the museum.
G: Perfect. Let's get started.

10 위 대화를 읽고 대답할 수 <u>없는</u> 것을 <u>모두</u> 고르시오. (2개)

① When are G and B going on a field trip?
② Who is going on a field trip with them?
③ How does G feel about the field trip?
④ What did G suggest B to do before the field trip?
⑤ What is the plan for the field trip?

11 What are G and B going to do afterwards?

① to find where the letter and the map are
② to search what kind of inventions there are in the museum
③ to hand over the school letter to parents
④ to make a plan for the field trip
⑤ to find out who is going to be on the same group

[01~02] 다음 대화를 읽고 물음에 답하시오.

G: John, look. The school is having an invention competition.

B: Really? That sounds interesting.

G: Yeah. You should enter that. You always have great ideas.

B: Does it say ___(A)___ the competition is?

G: Let me see.... It says it's November 11. That's two weeks from today.

B: I wonder ___(B)___ I have to do to enter the competition.

G: It says here you should talk to Mr. Harrison, the science teacher.

01 위 대화의 빈칸 (A)와 (B)에 들어갈 말을 쓰시오.

(A) _____ (B) _____

02 What does John have to do to enter the invention competition? (7 words)

➡ _____

[03~04] 다음 대화를 읽고 물음에 답하시오.

B: Look at this invention. It can help us cook without electricity.

(A) Wow. That would be really helpful when you go camping.

(B) Is that possible? I wonder how it works.

(C) It uses sunlight to cook food.

03 위 대화가 자연스럽게 이어지도록 순서대로 배열하시오.

➡ _____

04 What does the invention employ to cook? (6 words)

➡ _____

[05~07] 다음 글을 읽고 물음에 답하시오.

B: Hi, class. Have you ever heard about the Moai? They are tall, human-shaped stones in Chile. Most of the stones are four meters tall, but the tallest one is 20 meters tall. (A)저는 어떻게 사람들이 오래 전에 그것들을 옮겼는지 궁금했어요. (how / wondering / I / people / was / moved / long ago / them) So I searched the Internet and learned that they used ropes. Isn't that amazing?

05 위 글의 밑줄 친 (A)를 우리말에 맞게 나열하시오.

➡ _____

_____

06 다음 주어진 영영풀이에 맞는 단어를 위 글에서 찾아 쓰시오.

to look somewhere carefully in order to find something

➡ _____

07 According to the speaker, how did people in Chile move the stones? (7 words)

➡ _____

Grammar

교과서

① 가정법 과거: if + 주어 + 동사(과거형), 주어 + would + 동사원형

> • The water inside **would** quickly boil over **if** the lid **did** not have that hole.
> 만약 뚜껑에 저 구멍이 없다면, 안에 있는 물은 금방 끓어 넘칠 것이다.

■ 가정법 과거는 'If+주어+동사(과거형), 주어+would/should/could/might+동사원형'으로 쓰고 '만일 ~라면 …할 텐데.'로 해석하며, 현재 사실과 반대되는 일이나 상황을 가정한다.

  • **If** I **had** his phone number, I **would** call him. 만일 내가 그의 전화번호를 안다면 그에게 전화할 텐데.

■ If절의 동사(과거형)가 be동사일 경우 were를 쓰지만, 주어가 'I'나 '3인칭 단수'일 때는 구어체에서 was를 쓰기도 한다.

  • **If** I **were[was]** you, I **would** tell the truth. 만일 내가 너라면 진실을 말할 텐데.

■ 가정법 과거 표현에 as if를 활용한 것이 있는데 주절 동사의 시제에서 반대되는 상황이나 일을 표현하고자 할 때 사용하며 'S+V+as if+S+과거동사 ~'로 쓰고 '마치 ~인 것처럼'으로 해석한다.

  • He talks **as if** he **were[was]** rich. (= In fact, he is not rich.) 그는 마치 그가 부자인 것처럼 말한다.

  • He talked **as if** he **were** rich. (= In fact, he was not rich.) 그는 마치 그가 부자인 것처럼 말했다.

■ S+V+as if+S+had p.p./조동사 have p.p. ~: 마치 ~였던 것처럼

  • He talks **as if** he **had been** rich. 그는 마치 그가 부자였던 것처럼 말한다.
    (과거에 부자가 아니었는데 부자였던 것처럼 현재 말함.) (= In fact, he was not rich.)

  • He talked **as if** he **had been** rich. 그는 마치 그가 부자였던 것처럼 말했다.
    (말하는 과거 시점 이전에 부자가 아니었는데 부자였던 것처럼 말함.) (= In fact, he had not been rich.)

*가정법 과거완료: 과거 사실에 대한 반대되는 상황이나 일 표현

■ 가정법 과거완료는 'If+S+had p.p. ~, S+would/should/could/might+have p.p.'로 쓰고 '만일 ~했었다면, …했을 텐데.'로 해석하며, 과거 사실과 반대되는 일이나 상황을 가정한다.

  • If I **had studied** harder, I **could have passed** the test. 내가 공부를 열심히 했었더라면 시험에 통과했을 텐데.

핵심 Check

1. 다음 괄호 안에서 알맞은 말을 고르시오.

  (1) If I (get / got) up earlier, I would not be late for school.

  (2) I (would / will) be very glad if my son studied harder.

② so that 주어 can

- The hole also prevents the window from fogging up **so that** you **can** enjoy that fantastic view. 그 구멍은 또한, 당신이 멋진 경치를 즐길 수 있도록 창문에 김이 서리는 것을 막아 준다.

■ '주어 동사 so that 주어 can[could]'로 쓰고 '~ 할 수 있도록, ~하기 위해서'라고 해석한다. can 대신에 may를 쓰기도 하다.

- I go to bed early **so that** I **can** wake up early. 나는 일찍 일어날 수 있도록 일찍 잔다.

■ '~하기 위해서'는 'so that 주어 can' 뿐만 아니라 'to', 'so as to', 'in order to', 'in order that S V'로도 표현할 수 있다.

- She goes jogging every morning **so that** she **can**[**may**] stay healthy.
  그녀는 건강을 유지하기 위해 매일 아침 조깅을 한다.
- = She goes jogging every morning **to stay** healthy.
- = She goes jogging every morning **so as to stay** healthy.
- = She goes jogging every morning **in order to stay** healthy.
- = She goes jogging every morning **in order that** she **can**[**may**] stay healthy.

■ 그밖의 so that 용법

1) ~, so that S V: (결과) 그래서 ~하다

- It was freezing last weekend, **so that** I stayed at home all day.
  지난 주말에 너무 추워서 나는 하루 종일 집에 있었다.
- There was a car accident on my way to work, **so that** I was late for the meeting.
  출근길에 차 사고가 있어서, 나는 회의에 늦었다.

2) so 형용사/부사 that S V = such a 형용사+명사 that S V

- He is **so** wealthy **that** he can purchase a building in Gangnam.
  그는 너무 돈이 많아서 강남에 있는 빌딩을 살 수 있다.
- He is **such** a wealthy man **that** he can purchase a building in Gangnam.
- She is **so** kind **that** everyone likes her. 그녀는 너무 친절해서 모두가 그녀를 좋아한다.
- The grocery store near my house was **so** crowded **that** I had to go another store.
  집 근처에 있는 마트가 너무 사람이 많아서 나는 다른 마트에 가야 했다.
- He drank **so** much last night **that** he's suffering from a hangover today.
  어젯밤에 술을 너무 마셔서 그는 오늘 숙취로 고생하고 있다.

핵심 Check

2. 다음 괄호 안에서 알맞은 말을 고르시오.

(1) I study English hard (such / so) that I can speak English well.

(2) I will buy toys so (that / what) I can give them to my brother.

01 다음 문장에서 어법상 <u>어색한</u> 부분을 바르게 고쳐 쓰시오.

(1) If she has a pretty dress like yours, she wouldn't cry.

_____ ➡ _____

(2) If I were the President, I will support that policy.

_____ ➡ _____

(3) I study hard so what I can get a good grade.

_____ ➡ _____

(4) She practices the violin so that she can't play the violin without mistakes.

_____ ➡ _____.

02 다음 주어진 두 문장을 so that을 활용하여 한 문장으로 쓰시오.

(1) Jack is very tall. He can touch the ceiling.

➡ _____

(2) We worked hard. Everything will be ready in time.

➡ _____

(3) I got up early. I could catch the first bus.

➡ _____

(4) She works very hard. She deserves a vacation.

➡ _____

03 다음 우리말에 맞게 주어진 단어를 활용하여 영작하시오.

(1) 더 긴 팔을 가지고 있다면, 저 사과를 잡을 수 있을 텐데. (have, grab)

➡ _____

(2) 내가 만일 영국에 있다면, 영어를 더 잘 말할 수 있을 텐데. (be)

➡ _____

서답형

01 다음 문장에서 어법상 틀린 부분을 찾아 바르게 고쳐 쓰시오.

> If I had had time, I could gone there with you.

_____ ➡ _____

서답형

02 다음 문장과 같은 뜻이 되도록 As를 활용하여 바꿔 쓰시오.

> If he were rich, he would buy that car.

➡ _____

서답형

03 우리말에 맞게 괄호 안의 단어들을 알맞은 순서로 배열하시오.

> 얘기를 하게 좀 더 가까이 앉아라. (so, sit, little, we, closer, a, that, talk, a, have, can)

➡ _____

04 다음 문장과 같은 뜻을 지닌 문장을 고르시오.

> I gave her my phone number so that she could contact me.

① I gave her my phone number in order that she could contact me.
② I gave her my phone number if she could contact me.
③ I gave her my phone number that she doesn't know.
④ I gave her my phone number because she could contact me.
⑤ I gave her my phone number though she wanted to keep in touch with me.

중요

05 다음 중 어법상 어색한 문장을 고르시오.

① If Peter asked Karen out, she would say yes.
② If I had known, I would not done the work.
③ If I had a million dollars, I could buy my own helicopter.
④ If Diane was here right now, she would agree.
⑤ If I were not sick, I could go to the party.

06 다음 문맥상 빈칸에 들어갈 말로 알맞은 것을 고르시오.

> _____, I would tell you.

① If I knew her name
② If I had known her name
③ If I know her name
④ As I know her name
⑤ As I knew her name

서답형

07 빈칸에 들어갈 적절한 단어를 쓰시오.

> If I were you, I _____ not go there alone.

➡ _____

08 다음 중 빈칸에 들어갈 단어가 나머지와 <u>다른</u> 것을 고르시오.

① I need to study hard _____ I can get a full scholarship next semester.
② Turn it _____ I can see it.
③ We need the break _____ recharge.
④ Please bring him forward _____ we can have a closer look.
⑤ He has made a new plan _____ they can do that.

09 다음 빈칸에 들어갈 말로 알맞은 것을 고르시오.

> If the weather were fine, _____.

① I would have gone on a picnic
② I will go on a picnic
③ I have to go on a picnic
④ I would go on a picnic
⑤ I go on a picnic

10 다음 빈칸에 들어갈 말로 적절한 것을 고르시오.

> He works hard _____ support his family.

① in order   ② in order to
③ in order that   ④ in as to
⑤ so as

11 다음 빈칸에 들어갈 말끼리 알맞게 짝지어진 것을 고르시오.

> Can you move aside _____ I _____ pass?

① so that – can   ② so that – can't
③ so what – can   ④ so what – can't
⑤ so what – couldn't

12 다음 우리말을 영작한 것으로 어법상 알맞은 것을 고르시오.

> 내가 형이 있다면, 그와 함께 놀 텐데.

① If I had a brother, I would hang out with him.
② If I have a brother, I would hang out with him.
③ If I had a brother, I will hang out with him.
④ If I have a brother, I hang out with him.
⑤ If I had a brother, I hang out with him.

서답형

13 다음 우리말에 맞게 괄호 안의 표현을 활용하여 영작하시오.

> 그 여자는 추운 듯 팔짱을 꼈다.
> (as if, fold one's arm)

➡ _____

14 다음 중 어법상 <u>어색한</u> 것을 고르시오.

① She talked as if she were the queen.
② She ate them all as if she hungered for weeks.
③ She said it as if she had read my thought.
④ She looks as if she had seen a ghost.
⑤ She felt as if she is flying.

15 다음 문장과 같은 뜻을 지닌 문장을 <u>모두</u> 고르시오.

> He slept earlier than usual so that he could get up early the next day.

① He slept earlier than usual but he got up early the next day.

② He slept earlier than usual in order that he could get up early the next day.

③ He slept earlier than usual for he could get up early the next day.

④ He slept earlier than usual in order to get up early the next day.

⑤ He slept earlier than usual in order not to get up early the next day.

서답형

16 우리말에 맞게 괄호 안의 단어를 활용하여 빈칸을 채우시오.

> We went early _____ (so) get good seats.

➡ _____

서답형

17 다음 우리말에 맞게 괄호 안의 단어를 이용하여 영작하시오.

> 난 첫 기차를 놓치지 않으려고 일찍 일어났다. (in order to)

➡ _____

서답형

18 우리말에 맞게 괄호 안의 어휘들을 배열하여 영작할 때, 3번째 단어를 쓰시오. (바로 문장을 시작할 것.)

(1) 그가 더 열심히 운동한다면, 그는 좋은 운동 선수가 될 텐데. (harder, be, if, he, he, would, exercised, good, athlete, a)

➡ _____

(2) 가령 네가 내 입장이라면 어떻게 하겠니? (me, you, do, you, if, what, were, would)

➡ _____

(3) 만약 내가 아프지 않았더라면, 어제 함께 여행을 갔을 텐데. (been, had, if, would, gone, on, trip, a, I, not, sick, I, have, yesterday, together)

➡ _____

19 다음 빈칸에 공통으로 들어갈 말을 고르시오.

> • He then attended Johns Hopkins University _____ earn his doctorate.
> • We studied last night _____ pass the test.
>
> *doctorate 박사학위

① so that   ② so

③ in order that   ④ that

⑤ so as to

01 괄호 안의 단어를 활용하여 우리말을 영작하시오.

> 내가 그의 전화번호를 안다면 그에게 전화를 할 텐데. (phone number, call)

➡ _____

02 다음 문장과 같은 뜻이 되도록 as if를 활용하여 빈칸을 채우시오.

> In fact, I am not her younger brother.
> ➡ She helps me _____
> _____.

03 다음과 같은 뜻의 문장을 각 조건에 맞춰 영작하시오.

> She goes jogging every morning so that she can stay healthy.

(to부정사 사용)
➡ _____

(so as to 사용)
➡ _____
_____

(in order to 사용)
➡ _____
_____

(in order that 사용)
➡ _____
_____

04 다음 두 문장을 활용하여 가정법 과거문장으로 영작하시오.

> • She studies harder.
> • She can pass the test.

➡ _____

05 다음을 읽고 가정법 과거 문장으로 쓰시오.

> She wants to visit her friend's house, but she doesn't feel well.

➡ _____

06 다음 밑줄 친 부분과 같은 의미를 가진 3 단어를 쓰시오.

> I asked him out <u>in order to</u> know whether he had any interest in me.
> ➡ I asked him out _____ _____ _____ know whether he had any interest in me.

07 다음 빈칸에 공통으로 들어갈 말을 쓰시오.

> • I waited for an hour _____ _____ I could meet her.
> • My baby was born _____ small _____ he spent two weeks in an incubator.

08 다음 문장에서 <u>어색한</u> 곳을 바르게 고쳐 다시 쓰시오.

> In order to oversleep, I set the alarm for six o'clock.

➡ _____

_____

09 다음 우리말에 맞게 괄호 안의 단어를 참고하여 각 조건에 맞게 영작하시오.

> 그들은 시간을 낭비하지 않기 위해 택시를 탔다.
> (take, waste)

(to부정사 사용)

➡ _____

(in order to 사용)

➡ _____

(so as to 사용)

➡ _____

10 다음 우리말에 맞게 괄호 안의 단어를 활용하여 영작하시오.

> 만약 Bob이 그 팀에서 일한다면, 그렇게 스트레스를 받지 않을 것이다. (work, be, so)

➡ _____

_____

11 우리말에 맞게 다음 각 문장의 빈칸에 들어갈 말을 괄호 안의 단어를 활용하여 쓰시오.

(1) 내가 휴대 전화를 가지고 있다면 도움을 요청할 텐데. (call for)

➡ If I had a cell phone, _____

_____ _____ _____ .

(2) 만약 내가 배를 갖고 있다면 타고 갈 텐데. (boat)

➡ _____ _____ _____ _____

_____ , I would sail away.

(3) 따라서, 만약 당신이 그 날 화성을 향해 빛을 쏘았다면, 그것은 186초 만에 화성에 도달하였을 것이다. (reach)

➡ Thus, if you had turned a light toward Mars that day, _____

_____ _____ _____ in 186 seconds.

(4) 내가 새라면 날아갈 텐데. (be)

➡ _____ _____ _____ _____

_____ , I would fly away.

12 괄호 안의 단어를 활용하여 우리말에 맞게 영작하시오.

> 만약 내가 오늘 수업이 없다면, 놀이공원에 갈텐데. (have, go)

➡ _____

_____ (14 단어)

13 괄호 안의 단어를 활용하여 다음 우리말에 맞게 빈칸을 알맞게 채우시오.

(1) 라면이 불기 전에 가스렌지 불을 껐다.
(overcook, order to)

➡ I turned the range off _____

_____ _____ _____

the ramyon.

(2) 많은 시간을 가지려면 일찍 오너라.
(have, order to)

➡ Come early _____ _____

_____ plenty of time.

Hidden Holes

Think about a hole that you have seen recently. Was it a good hole or
현재완료 경험 용법

a bad hole? If it was a hole in your sock, it was bad. If it was a hole in
조건('만약 ~라면')을 의미   조건('만약 ~라면')을 의미

your shirt for a button, it was good. There are holes everywhere. Some

are so small you may not even notice them. They are well hidden, but
so ~ that: 너무 ~해서 …하다. you 앞에 접속사 that이 생략   hide의 과거분사형으로, 수동태 문장을 나타내기 위해 쓰였음.

many of these small holes are very important and make your life safe.

Take a pen. Look at it carefully. Do you see a small hole in the cap?

Do you know why it is there? The hole in a pen cap can help save
간접의문문(의문사+주어+동사)의 어순

lives. People, especially children, often put small things like pen caps
빈도부사(종종), 일반동사(put) 앞이나 'be동사' 뒤에 위치

in their mouths. Sometimes they even swallow them. This can stop

their breathing and cause death. A famous pen company started putting

a small hole in their pen caps. The hole in the cap lets air pass through
사역동사 let(~하게 하다): 목적격 보어 자리에 동사원형만 올 수 있다.

and has saved lives.
life의 복수형

recently 최근에
notice 알아채다. 의식하다
hide 숨기다. 숨다
especially 특히
swallow 삼키다
breathing 숨. 호흡
cause ~을 야기하다. 초래하다
death 죽음
pass through 거쳐 지나가다. 통과하다

📎 확인문제

● 다음 문장이 본문의 내용과 일치하면 T, 일치하지 않으면 F를 쓰시오.

1   If there is a hole in your sock, it is a bad hole. ☐

2   Many of the holes are so small that they aren't important. ☐

3   The hole in a pen cap can help save lives. ☐

4   Sometimes children even swallow large things. ☐

5   What children swallow can stop their breathing and cause death. ☐

6   Air can't pass through the hole in the cap. ☐

If you look around, you will see other holes that play a helpful role in
주격 관계대명사   play a role: 역할을 하다

your life. If you have ever cooked anything in a pot with a lid, perhaps
현재완료 경험 용법

you noticed a small hole in the lid. This hole, too, is there for safety.

When cooking something in a pot with a lid, the pressure inside the
= When you cook. 접속사가 있는 분사구문   'the pressure'를 수식하는 형용사구

pot builds up. The water inside would quickly boil over if the lid did
가정법 과거: if+주어+동사(과거형), 주어+조동사(과거형)+동사원형, 현재 사실에 반대되는 상황을 가정하는 문장

not have that hole. The hole lets steam out and keeps the water from
keep A from -ing: A가 ~하는 것을 막다

coming out.

Have you ever been on an airplane? Wasn't it exciting to look out the
수사의문문: 수사의문문은 강한 반어적 표현으로 부정형 수사의문문은 강한 긍정의 뜻을 포함한다.

window and see the world below? Surprisingly, there was a small hole
문장 전체를 수식하는 부사

in your window. Airplane windows are made up of three panes. There
~로 이루어지다

is a hole in the middle pane. It balances the air pressure. Without this
가주어   without+명사구, 주어+조동사(과거형)+동사원형: 가정법 과거

little hole, airplane windows might break in an emergency. The hole

also prevents the window from fogging up so that you can enjoy that
prevent A from -ing: A가 ~하지 않게 막다   so that … can ~: …가 ~할 수 있도록(목적)

fantastic view.

There are many more products that have small hidden holes. In the

future, when you see a little hole in something, ask yourself why it is

there. Maybe it is the result of a careful design to make your life safer.
to부정사의 형용사적 용법

lid 뚜껑

perhaps 아마, 어쩌면

pressure 압력

quickly 빨리, 빠르게

boil 끓다, 끓이다

steam 증기, 김

build up 점점 커지다

surprisingly 놀랍게도

pane 판유리

balance 균형을 유지하다

emergency 비상(사태)

prevent (~가 …하는 것을) 막다, 예방하다

fantastic 환상적인

product 생산물, 상품

fog up 김이 서리다

확인문제

● 다음 문장이 본문의 내용과 일치하면 T, 일치하지 않으면 F를 쓰시오.

1   All around you, there are other holes that play a helpful role in your life. ☐

2   When you cook something in a pot without a lid, the pressure inside the pot builds up. ☐

3   Thanks to a hole in the lid of a pot, steam can escape through it. ☐

4   There is a hole in the inner pane of airplane windows. ☐

5   The hole in the pane balances the air pressure. ☐

6   The hole in the airplane windows is too small to prevent the airplane windows from breaking in an emergency. ☐

● 우리말을 참고하여 빈칸에 알맞은 말을 쓰시오.

1 _____ Holes

2 Think about a hole that you _____ _____ _____.

3 Was it a _____ hole or a _____ hole?

4 If it was a hole _____ _____ _____, it was bad.

5 If it was a hole in your shirt _____ _____ _____, it was good.

6 There are holes _____.

7 Some are _____ _____ you may not even notice them.

8 They are _____ _____, but many of these small holes are very important and _____ _____ _____ _____.

9 _____ a pen.

10 _____ _____ it carefully.

11 Do you see _____ _____ _____ in the cap?

12 Do you know _____ _____ _____ _____?

13 The hole in a pen cap can _____ _____ _____.

14 People, especially children, often _____ small things like pen caps _____ their mouths.

15 Sometimes they even _____ _____.

16 This can _____ _____ _____ and cause death.

17 A famous pen company started _____ _____ _____ _____ in their pen caps.

18 The hole in the cap lets air _____ _____ and has saved lives.

1	숨겨진 구멍들
2	여러분이 최근에 본 구멍에 대해 생각해 보라.
3	그것은 좋은 구멍이었는가, 아니면 나쁜 구멍이었는가?
4	만약 그것이 여러분의 양말에 있는 구멍이었다면, 그것은 좋지 않은 것이었다.
5	만약 그것이 단추를 위해 셔츠에 있는 구멍이었다면, 그것은 좋은 것이었다.
6	구멍은 어디에나 있다.
7	어떤 것들은 너무 작아서 인지하지 못할 수도 있다.
8	그것들은 잘 숨겨져 있지만, 이 작은 구멍들 중 많은 것들이 매우 중요하고 여러분의 삶을 안전하게 해 준다.
9	펜을 꺼내라.
10	그것을 자세히 관찰해 보라.
11	뚜껑에 작은 구멍이 보이는가?
12	여러분은 왜 거기에 구멍이 있는지 아는가?
13	펜 뚜껑에 있는 구멍이 생명을 구하는 데 도움을 줄 수 있기 때문이다.
14	사람들, 특히 아이들은 종종 펜 뚜껑 같은 작은 것들을 그들의 입에 넣는다.
15	때때로 그들은 심지어 그것들을 삼키기도 한다.
16	이것은 그들의 호흡을 막고 죽음을 초래할 수도 있다.
17	유명한 펜 회사가 자사의 펜 뚜껑에 작은 구멍을 넣기 시작했다.
18	뚜껑에 있는 그 구멍은 공기를 통하게 해 주고 생명들을 구했다.

19 If you look around, you will see other holes that _____ _____ _____ _____ in your life.

20 If you have ever cooked anything in a pot _____ _____ _____, perhaps you _____ a small hole in the lid.

21 This hole, too, is there _____ _____.

22 _____ _____ something in a pot with a lid, the pressure inside the pot _____ _____.

23 The water inside would quickly _____ _____ if the lid did not have that hole.

24 The hole lets steam out and _____ the water _____ _____ out.

25 _____ you ever _____ on an airplane?

26 _____ _____ _____ to look out the window and see the world below?

27 _____, there was a small hole in your window.

28 Airplane windows _____ _____ _____ _____ three panes.

29 There is a hole _____ _____ _____ _____ _____.

30 It _____ the air pressure.

31 _____ this little hole, airplane windows might break _____ _____ _____.

32 The hole also _____ the window _____ _____ _____ so that you can enjoy that fantastic view.

33 There are many more products _____ _____ small hidden holes.

34 In the future, when you see a little hole in something, ask yourself _____ _____ _____ _____.

35 Maybe it is the result of a careful design _____ _____ _____ _____ _____.

19 여러분이 주위를 둘러본다면, 여러분의 생활에 도움을 주는 다른 구멍들을 보게 될 것이다.

20 만약 여러분이 뚜껑 있는 냄비에 어떤 것을 요리해 본 적이 있다면, 아마도 여러분은 뚜껑에 작은 구멍이 있다는 것을 알아챘을 수도 있다.

21 이 구멍 역시 안전을 위해 존재한다.

22 뚜껑이 있는 냄비에 무언가를 요리할 때, 냄비 안쪽의 압력이 상승한다.

23 만약 뚜껑에 그 구멍이 없다면, 그 안의 물은 금방 끓어 넘칠 것이다.

24 그 구멍이 수증기를 나가게 해 주고 물이 밖으로 넘치는 것을 막아 준다.

25 비행기를 타 본 적이 있는가?

26 창밖을 내다보고 아래에 있는 세상을 보는 것이 신나지 않았는가?

27 놀랍게도, 여러분의 창문에는 작은 구멍이 하나 있었다.

28 비행기 창문은 세 개의 유리판으로 구성되어 있다.

29 그 중간 유리판에 구멍이 있다.

30 그것은 기압의 균형을 맞춰 준다.

31 이 작은 구멍이 없다면, 비행기 창문은 비상시에 깨질 수 있다.

32 그 구멍은 또한, 멋진 경치를 즐길 수 있도록 창문에 김이 서리는 것을 막아 준다.

33 숨겨진 작은 구멍들이 있는 더 많은 제품들이 있다.

34 앞으로, 여러분이 어떤 물건에서 작은 구멍을 본다면, 왜 그것이 거기에 있는지 자신에게 물어보라.

35 아마도 그것은 여러분의 삶을 더 안전하게 만들려는 사려 깊은 디자인의 결과일 것이다.

● 우리말을 참고하여 본문을 영작하시오.

1 숨겨진 구멍들
➡ _____

2 여러분이 최근에 본 구멍에 대해 생각해 보라.
➡ _____

3 그것은 좋은 구멍이었는가, 아니면 나쁜 구멍이었는가?
➡ _____

4 만약 그것이 여러분의 양말에 있는 구멍이었다면, 그것은 좋지 않은 것이었다.
➡ _____

5 만약 그것이 단추를 위해 셔츠에 있는 구멍이었다면, 그것은 좋은 것이었다.
➡ _____

6 구멍은 어디에나 있다.
➡ _____

7 어떤 것들은 너무 작아서 인지하지 못할 수도 있다.
➡ _____

8 그것들은 잘 숨겨져 있지만, 이 작은 구멍들 중 많은 것들이 매우 중요하고 여러분의 삶을 안전하게 해 준다.
➡ _____

9 펜을 꺼내라.
➡ _____

10 그것을 자세히 관찰해 보라.
➡ _____

11 뚜껑에 작은 구멍이 보이는가?
➡ _____

12 여러분은 왜 거기에 구멍이 있는지 아는가?
➡ _____

13 펜 뚜껑에 있는 구멍이 생명을 구하는 데 도움을 줄 수 있기 때문이다.
➡ _____

14 사람들, 특히 아이들은 종종 펜 뚜껑 같은 작은 것들을 그들의 입에 넣는다.
➡ _____

15 때때로 그들은 심지어 그것들을 삼키기도 한다.
➡ _____

16 이것은 그들의 호흡을 막고 죽음을 초래할 수도 있다.
➡ _____

17 유명한 펜 회사가 자사의 펜 뚜껑에 작은 구멍을 넣기 시작했다.
➡ _____

18 뚜껑에 있는 그 구멍은 공기를 통하게 해 주고 생명들을 구했다.
➡ _____

19 여러분이 주위를 둘러본다면, 여러분의 생활에 도움을 주는 다른 구멍들을 보게 될 것이다.

➡ _____

20 만약 여러분이 뚜껑 있는 냄비에 어떤 것을 요리해 본 적이 있다면, 아마도 여러분은 뚜껑에 작은 구멍이 있다는 것을 알아챘을 수도 있다.

➡ _____

21 이 구멍 역시 안전을 위해 존재한다.

➡ _____

22 뚜껑이 있는 냄비에 무언가를 요리할 때, 냄비 안쪽의 압력이 상승한다.

➡ _____

23 만약 뚜껑에 그 구멍이 없다면, 그 안의 물은 금방 끓어 넘칠 것이다.

➡ _____

24 그 구멍이 수증기를 나가게 해 주고 물이 밖으로 넘치는 것을 막아 준다.

➡ _____

25 비행기를 타 본 적이 있는가?

➡ _____

26 창밖을 내다보고 아래에 있는 세상을 보는 것이 신나지 않았는가?

➡ _____

27 놀랍게도, 여러분의 창문에는 작은 구멍이 하나 있었다.

➡ _____

28 비행기 창문은 세 개의 유리판으로 구성되어 있다.

➡ _____

29 그 중간 유리판에 구멍이 있다.

➡ _____

30 그것은 기압의 균형을 맞춰 준다.

➡ _____

31 이 작은 구멍이 없다면, 비행기 창문은 비상시에 깨질 수 있다.

➡ _____

32 그 구멍은 또한, 멋진 경치를 즐길 수 있도록 창문에 김이 서리는 것을 막아 준다.

➡ _____

33 숨겨진 작은 구멍들이 있는 더 많은 제품들이 있다.

➡ _____

34 앞으로, 여러분이 어떤 물건에서 작은 구멍을 본다면, 왜 그것이 거기에 있는지 자신에게 물어보라.

➡ _____

35 아마도 그것은 여러분의 삶을 더 안전하게 만들려는 사려 깊은 디자인의 결과일 것이다.

➡ _____

[01~03] 다음 글을 읽고 물음에 답하시오.

Think about a hole that you have seen recently. (①) Was it a good hole or a bad hole? (②) If it was a hole in your sock, it was bad. (③) If it was a hole in your shirt for a button, it was good. (④) Some are so small you may not even notice them. (⑤) They are well hidden, but many of these small holes are very important and make your life safe.

01 위 글의 흐름으로 보아, 주어진 문장이 들어가기에 가장 적절한 곳은?

> There are holes everywhere.

①   ②   ③   ④   ⑤

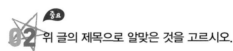

02 위 글의 제목으로 알맞은 것을 고르시오.

① Have You Ever Seen a Hole?
② Hidden but Important Holes
③ A Good Hole VS a Bad Hole
④ Oops, a Hole in the Sock
⑤ The Various Functions of Holes

03 According to the passage, which is NOT true?

① A hole in your sock is a bad hole.
② A hole in your shirt for a button is a good hole.
③ You can find holes everywhere.
④ Some holes are so small that you may not even notice them.
⑤ Many of the holes are so small that it can't keep your life safe.

[04~06] 다음 글을 읽고 물음에 답하시오.

Take a pen. Look at it carefully. Do you see a small hole in the cap? Do you know why it is there? The hole in a pen cap can help save lives. People, especially ①children, often put small things like pen caps in ②their mouths. ⓐSometimes ③they even swallow them. This can stop ④their breathing and cause death. A famous pen company started putting a small hole in ⑤their pen caps. The hole in the cap lets air pass through and has saved lives.

04 밑줄 친 ①~⑤ 중에서 가리키는 대상이 나머지 넷과 다른 것은?

①   ②   ③   ④   ⑤

05 위 글의 밑줄 친 ⓐSometimes와 바꿔 쓸 수 없는 말을 고르시오.

① Once in a while   ② Occasionally
③ From time to time ④ Frequently
⑤ Now and then

06 위 글의 주제로 알맞은 것을 고르시오.

① the size of the hole in the cap
② the role of the hole in the cap
③ the dangerous habit of children
④ the reason people stop their breathing
⑤ the strange sound of the air passing through the hole

[07~09] 다음 글을 읽고 물음에 답하시오.

If you look around, you will see other holes (A)that play a helpful role in your life. If you have ever cooked anything in a pot with a lid, perhaps you noticed a small hole in the lid. This hole, too, is there for ⓐ . When cooking something in a pot with a lid, the pressure inside the pot builds up. The water inside would quickly boil over if the lid did not have that hole. The hole lets steam out and (B)keeps the water from coming out.

서답형

07 주어진 영영풀이를 참고하여 빈칸 ⓐ에 철자 s로 시작하는 단어를 쓰시오.

> a state of being safe from harm or danger

➡ _____

08 위 글의 밑줄 친 (A)that과 문법적 쓰임이 같은 것을 모두 고르시오.

① He is the greatest novelist that has ever lived.

② It's true that we were a little late.

③ Are you sure she's that young?

④ There was no hope that she would recover her health.

⑤ This is the watch that I bought yesterday.

중요

09 위 글의 밑줄 친 (B)keeps와 바꿔 쓸 수 있는 말을 모두 고르시오.

① protects   ② stops

③ prevents   ④ denies

⑤ damages

[10~12] 다음 글을 읽고 물음에 답하시오.

ⓐHave you ever been on an airplane? Wasn't it exciting to look out the window and see the world below? Surprisingly, there was a small hole in your window. Airplane windows ⓑare made up of three panes. There is a hole in the middle pane. It balances the air pressure. Without this little hole, airplane windows might break in an emergency. The hole also prevents the window from fogging up so that you can enjoy that fantastic view.

There are many more products that have small hidden holes. ⓒIn the future, when you will see a little hole in something, ask yourself why it is there. Maybe it is the result of a careful design to make your life safer.

10 아래 〈보기〉에서 위 글의 밑줄 친 문장 ⓐ의 현재완료와 용법이 다른 것의 개수를 고르시오.

> ┤ 보기 ├
> ① She has already left for Paris.
> ② I have heard about the project before.
> ③ Mr. Smith has just bought this sweater.
> ④ I have known him for three years.
> ⑤ We have sold out all the tickets, so there are no more tickets available.

① 1개   ② 2개   ③ 3개   ④ 4개   ⑤ 5개

11 위 글의 밑줄 친 ⓑare made up of와 바꿔 쓸 수 있는 말을 모두 고르시오.

① are composed of   ② consist of

③ consist in   ④ deal with

⑤ are consisted of

서답형

12 위 글의 밑줄 친 ⓒ에서 어법상 틀린 부분을 찾아 고치시오.

_____ ➡ _____

[13~15] 다음 글을 읽고 물음에 답하시오.

If you look around, you will see (A)[another / other] holes that play a helpful ⓐrole in your life. If you have ever cooked anything in a pot with a lid, perhaps you noticed a small hole in the lid. This hole, too, is there for safety. When (B)[cooking / cooked] something in a pot with a lid, the pressure _____ⓑ_____ the pot builds up. The water inside would quickly boil over if the lid did not have that hole. The hole lets steam (C)[in / out] and keeps the water _____ⓒ_____ coming out.

서답형

13 위 글의 괄호 (A)~(C)에서 문맥이나 어법상 알맞은 낱말을 골라 쓰시오.

(A) _____ (B) _____ (C) _____

서답형

14 위 글의 밑줄 친 ⓐrole과 바꿔 쓸 수 있는 한 단어를 쓰시오.

➡ _____

15 위 글의 빈칸 ⓑ와 ⓒ에 들어갈 전치사가 바르게 짝지어진 것은?

	ⓑ	ⓒ		ⓑ	ⓒ
①	inside	– on	②	outside	– to
③	on	– to	④	inside	– from
⑤	outside	– from			

16 주어진 글 다음에 이어질 글의 순서로 가장 적절한 것은?

Take a pen. Look at it carefully. Do you see a small hole in the cap?

(A) This can stop their breathing and cause death. A famous pen company started putting a small hole in their pen caps. The hole in the cap lets air pass through and has saved lives.
(B) Do you know why it is there? The hole in a pen cap can help save lives.
(C) People, especially children, often put small things like pen caps in their mouths. Sometimes they even swallow them.

① (A) – (C) – (B) ② (B) – (A) – (C)
③ (B) – (C) – (A) ④ (C) – (A) – (B)
⑤ (C) – (B) – (A)

[17~19] 다음 글을 읽고 물음에 답하시오.

Think about a hole that you have seen recently. Was it a good hole or a bad hole? If it was a hole in your sock, it was bad. If it was a hole in your shirt for a button, it was good. There are holes everywhere. ⓐ어떤 것들은 너무 작아서 인지하지 못할 수도 있다. They are well hidden, but ⓑmany of these small holes are very important and make your life safely.

서답형

17 위 글의 밑줄 친 ⓐ의 우리말에 맞게 주어진 어휘를 알맞게 배열하시오.

notice / small / may / are / them / not / you / even / some / so

➡ _____

서답형

18 위 글의 밑줄 친 ⓑ에서 어법상 틀린 부분을 찾아 고치시오.

_____ ➡ _____

중요

19 Which question CANNOT be answered after reading the passage?

① If a hole is in your sock, is it a good hole?

② If a hole is in your shirt for a button, is it a good hole?

③ Where can we find holes?

④ Are the holes that we see around us all hidden?

⑤ How many kinds of holes are there in the world?

[20~21] 다음 글을 읽고 물음에 답하시오.

Take a pen. Look ____ⓐ____ it carefully. Do you see a small hole in the cap? Do you know why it is there? The hole in a pen cap can help (A)save lives. People, especially children, often put small things like pen caps ____ⓑ____ their mouths. Sometimes they even swallow them. This can stop their breathing and cause death. A famous pen company started putting a small hole in their pen caps. The hole in the cap lets air pass through and has saved lives.

20 위 글의 빈칸 ⓐ와 ⓑ에 들어갈 전치사가 바르게 짝지어진 것은?

	ⓐ	ⓑ		ⓐ	ⓑ
①	for	to	②	at	on
③	at	in	④	for	on
⑤	on	in			

중요

21 위 글의 밑줄 친 (A)save와 같은 의미로 쓰인 것을 고르시오.

① We'll eat some now and save some for tomorrow.

② You should save a little each week.

③ Doctors were unable to save her.

④ We should try to save water.

⑤ Save data frequently.

[22~23] 다음 글을 읽고 물음에 답하시오.

Have you ever been on an airplane? Wasn't ⓐit exciting to look out the window and see the world below? Surprisingly, there was a small hole in your window. Airplane windows are made up of three panes. There is a hole in the middle pane. ⓑIt balances the air pressure. Without this little hole, airplane windows might break in an emergency. The hole also prevents the window from fogging up so that you can enjoy that fantastic view.

22 위 글의 밑줄 친 ⓐit과 문법적 쓰임이 같은 것을 고르시오.

① I think it strange that she doesn't want to go.

② It's two miles from here to the beach.

③ It is not easy to climb the mountain.

④ When the factory closes, it will mean 500 people losing their jobs.

⑤ It was she that told me the story.

서답형

23 위 글의 밑줄 친 ⓑit이 가리키는 것을 영어로 쓰시오.

➡ _____

[01~04] 다음 글을 읽고 물음에 답하시오.

Think about a hole that you have seen recently. Was (A)it a good hole or a bad hole? If it was a hole in your sock, it was bad. If it was a hole in your shirt for a button, it was good. There are holes everywhere. (B)Some are so small you may not even notice them. They are well ⓐ , but many of these small holes are very important and make your life safe.

01 위 글의 빈칸 ⓐ에 hide를 알맞은 형태로 쓰시오.

➡ _____

02 위 글의 밑줄 친 (A)it이 가리키는 것을 본문에서 찾아 쓰시오.

➡ _____

03 위 글의 밑줄 친 문장 (B)에 생략된 접속사를 넣어 문장을 다시 쓰시오.

➡ _____

04 위 글의 내용을 다음과 같이 정리하고자 한다. 빈칸 (A)~(C)에 들어갈 알맞은 단어를 본문에서 찾아 쓰시오.

Everywhere you can find holes. Some of which are too (A)_____ to notice. But many of these small holes are very (B)_____ ones and thanks to them, your life becomes (C)_____.

[05~07] 다음 글을 읽고 물음에 답하시오.

If you look around, you will see other holes that play a helpful role in your life. If you have ever cooked anything in a pot with a lid, perhaps you noticed a small hole in the lid. This hole, too, is there for safety. ⓐ When cooking something in a pot with a lid, the pressure inside the pot builds up. ⓑThe water inside would quickly boil over if the lid did not have that hole. The hole lets steam out and keeps the water from coming out.

05 위 글의 밑줄 친 분사구문 ⓐ를 다음과 같이 바꿔 쓸 때 빈칸에 들어갈 알맞은 말을 두 단어로 쓰시오.

When _____ _____ something in a pot with a lid

06 위 글의 밑줄 친 ⓑ를 접속사 as를 사용하여 직설법으로 고치시오.

➡ _____
_____

07 다음 빈칸 (A)와 (B)에 알맞은 단어를 넣어 '냄비 뚜껑에 있는 작은 구멍의 역할'을 완성하시오.

When you cook something in a pot with a lid, the water inside doesn't quickly boil over thanks to the (A)_____ _____ in the lid. It lets (B)_____ and keeps the water from coming out.

[08~11] 다음 글을 읽고 물음에 답하시오.

Take a pen. Look at it carefully. Do you see a small hole in the cap? Do you know why ⓐ it is there? ⓑ펜 뚜껑에 있는 구멍이 생명을 구하는 데 도움을 줄 수 있기 때문이다. People, especially children, often put small things like pen caps in their mouths. Sometimes they even swallow them. This can stop their breathing and cause death. A famous pen company started putting a small hole in their pen caps. ⓒThe hole in the cap lets air pass through and has saved lives.

08 위 글의 밑줄 친 ⓐit이 가리키는 것을 본문에서 찾아 쓰시오.

➡ _____

중요

09 위 글의 밑줄 친 ⓑ의 우리말에 맞게 주어진 어휘를 알맞게 배열하시오.

can / in a pen cap / help / lives / the hole / save

➡ _____

10 위 글의 밑줄 친 ⓒ를 다음과 같이 바꿔 쓸 때 빈칸에 들어갈 알맞은 말을 두 단어로 쓰시오.

The hole in the cap allows air _____ _____ through and has saved lives.

고난이도

11 How can the hole in the pen cap save a life if someone swallows a pen cap? Fill in the blanks (A) and (B) with suitable words.

If someone swallows a pen cap, it can stop the person's (A)_____ and cause death. If there is a hole in the pen cap, however, it lets (B)_____ pass through and can save a life.

[12~14] 다음 글을 읽고 물음에 답하시오.

Have you ever been on an airplane? Wasn't it exciting to look out the window and (A)[saw / see] the world below? Surprisingly, there was a small hole in your window. Airplane windows are made up of three panes. There is a hole in the middle pane. It balances the air (B)[pleasure / pressure]. ⓐWithout this little hole, airplane windows might break in an (C)[emergence / emergency]. The hole also prevents the window from fogging up so that you can enjoy that fantastic view.

There are many more products that have small hidden holes. In the future, when you see a little hole in something, ask yourself why it is there. Maybe it is the result of a careful design to make your life safer.

중요

12 위 글의 괄호 (A)~(C)에서 문맥이나 어법상 알맞은 낱말을 골라 쓰시오.

(A) _____ (B) _____ (C) _____

13 위 글의 밑줄 친 ⓐ를 If로 시작하여 고칠 때, 빈칸에 들어갈 알맞은 말을 쓰시오.

If _____ _____ _____ _____ this little hole,

14 다음 빈칸 (A)와 (B)에 알맞은 단어를 넣어 '비행기 창문'에 대한 소개를 완성하시오.

Airplane windows consist of (A)_____ _____ and a hole in the middle pane balances the (B)_____ _____.

교과서

구석구석

After You Read B

1. It lets the air <u>pass</u> through even when people swallow the pen cap.
사역동사 'let'의 목적격 보어 자리에 동사원형만 올 수 있다.

2. It balances the <u>air pressures</u>.
기압

3. It lets steam out and <u>prevents</u> the water in the pot <u>from boiling</u> over.
prevent A from –ing: A가 ~하는 것을 막다

구문해설 • swallow: 삼키다 • pass through: 거쳐 지나가다, 통과하다 • balance: 균형을 유지하다
• steam: 증기, 김 • boil: 끓다, 끓이다

Work Together

Sweet Dream Helmet

This invention <u>helps people dream</u> sweet dreams. <u>If you use the Sweet Dream</u>
사역동사+목적어+목적격보어   단순 조건문 If S 현재시제 동사. S will 동사원형

<u>Helmet, you will have</u> a sweet dream every night. You can even select the type

of <u>dream you</u> want to dream <u>so that you can</u> have different experiences <u>while</u>
dream (that) you   so that S can 동사원형 ~: ~하기 위해서   ~하는 동안

you are sleeping.

구문해설 • invention: 발명(품) • select: 고르다, 선택하다 • so that: ~하도록 • experience: 경험
• while: ~하는 동안

Writing Workshop

A Refrigerator

Can you imagine without a refrigerator? We use <u>it</u> every day <u>so that we can</u>
= a refrigerator   ~할 수 있도록, ~하기 위해

<u>keep food cool and fresh</u>. In 1755, William Cullen invented the first form of
keep+목적어+형용사: ~을 …하게 유지하다

the refrigerator. After that, it developed <u>through the years</u> and <u>has become</u> a
수년에 걸쳐   현재완료

necessary part of modern life. <u>If we did</u> not have refrigerators in today's world,
가정법 과거: If+주어+동사의 과거형 ~, 주어+조동사의 과거형+동사원형 …

we <u>would</u> not <u>be</u> able to enjoy ice cream on hot summer days.

구문해설 • imagine: 상상하다 • invent: 발명하다 • develop: 발전하다 • necessary: 필요한
• modern: 현대의 • be able to: ~할 수 있다

해석

1. 사람들이 펜 뚜껑을 삼킬 때도 그것은 공기를 통하게 해 준다.
2. 그것은 기압의 균형을 맞춰 준다.
3. 그것은 수증기를 나가게 해 주고 냄비 안의 물이 끓어 넘치는 것을 막아 준다.

단 잠 헬멧
이 발명품은 사람들이 단 잠을 잘 수 있도록 돕는다. 만약 단 잠 헬멧을 사용한다면, 당신은 매일 밤 행복한 꿈을 꿀 것입니다. 당신이 잠든 동안 다양한 경험을 할 수 있기 위해 당신은 심지어 당신이 꿈꾸고 싶은 꿈의 형태를 고를 수 있습니다.

냉장고
여러분은 냉장고가 없는 세상을 상상할 수 있나요? 우리는 음식을 차갑고 신선하게 보관하기 위해 이것을 매일 사용합니다. 1755년, 윌리엄 컬런이 초기 형태의 냉장고를 발명했습니다. 그 이후, 이것은 수년 동안 발전했고, 현대의 생활에서 필수적인 부분이 되었습니다. 만약 우리에게 오늘날 냉장고가 없다면, 더운 여름날 아이스크림을 즐겨 먹을 수 없을 것입니다.

Words & Expressions

01 다음 짝지어진 단어의 관계가 같도록 빈칸에 알맞은 말을 쓰시오.

> repair : mend = perhaps : _____

02 다음 중 밑줄 친 부분의 뜻풀이가 바르지 <u>않은</u> 것은?

① Watch the pot! The soup is about to <u>boil over</u> soon. (끓어 넘치다)
② The temperature difference makes the windows <u>fog up</u>. (김이 서리다)
③ You should <u>look out</u> for yourself from now on. (내다보다)
④ The fire extinguisher should only be used <u>in an emergency</u>. (비상 상황에서)
⑤ There will be a chance for parents to <u>look around</u> the school. (주위를 둘러보다)

03 다음 주어진 영영풀이가 가리키는 단어는?

> something that is made to be sold, usually something that is produced by an industrial process

① clothes　② product　③ present
④ pressure　⑤ invention

04 다음 우리말을 주어진 단어를 이용하여 영작하시오.

(1) 그것을 파손되지 않게 세심하게 포장하십시오.
(wrap, protect, carefully, against breakage)
➡ _____

(2) 우리들 중 몇몇은 우리의 재능을 잘 숨기라는 말을 종종 듣는다. (often, keep, well hidden)
➡ _____
_____

05 다음 주어진 문장의 밑줄 친 *notice*와 같은 의미로 쓰인 것은?

> The first thing you will <u>notice</u> about the room is the smell.

① Don't take any <u>notice</u> of his words.
② Prices may be changed without any <u>notice</u>.
③ You may <u>notice</u> redness and swelling after the injection.
④ There is a <u>notice</u> on the board saying the class is cancelled.
⑤ You must give one month's <u>notice</u>.

06 다음 빈칸에 들어갈 말로 가장 적절한 것은?

> The study suggests that salt may _____ in childhood obesity.

① be known for　② play a role
③ be made up of　④ think about
⑤ look at

Conversation

[07~09] 다음 대화를 읽고 물음에 답하시오.

B: Hi, Kate. Today's Saturday, so what about (A)[to go / going] to the Einstein Science Park today?

G: That sounds like a good idea. I heard that they (B)[have / had] special programs on Saturdays. I wonder what they are.

B: Let me see.... I saw an advertisement in the newspaper. Here it is.

G: What (C)[did / does] it say?

B: It says that today they have two shows: the Smart Design Show and the International Drone Show in Einstein Hall 101.

G: They both sound fantastic.

B: I'll call them and ask what time they start.

07 위 대화의 괄호 (A)~(C)에 들어갈 말이 바르게 짝지어진 것은?

      (A) (B)   (C)
① to go – had – did
② going – have – did
③ to go – have – did
④ going – have – does
⑤ to go – had – does

08 What will B do afterwards? (13 words)

➡ _____

    _____

09 Where does the two shows take place? (7 words)

➡ _____

10 다음 대화의 밑줄 친 부분의 의도로 가장 적절한 것은?

> A: <u>I wonder what the first plane looked like.</u>
>
> B: Look! There is a model. It looked like a big bird.

① 묘사하기   ② 조사하기
③ 감정 표현하기   ④ 선호 표현하기
⑤ 궁금증 표현하기

[11~13] 다음 대화를 읽고 물음에 답하시오.

G: We're going on a field trip tomorrow to the Invention Museum.

B: ① I've heard that (A)<u>it</u> has a lot of creative inventions. ②

G: ③ That's why I'm so excited. How about planning the tour before we go?

B: ④ Let me see.... I have the school letter and a map of the museum.

G: ⑤ Perfect. Let's get started.

11 위 대화의 ①~⑤ 중에서 주어진 문장이 들어가기에 가장 적절한 곳은?

> Good idea.

①   ②   ③   ④   ⑤

12 위 대화를 읽고 G의 심정으로 가장 적절한 것은?

① exhausted   ② terrified
③ disappointed   ④ touched
⑤ excited

13 위 대화의 밑줄 친 (A)it이 가리키는 것을 쓰시오.

➡ _____

14 어법상 빈칸에 들어갈 말로 적절한 것을 고르시오.

> If today's top rock singer released his or her next piece on the Internet, it would _____ like playing in a theater with 20 million seats.

① have been ② had been
③ was ④ were
⑤ be

15 다음 우리말에 맞게 괄호 안의 단어를 활용하여 빈칸을 채우시오.

> 나는 오늘 아침 피곤하지 않기 위해서 일찍 잠자리에 들었다. (so)
> ➡ _____ I wouldn't be tired this morning.

16 다음 중 so that 구문이 어법상 나머지와 다른 것을 고르시오.

① I stood the little girl on a chair <u>so that</u> she could see well.
② I was excited, <u>so that</u> I couldn't get to sleep.
③ The criminal went off <u>so that</u> no one could find him.
④ We have two ears and one mouth <u>so that</u> we can listen twice as much as we speak.
⑤ Jane has come here <u>so that</u> she can see what happened with her own eyes.

17 우리말과 같은 뜻이 되도록 괄호 안의 어휘를 배열하여 영작하시오.

> 내가 Robinson Crusoe라면 낚시를 하러 가기 위해 보트를 만들 거야. (were, would, I, Robinson Crusoe, If, I, make, go, boat, a, to, fishing)

➡ _____

_____

18 다음 우리말에 맞게 괄호 안의 단어를 활용하여 영작하시오.

> 그녀는 자기의 개들을 마치 자기의 아이들인 것처럼 사랑한다. (be, as if, kids)

➡ _____

19 우리말에 맞게 괄호 안의 어휘들을 배열하여 영작할 때, 5번째 단어를 쓰시오.

> 내 친구는 그의 어머니가 노년을 즐길 수 있도록 열심히 일했다. (worked, that, my, his, mother, friend, hard, so, her, might, enjoy, old, age)

➡ _____

Reading

[20~22] 다음 글을 읽고 물음에 답하시오.

Think about a hole that you ⓐhave seen recently. Was it a good hole or a bad hole? If it was a hole in your sock, it was bad. If it was a hole in your shirt for a button, it was good. There are holes everywhere. Some are so small you may not even notice them. They are well hidden, but many of these small holes are very important and make your life safe.

20 위 글의 밑줄 친 ⓐhave seen과 현재완료의 용법이 같은 것을 모두 고르시오.

① I have never visited Paris.
② I have studied English since the third grade of elementary school.
③ Have the children finished their lunch yet?
④ She has watched the movie twice.
⑤ It has just stopped snowing.

21 다음 빈칸에 알맞은 단어를 넣어 '좋은 구멍'의 한 예를 완성하시오.

> If a hole is in your shirt for _____
> _____, it is a good hole.

➡ _____

22 What's the reason why you may not even notice holes? Fill in the blank with a suitable word.

> Because some of the holes are too _____ for you to notice.

➡ _____

[23~24] 다음 글을 읽고 물음에 답하시오.

If you look around, you will see other holes that play a helpful role in your life. If you have ever cooked anything in a pot with a lid, perhaps you noticed a small hole in the lid. This hole, too, is ⓐthere for safety. When cooking something in a pot with a lid, the pressure inside the pot builds up. The water inside would quickly boil over if the lid did not have that hole. The hole lets steam out and keeps the water from coming out.

23 위 글의 밑줄 친 ⓐthere가 지칭하는 것을 본문에서 찾아 쓰시오.

➡ _____

24 According to the passage, which is NOT true?

① All around you, there are other holes that play a helpful role in your life.
② A small hole in the lid of a pot is also there for safety.
③ When you cook something in a pot without a lid, the pressure inside the pot builds up.
④ The water inside the pot doesn't quickly boil over as the lid has a hole.
⑤ Thanks to a hole in the lid of a pot, steam can escape through it.

[25~27] 다음 글을 읽고 물음에 답하시오.

Have you ever been on an airplane? (①) Wasn't it exciting to look out the window and see the world below? (②) Surprisingly, there was a small hole in your window. (③) Airplane windows are made up of three panes. (④) It balances the air pressure. (⑤) Without this little hole, airplane windows might break in an emergency. The hole also prevents the window from fogging up so that you can enjoy that fantastic view.

25 위 글의 흐름으로 보아, 주어진 문장이 들어가기에 가장 적절한 곳은?

There is a hole in the middle pane.

①   ②   ③   ④   ⑤

26 위 글의 제목으로 알맞은 것을 고르시오.

① Have You Ever Been on an Airplane?
② The Exciting View from the Airplane
③ What Does the Hole in the Middle Pane Do?
④ Wow! Airplane Windows Are Made Up of Three Panes!
⑤ Many Products That Have Small Hidden Holes

27 Which question CANNOT be answered after reading the passage?

① How many panes do airplane windows consist of?
② Why are airplane windows made up of three panes?
③ Where is a small hole in the three panes of airplane windows?
④ If it were not for a small hole in the airplane windows, would it be possible to balance the air pressure in an emergency?
⑤ What prevents the window from fogging up in an airplane?

[28~29] 다음 글을 읽고 물음에 답하시오.

A Refrigerator

Can you imagine life without a refrigerator? We use it every day so that we can keep food cool and fresh. In 1755, William Cullen invented the first form of the refrigerator. After ⓐthat, it developed through the years and has become a necessary part of modern life. ⓑIf we did not have refrigerators in today's world, we will not be able to enjoy ice cream on hot summer days.

28 위 글의 밑줄 친 ⓐthat이 가리키는 것을 본문에서 찾아 쓰시오.

➡ _____

_____

29 위 글의 밑줄 친 ⓑ에서 어법상 틀린 부분을 찾아 고치시오.

_____ ➡ _____

출제율 90%

01 다음 영영풀이가 가리키는 것을 고르시오.

> the process to take air into the lungs and let it out again

① death   ② steam   ③ swallow
④ breathing   ⑤ pressure

출제율 95%

02 주어진 문장에 들어갈 단어로 가장 알맞은 것은?

> Doctors say that back pains can be _____ bad posture.

① in front of   ② built up
③ came out   ④ prevented from
⑤ the result of

[03~05] 다음 대화를 읽고 물음에 답하시오.

G: I like these crackers. They're really good.
B: Yeah, me, too. I wonder why crackers have these little holes in them.
G: I don't know. Let me think.... Um... well... maybe it's because the holes make the crackers look tastier.
B: That's possible, but there (A)<u>must</u> be some other reasons.
G: Let's look up crackers on the Internet and see what it says.
B: Okay. Oh, look at this.
G: It says during baking, steam comes out through the holes and (B)<u>that</u> makes the crackers thin.
B: It also says that the holes make the crackers crispy.
G: Wow! (C)그래서 그게 구멍을 갖고 있는 이유구나!

출제율 90%

03 위 대화의 밑줄 친 (A)<u>must</u>와 같은 의미로 쓰인 것은?

① You <u>must</u> finish this work toady.
② I <u>must</u> go to the bank and get some money.
③ You <u>must</u> be hungry after all that walking.
④ Cars <u>must</u> not park in front of the entrance.
⑤ You <u>must</u> not say things like that.

출제율 95%

04 위 대화의 밑줄 친 (B)<u>that</u>이 가리키는 것을 찾아 쓰시오. (6 words)

➡ _____

출제율 90%

05 위 대화의 밑줄 친 (C)의 우리말을 바르게 영작하시오. (6 words)

➡ _____

[06~07] 다음 대화를 읽고 물음에 답하시오.

B: Look at ⓐthis invention. ⓑIt can help us cook without electricity.
G: Is ⓒthat possible? I wonder how ⓓit works.
B: ⓔIt uses sunlight to cook food.
G: Wow. (A)캠핑을 갈 때 그건 정말 도움이 될 것 같아. (when / would / really / that / helpful / you / be / go camping)

출제율 90%

06 위 대화의 밑줄 친 (A)의 우리말에 맞게 주어진 어구를 바르게 나열하시오.

➡ _____

출제율 100%

07 위 대화의 밑줄 친 ⓐ~ⓔ 중 가리키는 것이 <u>다른</u> 하나는?

① ⓐ   ② ⓑ   ③ ⓒ   ④ ⓓ   ⑤ ⓔ

[08~10] 다음 대화를 읽고 물음에 답하시오.

> G: John, look. The school is having an invention competition.
> B: Really? That sounds interesting.
> G: Yeah. You should enter that. You always have great ideas.
> B: Does it say when the competition is?
> G: (A)Let me see.... It says it's November 11. That's two weeks from today.
> B: (B)그 대회에 참가하기 위해 내가 뭘 해야 하는지 궁금해. (have, enter)
> G: It says here you should talk to Mr. Harrison, the science teacher.

출제율 95%

08 위 대화의 밑줄 친 (A)의 의도로 가장 적절한 것은?

① 생각할 시간 요청하기
② 아이디어 요청하기
③ 발명품 살펴보기
④ 지도 살펴보기
⑤ 계획 제안하기

출제율 90%

09 위 대화의 밑줄 친 (B)의 우리말을 주어진 단어를 이용해 바르게 영작하시오. (11 words)

➡ _____

출제율 100%

10 위 대화를 읽고 답할 수 <u>없는</u> 질문은?

① When will the invention competition take place?
② Why did G encourage B to enter the competition?
③ What is the prize for the winner of the competition?
④ What is Mr. Harrison?
⑤ What will B do afterwards?

출제율 90%

11 다음 빈칸에 공통으로 들어갈 말을 쓰시오.

> • I'll go by car _____ I can take more luggage.
> • We left a message with his neighbor _____ he would know we'd called.

➡ _____

출제율 95%

12 다음 우리말에 맞게 괄호 안의 단어를 활용하여 as if 구문으로 영작하시오.

> (millionaire)

(1) 그는 백만장자인 듯이 말한다.

➡ _____

(2) 그는 백만장자인 듯이 말했다.

➡ _____

13 다음 밑줄 친 부분이 나머지 넷과 <u>다른</u> 의미를 지닌 것을 고르시오.

① I wrote a report correctly <u>so that</u> you could understand it.

② Teamwork is required <u>in order to</u> achieve these aims.

③ The grocery store near my house was <u>so</u> crowded <u>that</u> I had to go to another store.

④ I signed up for the fitness club <u>so as to</u> get into shape.

⑤ <u>In order that</u> training should be effective, it must be planned systematically.

14 괄호 안의 단어를 활용하여 우리말에 맞게 빈칸을 채우시오.

(1) 만약 내가 UFO를 본다면 그것을 사진 찍을 텐데. (take)

➡ If I saw a UFO, I _____ of it.

(2) 만약 하나라도 깨지지 않은 화병이 있다면 그것을 송도로 가져갈 수 있을 텐데. (one, have)

➡ _____, I could take it to Songdo.

15 다음 주어진 단어를 활용하여 우리말에 맞게 영작하시오.

나는 그녀가 나에게 연락할 수 있도록 그녀에게 나의 전화번호를 주었다. (so that, contact)

➡ _____

_____

[16~18] 다음 글을 읽고 물음에 답하시오.

Take a pen. Look at it carefully. (①) Do you see a small hole in the cap? (②) The hole in a pen cap can help save lives. (③) People, especially children, often put small things like pen caps in their mouths. (④) Sometimes they even swallow them. (⑤) This can stop their breathing and cause death. A famous pen company started ⓐputting a small hole in their pen caps. The hole in the cap lets air pass through and has saved lives.

16 위 글의 흐름으로 보아, 주어진 문장이 들어가기에 가장 적절한 곳은?

Do you know why it is there?

①   ②   ③   ④   ⑤

17 위 글의 밑줄 친 ⓐputting과 문법적 쓰임이 같은 것을 <u>모두</u> 고르시오.

① Would you mind <u>opening</u> the window?

② His job is <u>selling</u> cars.

③ I found Tom <u>crying</u>.

④ He is good at <u>playing</u> tennis.

⑤ The man <u>working</u> in the garden is my father.

18 위 글을 읽고 알 수 <u>없는</u> 것을 고르시오.

① the reason why a small hole is in the cap of a pen

② the thing people often put in their mouths

③ who started putting a small hole in their pen caps

④ the common material used to make the pen cap

⑤ the function of the hole in the cap

[19~20] 다음 글을 읽고 물음에 답하시오.

If you look around, you will see other holes that play a helpful role in your life. If you have ever cooked anything in a pot with a lid, perhaps you noticed a small hole in the lid. This hole, too, is there for safety. When cooking something in a pot with a lid, the pressure inside the pot builds up. The water inside would quickly boil over if the lid did not have that hole. ⓐ그 구멍이 수증기를 나가게 해 주고 물이 밖으로 넘치는 것을 막아 준다.

19 위 글의 밑줄 친 ⓐ의 우리말에 맞게 주어진 어휘를 이용하여 12 단어로 영작하시오.

> lets, keeps, coming

➡ _____

_____

20 위 글의 주제로 알맞은 것을 고르시오.

① other holes that play a helpful role in your life
② the role of a small hole in the lid of a pot
③ how to cook something in a pot with a lid
④ the increasing pressure inside the pot
⑤ the importance of preventing the water inside the pot from boiling over

[21~23] 다음 글을 읽고 물음에 답하시오.

Have you ever been on an airplane? Wasn't it exciting to look out the window and see the world below? Surprisingly, there was a small hole in your window. Airplane windows are made up of three panes. There is a hole in the middle pane. It balances the air pressure. ⓐ With this little hole, airplane windows might break in an emergency. The hole also prevents the window from fogging up so that you can enjoy that fantastic view.

21 위 글의 밑줄 친 ⓐ에서 흐름상 어색한 부분을 찾아 고치시오.

_____ ➡ _____

22 본문의 내용과 일치하도록 다음 빈칸 (A)와 (B)에 알맞은 단어를 쓰시오.

> Were it not for (A)_____ _____ in the middle pane of airplane windows, you could not enjoy the fantastic view from an airplane because the window would (B)_____ _____.

23 According to the passage, which is NOT true?

① There is a small hole in an airplane window.
② Airplane windows consist of three panes.
③ There is a hole in the inner pane of airplane windows.
④ The hole in the pane balances the air pressure.
⑤ A small hole in the airplane windows can prevent the airplane windows from breaking in an emergency.

[01~02] 다음 대화를 읽고 물음에 답하시오.

> G: We're going on a field trip tomorrow to the Invention Museum.
> B: I've heard that it has a lot of creative inventions.
> G: That's why I'm so excited. How about planning the tour before we go?
> B: Good idea. Let me see.... I have the school letter and a map of the museum.
> G: Perfect. Let's get started.

01 What is the relationship between the speakers? (3 words)

➡ _____

02 What did B hear about the Invention Museum? (10 words)

➡ _____

[03~04] 다음 글을 읽고 물음에 답하시오.

> B: Hi, class. Have you ever heard about the Moai? They are tall, human-shaped stones in Chile. Most of the stones are four meters tall, but the tallest one is 20 meters tall. I was wondering how people moved them long ago. So I searched the Internet and learned that they used ropes. Isn't that amazing?

03 Describe what the tallest Moai looks like. (Include two different features.)

➡ _____
_____

04 How did the speaker find out how people moved the stones?

➡ _____

05 다음 문장의 단어들을 활용하여 예상 가능한 가정법 과거 문장을 쓰시오.

> I'd like to lose weight by exercising every day. But It's not easy to practice every day.

➡ _____

06 다음 문장의 단어들을 활용하여 가능한 가정법 과거 문장을 〈조건〉에 맞게 쓰시오.

> ┤ 조건 ├
> 1. 명령문으로 시작할 것.
> 2. as if와 in one's place(~의 입장에서)를 이용할 것.

> I agree that "The rich have to help the poor." But my friend Joel doesn't agree to my thought. In this case, I could say to Joel, "_____"

➡ _____

07 괄호 안의 단어를 활용하여 두 문장 중 한 문장이 목적의 의미를 나타내도록 한 문장으로 바꿔 쓰시오.

> • I worked hard. • I could succeed.

➡ (so) _____

➡ (in) _____

08 다음 우리말에 맞게 괄호 안의 단어를 어법에 맞게 배열하시오.

> 그는 마치 지난밤에 귀신을 봤던 것처럼 말했다.
> (talked, seen, he, if, ghost, a, as, he, had, last, night)

➡ _____

[09~11] 다음 글을 읽고 물음에 답하시오.

> Take a pen. Look at it carefully. Do you see a small hole in the cap? ⓐ여러분은 왜 거기에 구멍이 있는지 아는가? The hole in a pen cap can help save lives. People, especially children, often put small things like pen caps in their mouths. Sometimes they even swallow them. This can stop their breathing and cause death. A famous pen company started putting a small hole in ⓑtheir pen caps. The hole in the cap lets air pass through and has saved lives.

09 위 글의 밑줄 친 ⓐ의 우리말에 맞게 주어진 어휘를 이용하여 7 단어로 영작하시오.

> it, there

➡ _____

10 위 글의 밑줄 친 ⓑ가 가리키는 것을 본문에서 찾아 쓰시오.

➡ _____

11 Why is there a small hole in the pen cap? Fill in the blanks (A) and (B) with suitable words.

> There is a small hole in the pen cap to let air (A)_____ _____ and (B)_____ a life if someone swallows it.

[12~13] 다음 글을 읽고 물음에 답하시오.

> Have you ever been (A)[on / to] an airplane? Wasn't it exciting to look out the window and see the world below? Surprisingly, there was a small hole in your window. Airplane windows are made up of three panes. There is a hole in the middle pane. It balances the air pressure. Without this little hole, airplane windows might break in an emergency. The hole also prevents the window from fogging up ⓐso that you can enjoy that fantastic view.
>
> There are many more products that have small hidden holes. In the future, when you see (B)[a few / a little] hole in something, ask yourself why it is there. Maybe it is the result of a careful design to make your life (C)[more safely / safer].

12 위 글의 괄호 (A)~(C)에서 문맥이나 어법상 알맞은 낱말을 골라 쓰시오.

(A) _____ (B) _____ (C) _____

13 위 글의 밑줄 친 ⓐ를 다음과 같이 바꿔 쓸 때 빈칸에 들어갈 알맞은 말을 두 단어로 쓰시오.

> for you _____ _____ that fantastic view

01 다음은 아래 그림의 발명품에 대한 글이다. 다음 정보를 활용하여 빈칸을 채우시오.

- The Role
 - We use a telephone every day.
 - We can talk to people who are far away from us.
- The Information
 - In 1876, Alexander Bell invented the first practical form of the telephone.
 - Without telephones, we wouldn't be able to have a chat with friends living in another city.

Can you imagine life without a telephone? _____
_____.
In 1876, _____.
After that, it developed quickly through the years and has become a necessary part of modern life. _____ in today's world, _____
_____.

---

02 다음 내용을 바탕으로 발명품을 소개하는 글을 쓰시오.

A Refrigerator
- The Role: We use a refrigerator every day so that we can keep food cool and fresh.
- The Information: In 1755, William Cullen invented the first form of the refrigerator. After the invention, it developed through the years and has become a necessary part of modern life. As we have refrigerators in today's world, we are able to enjoy ice cream on hot summer days.

A Refrigerator
 Can you imagine life without a refrigerator? We use it every day so that we can keep food (A)_____. In 1755, (B)_____ invented the first form of the refrigerator. After that, it developed through the years and has become (C)_____. If we did not have refrigerators in today's world, we would not be able to enjoy (D)_____ on hot summer days.

단원별 모의고사

01 다음 영영풀이가 가리키는 것은?

> to be in a position where you will stand without falling to either side, or to put something in this position

① weigh   ② expect   ③ balance
④ stand   ⑤ calculate

02 다음 주어진 문장의 빈칸에 가장 알맞은 단어는?

> _____ it would be better if you came back at once.

① Even though   ② Although
③ Despite   ④ Perhaps
⑤ Not only

03 다음 주어진 문장의 빈칸에 알맞은 말을 쓰시오.

(1) 우리는 독감이 퍼지는 것을 막기 위해 손을 최대한 자주 씻어야 한다.
➡ We need to wash hands as often as possible to _____ the flu _____ spreading.

(2) 우리가 지금 취하는 결정은 미래의 사태에 영향을 미칠 수도 있다.
➡ The decisions we take now may influence events _____ _____ _____.

[04~05] 다음 대화를 읽고 물음에 답하시오.

> G: Look at the number. It's going up quickly.
> B: (A)사람들이 지나갈 때 그 숫자가 증가해.
> G: Oh, you're right. What does the number mean?
> B: Let me see.... Oh, when people step on the floor, energy is made. It shows the amount of energy that is made.
> G: Wow, that's amazing!

04 위 대화의 밑줄 친 (A)의 우리말을 주어진 단어를 사용하여 영작하시오. (7 words)

➡ _____

05 위 대화에서 주어진 영영풀이에 맞는 단어를 찾아 쓰시오.

> the degree to which something is a lot or a little; how much something is

➡ _____

[06~08] 다음 대화를 읽고 물음에 답하시오.

> G: I like these crackers. They're really good.
> B: Yeah, me, too. I wonder why crackers have these little holes in them.
> G: I don't know. (A)어디 보자... Um... well... maybe it's because the holes make the crackers look tastier.
> B: That's possible, but there must be some other reasons.
> G: Let's look up crackers on the Internet and see what it says.
> B: Okay. Oh, look at this.

G: It says during baking, steam comes out through the holes and that makes the crackers thin.

B: It also says that the holes make the crackers crispy.

G: Wow! So that's why they have holes!

06 위 글의 밑줄 친 (A)를 영작한 표현으로 적절하지 <u>않은</u> 것은?

① Let me think ② Let me see

③ Let me check ④ Just a second

⑤ Just a minute

07 위 대화에 드러난 B와 G의 심경 변화로 가장 적절한 것은?

① excited → worried

② surprised → relieved

③ curious → stressed

④ excited → disappointed

⑤ curious → satisfied

08 Explain the reason why crackers have little holes in them. (11 words)

➡ _____

_____

09 주어진 대화가 자연스럽게 이어지도록 순서대로 배열하시오.

G: We're going on a field trip tomorrow to the Invention Museum.

(A) Good idea. Let me see.... I have the school letter and a map of the museum.

(B) That's why I'm so excited. How about planning the tour before we go?

(C) I've heard that it has a lot of creative inventions.

G: Perfect. Let's get started.

➡ _____

[10~11] 다음 대화를 읽고 물음에 답하시오.

B: Hi, Kate. Today's Saturday, so what about going to the Einstein Science Park today?

G: That sounds like a good idea. I heard that they have special programs on Saturdays. I wonder what they are.

B: Let me see···. I saw an advertisement in the newspaper. Here it is.

G: What does (A)it say?

B: It says that today they have two shows: the Smart Design Show and the International Drone Show in Einstein Hall 101.

G: They both sound fantastic.

B: I'll call them and ask what time they start.

10 위 대화의 밑줄 친 (A)it이 가리키는 것을 쓰시오. (5 words)

➡ _____

11 What kind of programs does the park have? (11 words)

➡ _____

_____

12 다음 중 짝지어진 대화가 어색한 것을 고르시오.

① A: What can we do with this drone?
   B: Well, let me see.... Maybe we can take pictures from the sky.
② A: How does this train start to move?
   B: Just a moment.... I think you can take it.
③ A: What can we do with this VR glasses?
   B: Just a minute.... We can play soccer.
④ A: What can we do with the smart watch?
   B: Let me think.... We can send text messages.
⑤ A: What do I have to do to enter the competition?
   B: Let me see.... You should talk to Ann.

13 다음 문장에서 어법상 어색한 부분을 고치시오. 어색하지 않은 것은 '없음'이라고 쓰시오.

(1) Olivia exercises every day so that she can stay healthy.
   _____ ➡ _____
(2) Joel is working hard so that he can't finish the project on time.
   _____ ➡ _____
(3) I moved my legs out of the way such that she could get past.
   _____ ➡ _____
(4) She hurried up so what she could get there on time.
   _____ ➡ _____

14 다음 빈칸에 들어갈 말로 알맞은 것을 고르시오.

> She acts as if she had known everybody.
> ➡ In fact, she _____ everybody.

① didn't know   ② hasn't known
③ knew   ④ doesn't know
⑤ knows

15 다음 중 어법상 어색한 것은?

① If I took some time off, I could have a rest on weekdays.
② If he had done the assignment, he would have gotten A$^+$.
③ If I had a time machine, I will go back to the 6th grade.
④ If I met a famous singer, I would take a picture with him.
⑤ If you had contacted me, you could have understood it.

16 다음 우리말에 맞게 괄호 안의 단어를 활용하여 영작하시오.

> 당신이 제 입장이라면 기분이 어떻겠어요? (in my situation)

➡ _____, how would you feel?

17 빈칸에 들어갈 말로 적절한 것을 쓰시오.

> Although Britney Spears makes much of her money through her worldwide tours, she recently said she wanted to stop traveling for a while _____ _____ she could take care of her new baby.

➡ _____

18 우리말에 맞게 괄호 안의 단어를 배열하시오.

> 나는 보기 위해 눈을 감는다. – Paul Gauguin
> (in, I, my, see, shut, order, eyes, to)

➡ _____

19 다음 우리말에 맞게 괄호 안의 단어를 이용하여 빈칸을 채우시오.

> Steve는 신선한 공기를 좀 마시기 위해 창문을 열었다. (so, some)
> ➡ Steve opened the window _____
> _____ .
> ➡ Steve opened the window _____
> _____ .

20 우리말에 맞게 괄호 안의 단어를 활용하여 빈칸에 들어갈 알맞은 말을 쓰시오.

(1) 만약 Jane이 노래를 잘 부른다면 노래 경연 대회에 출전할 텐데. (be, singing)

➡ _____ ,
Jane would enter the singing contest.

(2) 만약 아이돌 그룹이 학교에 온다면 나는 행복할 텐데. (come)

➡ _____ ,
I would be happy.

21 빈칸에 들어갈 말로 바르게 짝지어진 것끼리 고르시오.

> She decided to run for a parliamentary job _____ _____ she _____ help other North Korea defectors struggling to adjust to South Korean society.
> *run for: ~에 출마하다 *parliamentary job: 국회의원 *defector: 이탈자, 망명자

[22~23] 다음 글을 읽고 물음에 답하시오.

> Think about a hole that you have seen ⓐ recently. Was it a good hole or a bad hole? If it was a hole in your sock, it was bad. If it was a hole in your shirt for a button, it was good. There are holes everywhere. Some are so small you may not even notice them. They are well hidden, but many of these small holes are very important and make your life safe.

22 위 글의 밑줄 친 ⓐrecently와 바꿔 쓸 수 있는 말을 모두 고르시오.

① those days   ② lately
③ previously   ④ of late
⑤ of the other day

23 Are the holes that we see around us all good holes? If not, give an example beginning with "If".

➡ _____
_____
_____
_____

[24~25] 다음 글을 읽고 물음에 답하시오.

> Take a pen. Look at it carefully. Do you see a small hole in the cap? Do you know why it is ⓐthere? The hole in a pen cap can help save lives. People, especially children, often put small things like pen caps in their mouths. Sometimes they even swallow them. This can stop their breathing and cause death. A famous pen company started putting a small hole in their pen caps. The hole in the cap lets air pass through and has saved lives.

24 위 글의 밑줄 친 ⓐthere가 지칭하는 것을 본문에서 찾아 쓰시오.

➡ _____

25 According to the passage, which is NOT true?

① The hole in a pen cap can help save lives.

② Children often put pen caps in their mouths.

③ Sometimes children even swallow large things.

④ What children swallow can stop their breathing and cause death.

⑤ Air can pass through the hole in the cap.

[26~27] 다음 글을 읽고 물음에 답하시오.

If you look around, you will see other holes that play a helpful role in your life. (①) If you have ever cooked anything in a pot with a lid, perhaps you noticed a small hole in the lid. (②) When cooking something in a pot with a lid, the pressure inside the pot builds up. (③) The water inside would quickly boil over if the lid did not have that hole. (④) The hole lets steam out and keeps the water from coming out. (⑤)

26 위 글의 흐름으로 보아, 주어진 문장이 들어가기에 가장 적절한 곳은?

This hole, too, is there for safety.

①   ②   ③   ④   ⑤

27 Which question CANNOT be answered after reading the passage?

① Why is there a hole in the lid of a pot?

② When you cook something in a pot with a lid, what happens?

③ If there were no hole in the lid of a pot, what would happen?

④ What does the hole in the lid of a pot do?

⑤ How long does it take for the hole to let steam out?

[28~29] 다음 글을 읽고 물음에 답하시오.

There are many more products that have small hidden holes. In the future, when you see a little hole in something, ⓐ왜 그것이 거기에 있는지 자신에게 물어보라. Maybe it is the result of a careful design ⓑto make your life safer.

28 위 글의 밑줄 친 ⓐ의 우리말에 맞게 한 단어를 보충하여, 주어진 어휘를 알맞게 배열하시오.

why / ask / is / there / it

➡ _____

29 위 글의 밑줄 친 ⓑto make와 to부정사의 용법이 같은 것을 모두 고르시오.

① He was the first man to land on the moon.

② I went to his house to fix the radio.

③ There are interesting activities to play outdoors.

④ They decided to go there.

⑤ He is too young to travel alone.

MEMO

Lesson

8

Healthy Food Around the World

 의사소통 기능

- 반복 요청하기

  A: Have you ever tried *Rasmalai*?

  B: Sorry, could you say that again?

  A: *Rasmalai.*

- 추천하기

  A: Could you recommend a good traditional dish?

  B: Try Samgyetang. It'll give you energy.

 언어 형식

- not only A but also B

  Gogol-mogol is **not only** good for people with a cold **but also** popular as a dessert for healthy people.

- 접속사 While

  While people in Korea and Finland look for drinks when sick, many people in America want a bowl of chicken soup.

Words & Expressions

Key Words

- **add** [æd] 동 더하다, 첨가하다
- **blend** [blend] 동 섞다
- **boil** [bɔil] 동 끓다, 끓이다
- **cell phone** 휴대폰
- **chop** [tʃɑp] 동 잘게 썰다
- **cool** [kuːl] 동 식히다
- **dessert** [dizə́ːrt] 명 후식
- **dish** [diʃ] 명 요리
- **eastern** [íːstərn] 형 동쪽에 위치한
- **ginger** [dʒíndʒər] 명 생강
- **heat** [hiːt] 명 온도, 열
- **hold** [hould] 동 열다, 개최하다
- **honey** [hʌ́ni] 명 꿀
- **hurt** [həːrt] 동 아프다
- **lamb** [læm] 명 양고기
- **little sister** 여동생
- **local** [lóukəl] 형 지역의, 현지의
- **low** [lou] 형 낮은
- **medicine** [médisn] 명 약
- **melt** [melt] 동 녹다
- **mix** [miks] 동 섞다
- **mixture** [míkstʃər] 명 혼합물
- **often** [ɔ́ːfən] 부 자주
- **over** [óuvər] 전 ~ 위에
- **pain** [pein] 명 아픔, 통증
- **pepper** [pépər] 명 후추, 고추

- **pour** [pɔːr] 동 붓다, 따르다
- **recipe** [résəpi] 명 요리법
- **recommend** [rèkəménd] 동 추천하다
- **reduce** [ridjúːs] 동 줄이다
- **refrigerator** [rifrídʒəréitər] 명 냉장고
- **room temperature** 상온, 실온
- **seafood** [síːfud] 명 해산물
- **serve** [səːrv] 동 제공하다
- **smooth** [smuːð] 형 매끄러운, 고루 잘 섞인
- **sore** [sɔːr] 형 아픈, 따가운
- **stay** [stei] 동 그대로 있다
- **stir** [stəːr] 동 휘젓다
- **stuffy** [stʌ́fi] 형 코가 막힌, 답답한
- **taste** [teist] 명 맛
- **temperature** [témpərətʃər] 명 온도, 기온
- **thick** [θik] 형 두꺼운, 걸쭉한
- **throat** [θrout] 명 목구멍, 목
- **touching** [tʌ́tʃin] 형 감동적인
- **treasure** [tréʒər] 명 보물
- **vegetable** [védʒətəbl] 명 채소
- **warm** [wɔːrm] 동 따뜻하게 하다 형 따뜻한
- **wear** [wɛər] 동 입다
- **weather** [wéðər] 명 날씨
- **while** [hwail] 접 반면에, ~하는 동안에
- **yogurt** [jóuɡərt] 명 요구르트

Key Expressions

- **a bottle of** ~ 한 병
- **a bowl of** ~ 한 그릇
- **a cup of** ~ 한 컵
- **a plate of** ~ 한 접시
- **as well as** ~에 더하여, 게다가
- **be different from** ~와 다르다
- **be good for** ~에 좋다
- **be made with** ~로 만들어지다
- **breathe through** ~를 통해서 숨쉬다
- **catch a cold** 감기에 걸리다
- **find out** 알아내다, 발견하다
- **for the first time** 처음으로
- **get sick** 병에 걸리다

- **half an hour** 30분
- **have a runny nose** 콧물이 흐르다
- **look for** 찾다, 기대하다
- **look like** ~처럼 보이다
- **not only A but also B** A뿐만 아니라 B도
- **of course** 당연히
- **put on** 몸에 걸치다
- **show A around B** A에게 B를 둘러보도록 안내하다
- **such as A** A와 같은
- **take a picture** 사진을 찍다
- **take a walk** 산책하다
- **turn off** 끄다

Word Power

※ 서로 비슷한 뜻을 가진 어휘

- ☐ **blend** 섞다 – **compound** 혼합하다, 섞어서 만들다
- ☐ **medicine** 약 – **medication** 약제, 약물
- ☐ **pain** 아픔, 통증 – **ache** 아픔, 쑤심
- ☐ **touching** 감동적인 – **moving** 감동시키는, 심금을 울리는
- ☐ **local** 지역의, 현지의 – **regional** 지방의, 지방적인
- ☐ **often** 자주 – **frequently** 종종, 빈번히
- ☐ **stay** 그대로 있다 – **remain** 계속 ∼이다
- ☐ **while** 반면에 – **whereas** 반면에

※ 서로 반대의 뜻을 가진 어휘

- ☐ **add** 더하다, 첨가하다 ↔ **remove** 제거하다, 줄이다
- ☐ **low** 낮은 ↔ **high** 높은
- ☐ **smooth** 매끄러운 ↔ **rough** 거칠거칠한
- ☐ **cool** 식히다 ↔ **warm** 따뜻하게 하다
- ☐ **reduce** 줄이다 ↔ **increase** 증가하다, 늘다
- ☐ **thick** 두꺼운, 걸쭉한 ↔ **thin** 얇은, 가는

※ 접두사 re + 동사

- ☐ **re** + **consider** → **reconsider** 재고하다
- ☐ **re** + **form** → **reform** 개혁하다
- ☐ **re** + **generate** → **regenerate** 재건하다
- ☐ **re** + **make** → **remake** 새로 만들다, 리메이크하다
- ☐ **re** + **organize** → **reorganize** 재조직하다
- ☐ **re** + **touch** → **retouch** 수정하다
- ☐ **re** + **focus** → **refocus** 다시 집중하다
- ☐ **re** + **gain** → **regain** 되찾다
- ☐ **re** + **join** → **rejoin** 다시 합류하다
- ☐ **re** + **order** → **reorder** 재주문하다
- ☐ **re** + **produce** → **reproduce** 다시 만들어 내다
- ☐ **re** + **use** → **reuse** 재사용하다

English Dictionary

- ☐ **boil** 끓다, 끓이다
  - → to change from a liquid to a gas as a result of heat
    열의 결과로 액체에서 기체로 변하다
- ☐ **chop** 잘게 썰다
  - → to cut into smaller pieces
    더 작은 조각들로 자르다
- ☐ **ginger** 생강
  - → a reed-like plant originally from Southeast Asia but now grown in most warm countries, having a strong-smelling and spicy root used in cookery and medicine
    동남 아시아에서 왔지만 현재 대부분의 따뜻한 나라에서 자라는 갈대 모양의 식물로, 요리와 의학에 사용되고 강한 향과 매운 뿌리를 가지고 있는 식물
- ☐ **local** 지역의, 현지의
  - → relating to a city, town or small district rather than an entire state or country
    전체 주 또는 국가가 아닌 도시, 마을 또는 작은 구역에 관련된
- ☐ **pain** 아픔, 통증
  - → physical suffering
    육체적 고통
- ☐ **pour** 붓다, 따르다
  - → to flow, as from one container to another, or into, over, or on something
    어떤 것 안에 혹은 위에, 혹은 하나의 용기에서 다른 용기로 흐르다
- ☐ **recommend** 추천하다
  - → to urge or suggest as proper, useful or beneficial
    적절하거나 유용하거나 혹은 유익하다고 제안하거나 권고하다
- ☐ **stay** 그대로 있다
  - → to remain over a length of time, as in a place or situation
    한 장소나 상황에서 오랜 시간 동안 머무르다
- ☐ **temperature** 온도, 기온
  - → a measure of the warmth of an object with reference to a standard scale
    표준 척도를 기준으로 한 물체의 온기 측정
- ☐ **thick** 두꺼운
  - → having a great distance from one surface to the opposite
    한 표면에서 반대편까지 큰 거리가 있는
- ☐ **touching** 감동적인
  - → causing strong emotion
    강한 감동을 유발하는
- ☐ **treasure** 보물
  - → anything or person greatly valued
    매우 가치가 있는 것 또는 사람

서답형

01 다음 짝지어진 단어의 관계가 같도록 빈칸에 알맞은 말을 쓰시오.

> low : high = reduce : _____

02 다음 영영풀이가 가리키는 것을 고르시오.

> causing strong emotion

① injured   ② touching
③ stuffy   ④ painful
⑤ hurting

03 다음 중 밑줄 친 부분의 뜻풀이가 바르지 않은 것은?

① The heat and the wine made her sleepy. (열, 열기)
② The doctor has given me some medicine to take. (약)
③ The back pain got progressively worse. (통증)
④ How did this dish get broken? (요리)
⑤ I experimented until I got the recipe just right. (요리법)

서답형

04 다음 우리말을 주어진 어휘를 이용하여 영작하시오.

(1) 당신의 사무실 근처에 있는 호텔을 추천해 주시 겠어요? (recommend)

➡ _____

(2) Sam의 식당은 훌륭한 프랑스 요리를 제공한다. (good, French cuisine)

➡ _____

(3) 눈은 언제 녹기 시작할까요? (start, melt)

➡ _____

서답형

05 다음 문장의 빈칸에 들어갈 말을 〈보기〉에서 골라 쓰시오. (필요하면 어형 변화를 할 것.)

> ┤ 보기 ├
> put on / get sick / find out /
> be different from

(1) American English _____ significantly _____ British English.
(2) It would be better to _____ my sweater in weather like today.
(3) The children were malnourished and _____ often. ※malnourished: 영양실조의

중요

06 다음 문장의 빈칸 (A)와 (B)에 각각 공통으로 들어갈 말이 바르게 짝지어진 것은?

> • She speaks French as well ___(A)___ English.
> • Organizations such ___(A)___ schools and clubs bind a community together.
> • The accident happened as the airplane was about to take ___(B)___.
> • Please turn ___(B)___ your cellphones during the meeting.

① on – up   ② on – off
③ as – up   ④ as – off
⑤ like – on

⭐️ 중요 01 다음 짝지어진 단어의 관계가 같도록 빈칸에 알맞은 말을 쓰시오.

```
pain : ache = touching : _____
```

02 다음 주어진 영영풀이에 맞는 단어를 쓰시오.

(1) having a great distance from one surface to the opposite

➡ _____

(2) anything or person greatly valued

➡ _____

⭐️ 중요 03 다음 문장의 빈칸에 들어갈 말을 〈보기〉에서 골라 쓰시오. (필요하면 어형 변화를 할 것.)

┌─ 보기 ─┐
look like / show around / of course /
for the first time
└────────┘

(1) She slept well _____ in a long time.

(2) New employees will be _____ by the HR manager.

(3) He may not _____ it, but he's a big eater.

04 우리말과 일치하도록 주어진 어구를 모두 배열하여 영작하시오.

(1) 그들은 산책을 하기 위해 공원에 갔다.
(went / a walk / they / to / to / the park / take)

➡ _____

(2) 난 콧물이 나고 목이 아프다.
(I / and / a sore throat / a runny nose / have)

➡ _____

고난이도 05 다음 우리말에 맞게 주어진 단어를 사용하여 영작하시오.

(1) 우리는 기온 차이를 먼저 측정했다.
(temperature, measure)

➡ _____

(2) 그 껍데기는 안쪽 면이 매끄럽다.
(smooth, the shell, on)

➡ _____

06 다음 우리말에 맞게 빈칸에 알맞은 말을 쓰시오.

```
Smith 부부는 책임이 있을 뿐만 아니라 고학력
자이다.

➡ Mr. and Mrs. Smith are _____
responsible _____ highly educated.
```

Conversation

1 반복 요청하기

> **A** Have you ever tried *Rasmalai*? 라스말라이 먹어 봤니?
> **B** Sorry, could you say that again? 미안, 다시 말해 줄래?
> **A** *Rasmalai*. 라스말라이.

- 'Could you say that again?'은 '다시 말해 줄래요?'라는 뜻으로 상대방에게 했던 말을 반복해 달라고 요청할 때 사용하는 표현이다.

- 비슷한 표현으로는 'Pardon?', 'I beg your pardon?', 'Pardon me?', 'Excuse me?', 'I'm sorry?', 'What did you say?', 'Say that again, please?', 'I can't hear you.', 'Could you speak a little louder, please?' 등이 있다.

- 반복을 요청할 때 정중한 표현과 덜 정중한 표현이 있으므로 사용에 유의한다. 'Pardon?', 'I beg your pardon?', 'Pardon me?', 'Excuse me?' 등은 상대적으로 정중한 표현이다. 'I'm sorry?', 'What did you say?', 'Say that again, please?', 'I can't hear you.', 'Could you speak a little louder, please?' 등은 앞의 표현들보다는 덜 정중한 표현이다.

핵심 Check

1. 다음 대화에서 밑줄 친 부분과 바꿔 쓸 수 <u>없는</u> 것은?

A: Have you ever tried *macaron*?

B: Sorry, <u>could you say that again?</u>

A: *Macaron*. It's a traditional dessert in France.

① I beg your pardon?　　　　② Excuse me?

③ I'm sorry?　　　　　　　　④ What did you say?

⑤ I can hear you.

② 추천하기

> **A** Could you recommend a good traditional dish? 괜찮은 전통 음식을 추천해 주시겠어요?
>
> **B** Try Samgyetang. It'll give you energy. 삼계탕을 드셔 보세요. 기운을 북돋아 줄 겁니다.

■ 'Could you recommend ~?'는 '~를 추천해 주시겠어요?'라는 뜻으로 상대방에게 추천해달라고 요청할 때 사용하는 표현이다.

■ 이와 같은 표현으로는, 'Can you recommend ~?', 또는 'Can/Could you give me a recommendation for ~?' 등이 있다. 반대로 상대방에게 추천해 줘도 되냐고 물어볼 때는 'Can I recommend something for you?', 'Can I make a recommendation?' 등의 표현을 쓸 수 있다.

■ 따라서 상대방에게 추천해 줄 때 'How about ~?', 'What about ~?', 'I recommend ~.', 'I'd recommend ~.', 'Try ~.'라고 말할 수 있다.

- How about ~? ~은 어때요?
- What about ~? ~은 어때요?
- I recommend ~. 전 ~를 추천합니다.
- I'd recommend ~. 전 ~를 추천할게요.
- Try ~. ~를 시도해 보세요.

 핵심 Check

2. 다음 대화에서 밑줄 친 부분을 영작하시오.

A: 제 여동생을 위해 좋은 책을 추천해 주시겠어요?

B: I recommend this one. The story is touching.

➡ _____

Real-Life Zone

M: Good afternoon. ❶A table for two?

B: Yes.

M: ❷This way please. Here is the menu. I'll be back in a few minutes and ❸take your order.

B: Okay. Thank you.

G: I don't know ❹much about Korean food. ❺Could you recommend something?

B: Well, I'd recommend the Bibimbap.

G: I'm sorry. ❻Could you say that again, please?

B: This one. Bi-bim-bap. It's made with lots of vegetables, beef and an egg over rice. It's tasty and it's also ❼good for your health.

G: That sounds great. ❽I'll try it.

B: It's served with a spicy red pepper sauce. Is that okay?

G: No problem. I like spicy food.

M: 안녕하세요. 두 분이신가요?
B: 네.
M: 이쪽으로 오십시오. 메뉴는 여기 있습니다. 잠시 후에 와서 주문 받겠습니다.
B: 알겠습니다. 감사합니다.
G: 나 한국 음식에 대해서 잘 알지 못해. 네가 추천해 줄래?
B: 음, 나는 비빔밥을 추천할게.
G: 미안, 다시 한 번 말해 줄래?
B: 이거. 비-빔-밥. 그것은 밥 위에 많은 야채들과 소고기, 그리고 계란을 얹어 만들어. 맛있고 건강에도 좋아.
G: 굉장한데. 난 그거 먹어 볼래.
B: 매운 고추장 양념이랑 같이 나오는 거야. 괜찮겠니?
G: 문제 없어. 나 매운 음식을 좋아해.

❶ 직역하면 '두 사람을 위한 테이블이신가요?'라는 뜻으로 식당에 갔을 때 몇 사람이냐고 물을 때 사용하는 표현이다. ❷ '이쪽입니다'라는 뜻으로, 이 상황에선 웨이터가 손님에게 따라오라고 할 때 사용된다. ❸ take one's order 주문을 받다 ❹ much (셀 수 없는 명사 앞에 쓰여서) 많이 ❺ '~를 추천해 주시겠어요?'라는 뜻으로 상대방에게 추천해달라고 요청할 때 사용하는 표현이다. ❻ '다시 말해 주세요.'라는 뜻으로 상대방에게 했던 말을 반복해 달라고 요청할 때 사용하는 표현이다. ❼ good for ~에 좋은 ❽ '그걸 시도해 볼게.'라는 뜻으로 이때 대명사 it은 앞서 말한 비빔밥을 가리킨다.

Check(√) True or False

(1) Both G and B have not tried Korean food before.　　　　　T ☐ F ☐

(2) It's the first time G tries spicy Korean food because G does not like spicy food.　　T ☐ F ☐

Wrap Up 1-2

B: Tomorrow is my birthday.

G: I know. Are you going to ❶have a birthday party, Alex?

B: Yes. ❷Can you recommend a good place to have the party?

G: ❸I'd recommend the Happy Snack House. The food is really good and it'll be large enough.

B: ❹What dish would you recommend?

G: I'd recommend the onion rings. They're fantastic!

B: Oh, ❺just thinking about ❻them makes my mouth water.

B: 내일은 내 생일이야.
G: 알고 있어. Alex, 생일 파티할 거니?
B: 응. 파티 열기에 좋은 장소 추천해 줄래?
G: 나는 Happy Snack House를 추천할게. 음식이 정말 맛있고 장소도 충분히 넓어.
B: 넌 무슨 음식을 추천해 줄래?
G: 나는 양파 튀김을 추천할게. 정말 환상적이야!
B: 오, 그거 생각하는 것만으로도 침이 고인다.

❶ have a party 파티를 열다 ❷ '~를 추천해 주시겠어요?'라는 뜻으로 상대방에게 추천해달라고 요청할 때 사용하는 표현으로, 같은 표현으로는 'Can/Could you give me a recommendation for ~?' 등이 있다. ❸ 상대방에게 추천해 줄 때 사용할 수 있는 표현이다. ❹ '어떤 음식을 추천해 줄래?'라는 뜻으로 의문사 what이 쓰인 의문문이다. ❺ 동명사가 쓰인 구문으로 thinking about them 전체가 주어이다. ❻ 대명사 them은 앞서 언급한 음식 the onion rings를 가리킨다.

Check(√) True or False

(3) B is going to throw a birthday party.　　　　　T ☐ F ☐

(4) The place that G recommends for the party is called the Happy Snack House.　　T ☐ F ☐

Listen & Speak 1 Listen 1

B: Hi, Grace. ❶Those are pretty. What are they called?

G: They're ❷called *dango*.

B: I'm sorry. ❸Could you say that again?

G: *Dan-go*. They're sweet and ❹made with rice cake powder. They're from Japan.

❶ Those는 대명사 that의 복수형이다.
❷ call ~라고 부르다
❸ '다시 말해 주겠니?'의 뜻이다.
❹ made with ~로 만들어진

Listen & Speak 1 Listen 2

B: Alice, ❶what's that you're eating?

G: It's *rasmalai*.

B: Ra.... Could you say that again?

G: *Ras-ma-lai*. It's like a cheesecake in a sweet cream. It's a ❷traditional food in India.

❶ '네가 먹고 있는 그것은 뭐니?'라는 뜻이다.
❷ traditional 전통적인

Listen & Speak 1 Listen 3

G: What's that you're eating, David? It ❶looks like a chocolate ball.

B: It's *brigadeiro*.

G: ❷Sorry? Could you say that again?

B: *Bri-ga-dei-ro*. It's sweet and ❸tasty. It's popular in Brazil.

❶ look like ~처럼 보이다
❷ 이때 사용된 'Sorry?'는 미안하다는 뜻이 아니라 상대방이 했던 말을 반복해 주기를 요청하는 표현이다.
❸ tasty 맛있는

Listen & Speak 1 A-1

G: My ❶favorite Korean traditional drink is Maesil-tea. ❷What about you, Jinsu?

B: Well, my favorite traditional drink is Sikhye.

G: Sik.... Can you say that again?

B: Sik-hye. It's sweet and cool.

G: I want to ❸try it.

❶ favorite 가장 좋아하는
❷ '너는 어때?'라는 뜻으로, 'How about you?'와 바꿔 쓸 수 있다.
❸ try (좋은지 보려고) 먹어 보다, 써 보다, 해 보다

Listen & Speak 1 A-2

B: ❶Have you ever tried *poke*?

G: Sorry, could you say that again, please?

B: *Po-ke*. It's a salad ❷that is popular in Hawaii.

G: What's so special about it?

B: It's made with rice and fish. It's ❸not only delicious but also very healthy.

❶ 현재완료의 경험 용법이 사용된 문장으로, '~해 본 적 있니?'라고 해석한다.
❷ 이때 that은 대명사가 아니라 접속사로 사용되었다.
❸ not only A but also B A뿐만 아니라 B도

Listen & Speak 1 B

1. **A:** Have you ever ❶tried *rasmalai*?
   B: Sorry, ❷could you say that again?
   A: *Rasmalai*. It's a traditional dessert in India.

2. **A:** Have you ever tried *brigadeiro*?
   B: Sorry, could you say that again?
   A: *Brigadeiro*. It's a ❸traditional dessert in Brazil.

3. **A:** Have you ever tried *macaron*?
   B: Sorry, could you say that again?
   A: *Macaron*. It's a traditional ❹dessert in France.

❶ try 써 보다, 해 보다, 먹어 보다
❷ '다시 말해 주시겠어요?'라는 뜻이다.
❸ traditional 전통적인
❹ dessert 디저트, 후식 *cf.* desert 사막, 버리다

Listen & Speak 2 Listen

1. B: Could you recommend a good traditional ❶dish?

   W: ❷Try Samgyetang. It'll give you energy.

2. G: Could you recommend a good book for my little sister?

   M: ❸I recommend this one. The story is ❹touching.

3. B: Could you recommend a guitar for beginners?

   W: ❺How about this one? Many beginners play it.

4. G: Could you recommend a snack for my dog?

   M: Sure. How about this? Dogs really like it.

❶ dish 음식
❷ 상대방에게 추천해 줄 때 쓰는 표현으로, '먹어 보세요.'라고 해석한다.
❸ 이와 같은 표현으로 'How about ~?', 'What about ~?', 'I'd recommend ~.', 'Try ~.'라고 말할 수 있다.
❹ touching 감동적인
❺ 상대방에게 추천해 줄 때 사용하는 표현이다.

Listen & Speak 2 A-2

M: Welcome to the Sydney Information Center. Sydney has many places ❶you will want to visit. The Rocks Markets is one of ❷them. There you can buy art, clothing, books and many other things. You can also eat fresh, tasty local food. We ❸recommend visiting the Rocks Markets and enjoying the food and the fun there.

❶ 관계대명사 that이나 which가 생략된 문장으로 many places를 꾸며 준다.
❷ 대명사 them은 앞선 문장에서 언급된 many places in Sydney를 가리킨다.
❸ recommend는 목적어로 동명사(~ing)를 취한다.

Listen & Speak 2 A-1

B: Tomorrow is my dad's birthday. ❶I'd like to do something special for him.

G: ❷How about cooking something for him? He would really like that.

B: That sounds great. Can you recommend ❸something easy to cook?

G: Umm. How about Gimchijeon? It's ❹easy to make and it's delicious.

B: Oh, that's a good idea. He'll love ❺it.

❶ would like to ~하고 싶다
❷ 'How about ~?'는 상대방에게 무언가를 제안하거나 추천할 때 쓰는 표현으로 'What about ~?'과 바꿔 쓸 수 있다.
❸ something은 형용사가 뒤에서 수식하기 때문에 형용사 easy가 something 뒤에 위치한다.
❹ easy to ~ ~하기 쉬운
❺ 대명사 it은 B가 만들 김치전을 가리킨다.

Listen & Speak 2 B

1. A: ❶Could you recommend a good traditional dish?

   B: ❷Try Samgyetang. It'll give you energy.

2. A: Could you recommend a good book for my little sister?

   B: I recommend ❸this one. The story is touching.

3. A: Could you recommend ❹a cell phone for my grandmother?

   B: How about this phone? It's ❺easy to use.

❶ 'Can you recommend ~?', 또는 'Can/Could you give me a recommendation for ~?' 등의 표현으로 대체할 수 있다.
❷ '삼계탕을 드셔 보세요.'라는 뜻으로, 'Try ~.' 이외에도 상대방에게 추천해 줄 때 'How about ~?', 'What about ~?', 'I recommend ~.', 'I'd recommend ~.' 등을 쓸 수 있다.
❸ 이때 this one은 책을 가리킨다.
❹ cell phone 휴대폰
❺ easy to use 사용하기 쉬운

● 다음 우리말과 일치하도록 빈칸에 알맞은 말을 쓰시오.

해석

Listen & Speak 1 Listen 1

B: Hi, Grace. Those are pretty. What are _____ called?

G: They're _____ *dango*.

B: I'm sorry. _____ you say that _____?

G: *Dan-go.* They're sweet and _____ with rice cake powder. They're _____ Japan.

B: Grace, 안녕. 그거 예쁘다. 그거 뭐라고 불리니?
G: 당고라고 불러.
B: 미안, 다시 말해 줄래?
G: 당−고. 달고 쌀가루로 만들어진 거야. 일본에서 온 거야.

Listen & Speak 1 Listen 2

B: Alice, what's that you're _____?

G: It's *rasmalai*.

B: *Ra....* Could you _____ that again?

G: *Ras-ma-lai.* It's _____ a cheesecake in a sweet cream. It's a traditional _____ in India.

B: Alice, 네가 먹고 있는 것은 무엇이니?
G: 라스말라이야.
B: 라… 다시 한 번 말해 줄래?
G: 라스−마−라이. 달콤한 크림 안에 있는 치즈케이크 같은 거야. 인도의 전통 음식이지.

Listen & Speak 1 Listen 3

G: What's _____ you're eating, David? It _____ like a chocolate ball.

B: It's *brigadeiro*.

G: _____? Could you say that _____?

B: B*ri-ga-dei-ro.* It's sweet and tasty. It's _____ in Brazil.

G: David, 뭐 먹고 있니? 그거 초콜릿 볼처럼 생겼다.
B: 브리가데이로야.
G: 뭐라고? 다시 한 번 말해 줄래?
B: 브리−가−데이−로. 달고 맛있어. 브라질에서 인기 많아.

Listen & Speak 1 A-1

G: My _____ Korean traditional drink is Maesil-tea. _____ about you, Jinsu?

B: Well, my favorite _____ drink is Sikhye.

G: Sik.... Can you _____ that _____?

B: Sik-hye. It's _____ and cool.

G: I want to _____ it.

G: 내가 제일 좋아하는 한국 전통 음료는 매실차야. 진수, 너는 뭐니?
B: 음, 내가 제일 좋아하는 음료는 식혜야.
G: 식… 다시 말해 줄래?
B: 식−혜. 달고 시원해.
G: 먹어 보고 싶다.

Listem & Speak 1 A-2

B: Have you ever _____ *poke*?

G: Sorry, _____ you say that again, please?

B: *Po-ke*. It's a _____ that is _____ in Hawaii.

G: What's so _____ about it?

B: It's made _____ rice and fish. It's not _____ delicious _____ also very _____.

Listen & Speak 1 B

1. A: _____ you ever tried *rasmalai*?

   B: _____, could you say that again?

   A: *Rasmalai*. It's a traditional _____ in India.

2. A: Have you ever _____ *brigadeiro*?

   B: Sorry, could you say that again?

   A: *Brigadeiro*. It's a _____ dessert in Brazil.

3. A: Have you _____ tried *macaron*?

   B: Sorry, could you say _____ again?

   A: *Macaron*. It's a traditional dessert _____ France.

Listen & Speak 2 Listen

1. B: Could you _____ a good traditional dish?

   W: _____ Samgyetang. It'll give you energy.

2. G: _____ you recommend a good book _____ my little sister?

   M: I recommend this one. The story is _____.

3. B: Could you recommend a guitar for _____?

   W: How _____ this one? Many beginners play it.

4. G: Could you recommend a _____ for my dog?

   M: Sure. _____ about this? Dogs really like it.

Listen & Speak 2 A-1

B: Tomorrow is my dad's birthday. I'd like to do something _____ for him.

G: _____ about _____ something for him? He _____ really like that.

B: That sounds great. Can you _____ something _____ to cook?

G: Umm. How _____ Gimchijeon? It's _____ to make and it's delicious.

B: Oh, that's a good _____. He'll love it.

B: 너 포케 먹어 본 적 있니?
G: 미안, 다시 한 번 말해 줄래?
G: 포-케. 하와이에서 인기 많은 샐러드야.
G: 그게 뭐가 그렇게 특별한데?
G: 쌀이랑 생선으로 만들어. 맛도 있고 매우 건강한 음식이야.

1. A: 너 라스말라이 먹어 본 적 있니?
   B: 미안, 다시 말해 줄래?
   A: 라스말라이. 그건 인도의 전통 디저트야.
2. A: 너 브리가데이로 먹어 본 적 있니?
   B: 미안, 다시 말해 줄래?
   A: 브리가데이로. 그건 브라질의 전통 디저트야.
3. A: 너 마카롱 먹어 본 적 있니?
   B: 미안, 다시 말해 줄래?
   A: 마카롱. 그건 프랑스 전통 디저트야.

1. B: 좋은 전통 음식 추천해 줄 수 있니?
   W: 삼계탕을 먹어봐. 너에게 에너지를 줄 거야.
2. G: 내 여동생에게 좋은 책을 추천해 줄 수 있니?
   M: 이것을 추천해. 이야기가 감동적이야.
3. B: 초보자를 위한 기타를 추천해 줄 수 있니?
   W: 이거 어때? 많은 초보자들이 그걸 연주해.
4. G: 내 개를 위한 간식을 추천해 줄래?
   M: 물론, 이거 어때? 개들이 그걸 정말 좋아해.

B: 내일은 우리 아빠의 생신이야. 난 아빠를 위해 좀 특별한 것을 하고 싶어.
G: 아버지를 위해 무언가를 요리하는 건 어때? 정말 좋아하실 거야.
B: 그거 좋겠다. 요리하기 쉬운 것을 추천해 줄래?
G: 음, 김치전 어때? 만들기 쉽고 맛있어.
B: 오, 좋은 생각이다. 아빠가 좋아하실 거야.

Listen & Speak 2 B-2

M: _____ to the Sydney Information Center. Sydney has _____ places you will want to _____. The Rocks Markets is one of them. _____ you can buy art, clothing, books and many _____ things. You can also eat fresh, _____ _____ food. We _____ visiting the Rocks Markets and _____ the food and the fun there.

Real-Life Zone

M: Good afternoon. A table _____ two?

B: Yes.

M: This way please. _____ is the menu. I'll be _____ in a few minutes and _____ your order.

B: Okay. Thank you.

G: I don't know _____ about Korean food. Could you _____ something?

B: Well, I'd _____ the Bibimbap.

G: I'm sorry. _____ you say that again, please?

B: This one. Bi-bim-bap. It's _____ with lots of vegetables, beef and an egg over rice. It's tasty and it's also _____ for your _____.

G: That sounds great. I'll _____ it.

B: It's _____ with a spicy red pepper sauce. Is that _____?

G: No _____. I like spicy food.

Wrap Up 1-2

B: Tomorrow is my birthday.

G: I know. _____ you going to _____ a birthday party, Alex?

B: Yes. _____ you recommend a good _____ to have the party?

G: I'd _____ the Happy Snack House. The food is really good and it'll be large _____.

B: What dish _____ you _____?

G: I'd recommend the onion rings. They're _____!

B: Oh, just _____ about them makes my mouth _____.

M: 시드니 여행 정보 센터에 오신 걸 환영합니다. 시드니는 여러분께서 방문하시고 싶으실 만한 장소들이 많습니다. Rocks Markets은 그 중의 하나죠. 그곳에선 예술 작품과 의류, 책 그리고 다른 많은 것들을 사실 수 있습니다. 또한 신선하고 맛있는 지역 음식도 드실 수 있습니다. 저희는 Rocks Markets에 가시는 것을 추천해 드리며 그곳에서 음식과 재미를 즐기시기를 추천합니다.

M: 안녕하세요. 두 분이신가요?
B: 네.
M: 이쪽으로 오십시오. 메뉴는 여기 있습니다. 잠시 후에 와서 주문 받겠습니다.
B: 알겠습니다. 감사합니다.
G: 나 한국 음식에 대해서 잘 알지 못해. 네가 추천해 줄래?
B: 음, 나는 비빔밥을 추천할게.
G: 미안, 다시 한 번 말해 줄래?
B: 이거. 비-빔-밥. 그것은 밥 위에 많은 야채들과 소고기, 그리고 계란을 얹어 만들어. 맛있고 건강에도 좋아.
G: 굉장한데. 난 그거 먹어 볼래.
B: 매운 고추장 양념이랑 같이 나오는 거야. 괜찮겠니?
G: 문제 없어. 나 매운 음식을 좋아해.

B: 내일은 내 생일이야.
G: 알고 있어. Alex, 생일 파티할 거니?
B: 응. 파티 열기에 좋은 장소 추천해 줄래?
G: 나는 Happy Snack House를 추천할게. 음식이 정말 맛있고 장소도 충분히 넓어.
B: 넌 무슨 음식을 추천해 줄래?
G: 나는 양파 튀김을 추천할게. 정말 환상적이야!
B: 오, 그거 생각하는 것만으로도 침이 고인다.

[01~02] 다음 대화를 읽고 물음에 답하시오.

> B: Hi, Grace. Those are pretty. What are they called?
>
> G: They're called *dango*.
>
> B: I'm sorry. _____(A)_____
>
> G: *Dan-go*. They're sweet and (B)make with rice cake powder. They're from Japan

01 위 대화의 빈칸 (A)에 알맞지 <u>않은</u> 것은?

① Can you say that again?

② Could you say that again?

③ Why did you say that again?

④ Excuse me?

⑤ Pardon me?

02 위 대화의 밑줄 친 (B)를 알맞은 형으로 고치시오.

➡ _____

[03~04] 다음 대화를 읽고 물음에 답하시오.

> B: Tomorrow is my dad's birthday. I'd like to do ⓐ<u>special something</u> for him.
>
> G: How about ⓑ<u>cooking</u> something for him? He ⓒ<u>would</u> really like that.
>
> B: That sounds ⓓ<u>great</u>. (A)요리하기 쉬운 것을 추천해 줄래?(can, something)
>
> G: Umm. How about Gimchijeon? It's easy ⓔ<u>to make</u> and it's delicious.
>
> B: Oh, that's a good idea. He'll love it.

03 위 대화의 밑줄 친 ⓐ~ⓔ 중에서 <u>어색한</u> 부분을 찾아 바르게 고치시오.

_____ ➡ _____

04 위 대화의 밑줄 친 (A)의 우리말을 주어진 단어를 이용해 영작하시오. (7 words)

➡ _____

[01~03] 다음 대화를 읽고 물음에 답하시오.

M: Good afternoon. A table for two?

B: Yes.

M: This way please. Here is the menu. I'll be back in (A)[few / a few] minutes and take your order.

B: Okay. Thank you.

G: I don't know much about Korean food. Could you recommend something?

B: Well, I'd recommend the Bibimbap.

G: I'm sorry. Could you say that again, please?

B: This one. Bi-bim-bap. It (B)[made / is made] with lots of vegetables, beef and an egg over rice. It's tasty and it's also good for your health.

G: That sounds great. I'll try it.

B: It (C)[served / is served] with a spicy red pepper sauce. Is that okay?

G: No problem. I like spicy food.

01 위 대화의 (A)~(C)에 알맞은 말이 바르게 짝지어진 것은?

① few – made – is served

② few – is made – served

③ a few – made – served

④ a few – is made – served

⑤ a few – is made – is served

02 위 대화에 나오는 M과 B의 관계로 적절한 것은?

① chef – critic   ② waiter – guest

③ chef – owner   ④ waiter – owner

⑤ critic – guest

서답형

03 According to B, describe what the Bibimbap is like. (8 words)

➡ _____

[04~05] 다음 대화를 읽고 물음에 답하시오.

B: Tomorrow is my birthday.

G: I know. Are you going to ⓐhave a birthday party, Alex?

B: Yes. Can you recommend a good place ⓑto have the party?

G: I'd recommend the Happy Snack House. The food is really good and (A)it'll be ⓒlarge enough.

B: What dish ⓓwould you recommend?

G: I'd recommend the onion rings. They're fantastic!

B: Oh, just ⓔthink about them makes my mouth water.

04 위 대화의 밑줄 친 ⓐ~ⓔ 중 어법상 어색한 것은?

① ⓐ   ② ⓑ   ③ ⓒ   ④ ⓓ   ⑤ ⓔ

서답형

05 위 대화의 밑줄 친 (A)it이 가리키는 것을 찾아 쓰시오. (4 words)

➡ _____

[06~08] 다음 대화를 읽고 물음에 답하시오.

> G: My favorite Korean traditional drink is Maesil-tea. What about you, Jinsu?
>
> B: Well, my favorite traditional drink is Sikhye.
>
> G: Sik.... (A)Can you say that again?
>
> B: Sik-hye. It's sweet and cool.
>
> G: I want to try (B)it.

06 위 대화의 밑줄 친 (A)와 바꾸어 쓰기에 어색한 것은?

① Pardon? ② Excuse me?
③ Sorry for that. ④ I can't hear you.
⑤ What did you say?

서답형
07 위 대화에서 주어진 영영풀이가 가리키는 것을 찾아 쓰시오.

> following or belonging to the ways of behaving or beliefs that have been established for a long time

➡ _____

서답형
08 위 대화에서 밑줄 친 (B)it이 가리키는 것을 찾아 쓰시오.

➡ _____

[09~11] 다음 글을 읽고 물음에 답하시오.

> M: Welcome to the Sydney Information Center. Sydney has (A)[many / much] places you will want to visit. The Rocks Markets is one of them. There you can buy art, clothing, books and many other things. You can also eat fresh, tasty local food. We recommend (B)[to visit / visiting] the Rocks Markets and enjoying the food and the fun there.

서답형
09 위 글의 (A)와 (B)에서 적절한 것을 골라 쓰시오.

(A) _____ (B) _____

서답형
10 위 글에서 다음 영영풀이가 뜻하는 것을 찾아 쓰시오.

> relating to a city, town or small district rather than an entire state or country

➡ _____

중요
11 위 글의 목적으로 가장 적절한 것은?

① to recommend ② to criticize
③ to demonstrate ④ to approve
⑤ to greet

[01~03] 다음 대화를 읽고 물음에 답하시오.

> B: Have you ever tried *poke*?
> (A) *Po-ke*. It's a salad that is popular in Hawaii.
> (B) Sorry, could you say that again, please?
> (C) What's so special about (a)it?
> B: It's made with rice and fish. It's not only delicious but also very healthy.

01 주어진 두 문장 사이의 대화가 자연스럽게 이어지도록 순서대로 배열하시오.

➡ _____

02 위 대화의 밑줄 친 (a)it이 가리키는 것을 쓰시오.

➡ _____

03 Why is *poke* so special and popular in Hawaii? (9 words)

➡ _____
_____

04 다음 대화의 밑줄 친 부분을 주어진 단어를 이용해 영작하시오. (9 words)

> A: 제 할머니를 위한 휴대폰을 추천해 주시겠어요?
> (could, cell phone)
> B: How about this phone? It's easy to use.

➡ _____
_____

[05~07] 다음 대화를 읽고 물음에 답하시오.

> B: Tomorrow is my birthday.
> G: I know. Are you going to have a birthday party, Alex?
> B: Yes. (A)파티를 열 수 있는 좋은 장소를 추천해 줄래?
> G: I'd recommend the Happy Snack House. The food is really good and it'll be large enough.
> B: What dish would you recommend?
> G: I'd recommend the onion rings. (B)They're fantastic!
> B: Oh, just thinking about them makes my mouth water.

05 위 대화의 밑줄 친 (A)의 우리말을 주어진 단어를 이용해 바르게 영작하시오. (10 words) (can, have)

➡ _____
_____

06 위 대화의 밑줄 친 (B)가 가리키는 것을 영어로 쓰시오.

➡ _____

07 Why does G recommend the restaurant for B's birthday party? (11 words)

➡ _____
_____

Grammar

1 상관접속사 not only ~ but also ...

> • *Gogol-mogol* is **not only** good for people with a cold **but also** popular as a dessert for healthy people.
> 고골모골은 감기에 걸린 사람들에게 좋을 뿐 아니라 건강한 사람들의 후식으로도 인기가 있다.
>
> • John can speak **not only** English **but also** Chinese.
> John은 영어뿐 아니라 중국어도 말할 수 있다.

■ 상관접속사 'not only A but also B'는 'A뿐만 아니라 B도 또한'이라는 뜻이며, 'B as well as A'로 바꿀 수 있다. 접속사이므로 A와 B 자리에 명사 뿐 아니라 동사, 형용사, 준동사 등 어떤 것이든 올 수 있으나 A와 B에는 같은 품사가 와야 한다.

- • Eric is **not only** a singer **but also** an actor.
  = Eric is an actor **as well as** a singer. Eric은 가수일 뿐 아니라 배우이기도 하다.
- • Sunny **not only** sings **but also** plays the piano. Sunny는 노래뿐 아니라 피아노도 친다.

■ 상관접속사의 종류와 주어로 쓰일 때의 수의 일치

(1) not only A but also B(= B as well as A): A뿐만 아니라 B도 또한 (B에 일치)
  - • **Not only** you **but also** he sees the girl. 너뿐만 아니라 그도 소녀를 본다.
    = He **as well as** you **sees** the girl.

(2) not A but B: A가 아니라 B (B에 일치)
  - • **Not** you **but** he **sees** the girl. 당신이 아니라 그가 소녀를 본다.

(3) both A and B: A와 B 둘 다 (복수 주어)
  - • **Both** you **and** he **see** the girl. 당신과 그 (사람) 둘 다 소녀를 본다.

(4) either A or B: A 또는 B 둘 중 하나 (동사와 가까운 주어에 일치)
  - • **Either** you **or** he **sees** the girl. 당신 또는 그 (사람) 둘 중 하나는 소녀를 본다.

(5) neither A nor B: A도 B도 아닌 (동사와 가까운 주어에 일치)
  - • **Neither** you **nor** he **sees** the girl. 당신도 그도 소녀를 보지 않는다.

■ not only가 문두에 올 경우, 의문문 형식의 도치가 일어난다.
  - • **Not only** is she smart, **but also** she is strong. 그녀는 똑똑할 뿐만 아니라 힘이 세다.
  - • **Not only** did he join the club, **but also** he helped the children.
    그는 그 클럽에 가입했을 뿐만 아니라, 그 아이들을 돕기도 했다.

■ not only에서 only 대신 just, simply도 가능하고, but 뒤의 also는 생략해서 쓰기도 한다.
  - • She bought **not just** his CDs **but** his posters. 그녀는 그의 CD뿐 아니라 포스터도 샀다.

핵심 Check

1. 다음 문장에서 어법상 틀린 곳을 찾아 바르게 고쳐 쓰시오.
  (1) Alex not only loves Jane but also respect her. _____ ➡ _____
  (2) Not only you but also she are going on the field trip. _____ ➡ _____

접속사 while

> • **While** people in Korea and Finland look for drinks when sick, many people in America want a bowl of chicken soup.
> 한국 사람들과 핀란드 사람들이 아플 때 음료를 찾는 반면, 미국의 많은 사람들은 닭고기 수프를 원한다.
>
> • My sister enjoys going out, **while** I enjoy staying home.
> 내 여동생은 나가는 것을 좋아하는데, 반면에 나는 집에 있는 것을 좋아한다.

■ 접속사 'while'은 부사절을 이끌며, 두 가지 뜻으로 사용된다.

(1) 다른 대상이나 상황을 비교 · 대조: '~인 반면에'

• **While** she is very good at science, she is so bad at literature.
그녀는 과학을 매우 잘하는 반면에, 문학은 아주 못 한다.

• My younger sister is very tall, **while** I am very short.
내 여동생은 매우 키가 크다. 반면에 나는 매우 작다.

(2) 시간: '~하는 동안에'

• Clean your room **while** your mom is preparing for dinner.
너의 엄마가 저녁 식사를 준비하시는 동안에 너의 방을 청소해라.

• Don't bother him **while** he's studying. 그가 공부하는 동안에 그를 귀찮게 하지 마라.

(주의) 전치사 during으로 바꿀 수 없다. Don't bother him ~~during~~ he's studying. (X)

■ while과 유사한 의미의 문장들을 다양하게 표현할 수 있다.

• **While** it is raining here, it is snowing in Daejeon. 여기는 비가 오는 반면에, 대전에는 눈이 온다.

= It is raining here, **but** it is snowing in Daejeon. (등위접속사 but으로 연결)

= It is raining here. **However**, it is snowing in Daejeon. (접속부사 however로 연결)

= **Though[Although]** it is raining here, it is snowing in Daejeon. (종속접속사 though로 연결)

핵심 Check

2. 다음 괄호 안에서 알맞은 말을 고르시오.

(1) He was watching TV (while / however) she was taking a shower.

(2) I am a late riser, (so / while) my brother is an early riser.

Grammar 시험대비 기본평가

01 다음 빈칸에 들어갈 말로 알맞은 것은?

> Ginger tea not only warms your body but also _____.

① comforting your sore throat
② simple and easy to drink at a time
③ good for a cold in winter
④ different from a family to another
⑤ helps reduce the pain in your throat

02 다음 두 문장을 한 문장으로 바꿔 쓸 때, 빈칸에 들어갈 말로 가장 적절한 것은?

> • People in Korea and Finland look for drinks when sick.
> • But many people in America want a bowl of chicken soup.
> ➡ _____ people in Korea and Finland look for drinks when sick, many people in America want a bowl of chicken soup.

① Since ② As ③ While
④ Until ⑤ Like

03 다음 중 어법상 어색한 것을 고르시오.

① The kids are interested either in swimming or in fishing.
② Sana has not only the character figure but also its house.
③ Doris' sisters not only dance well but sing well.
④ The gentleman is both generous and intelligent.
⑤ Mr. Kim not only speaks English but also handsome.

04 다음 빈칸에 공통으로 들어갈 말로 가장 적절한 것은? (대 · 소문자 무시.)

> • Drink the soup _____ it is still hot.
> • My sister enjoys going out _____ I enjoy reading books.
> • _____ many Koreans eat Samgyetang when they are sick, many people in India eat tomato soup.

① as ② because ③ though
④ before ⑤ while

 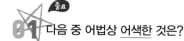

01 다음 중 어법상 어색한 것은?

① Not only his instruments but also my violin have that kind of problems.

② Jessy ate not only the bread but also the cookies that her brother had bought.

③ The cellist was not only kind to the young musicians but also influential to the members on the orchestra.

④ Not only the athletes but also the coach is working on the field.

⑤ My uncle has lived not only in Egypt but also in Italy.

[02~03] 다음 중 어법상 옳은 것을 고르시오.

02 ① The actor doesn't have neither a car nor a bike.

② Not only she was hungry but also couldn't walk any longer.

③ Both the animals and their owner is happy with the result.

④ Not only the girls but also the goose have lived in the farm since last year.

⑤ Mina bought her brother not only the books but also the bag.

03 ① Peter not only imagines but also making the plan of his holidays.

② Tell her not only what you like but also you want to buy.

③ Not only the employees but also the employer know what the product is.

④ Johnson not only teaches skiing but also sells a lot of ski boots.

⑤ Not only you but also Smith speak French well.

[04~05] 다음 우리말을 어법상 알맞게 영작한 것을 고르시오.

04
서양의 팬 케이크는 밀가루로 만들어지는 반면에, 녹두전은 간 녹두콩과 많은 다른 채소들로 만들어진다.

① While Nokdujeon is made with ground nokdu beans with many different vegetables, a western pancake is made with flour.

② Even though Nokdujeon is made with ground nokdu beans with many different vegetables, a western pancake is made with flour.

③ Since a western pancake is made with flour, Nokdujeon is made with ground nokdu beans with many different vegetables.

④ Whether a western pancake is made with flour, Nokdujeon is made with ground nokdu beans with many different vegetables.

⑤ While a western pancake is made with flour, Nokdujeon is made with ground nokdu beans with many different vegetables.

05

녹두전은 맛있을 뿐 아니라 영양가도 좋다.

① Nokdujeon is not delicious but nutritious.
② Nokdujeon not only is delicious but turns nutritious.
③ Nokdujeon is either delicious or also nutritious.
④ Nokdujeon is not only delicious but also nutritious.
⑤ Nokdujeon is delicious as well as nutritious.

06 다음 대화의 빈칸에 들어갈 말로 가장 적절한 것은?

A: What is Dave doing outside?
B: He is practicing basketball _____ it is raining.

① though   ② during   ③ like
④ since   ⑤ because

07 다음 두 문장을 한 문장으로 바꿔 쓸 때 적절하지 않은 것은?

① Susan can make a paper plane. + Or Jenny can make a paper plane.
   ➡ Either Susan or Jenny can make a paper plane.
② Michelle could grow fruits. + Michelle could make the juice as well.
   ➡ Not only could Michelle grow fruits but also make the juice.
③ Ellen likes the movie. + Yujin likes the movie, too.
   ➡ Not only Ellen but also Yujin likes the movie.
④ Cathy watches the TV program. + Mina watches the program, too.
   ➡ Both Cathy and Mina watches the TV program.
⑤ Bentley doesn't know the way to the supermarket. + His brothers don't know the way to the supermarket, either.
   ➡ Neither Bentley nor his brothers know the way to the supermarket.

08 다음 빈칸 (A)~(C)에 들어갈 알맞은 말이 바르게 짝지어진 것은?

• (A)_____ Hyejin wears glasses, Yuna does not.
• He wasn't late for class (B)_____ he got up late.
• Soyeon has long hair, (C)_____ Yeji has short hair.

   (A)   (B)   (C)
① Since – though – while
② Since – since – until
③ While – before – as
④ While – though – while
⑤ After – since – as

09 다음 〈보기〉의 문장과 가장 가까운 뜻을 가진 문장을 고르시오.

┤ 보기 ├
Not only Grace but also Ken doesn't like swimming as well as running.

① Neither Grace nor Ken doesn't like swimming but also running.
② Neither Grace nor Ken likes both swimming and running.
③ Either Grace or Ken doesn't like swimming nor running.

④ Both Grace and Ken like not swimming but running.

⑤ Both Grace and Ken don't like swimming but running.

서답형

10 다음 두 문장을 한 문장으로 표현할 때, 빈칸에 들어갈 알맞은 말을 쓰시오.

> • Sean began to work out at the gym two weeks ago.
> • Sean's classmates started working out at the gym two weeks ago as well.
> ➡ _____ _____ _____
> _____ his classmates have been working out at the gym for two weeks.

11 다음 두 문장을 접속사를 이용하여 한 문장으로 만들 때 가장 적절한 것은?

> • The virus came from China.
> • But some Chinese politicians blamed other countries.

① Since the virus came from China, some Chinese politicians blamed other countries.

② As some Chinese politicians blamed other countries, the virus came from China.

③ If the virus didn't come from China, some Chinese politicians would not blame other countries.

④ When some Chinese politicians blamed other countries, the virus came from China.

⑤ While the virus came from China, some Chinese politicians blamed other countries.

[12~13] 다음 중 어법상 옳은 문장은?

12 ① Not only the audience were surprised but also impressed.

② They can not only meet the Santa Clause but also sees the Rudolph in Finland.

③ Shakespeare only liked to write the plays but also acted himself.

④ Hermione had lost not only her husband's watch and also his ties.

⑤ The participants of the experiment not only arrived on time but also worked hard.

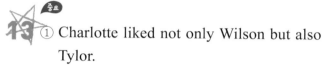

13 ① Charlotte liked not only Wilson but also Tylor.

② Can either you nor the doctor explain to me what made his condition worse?

③ Both Mina or her friend, Sana, watched the movie directed by the professor.

④ I think either Jade or her sister know how the problems were solved.

⑤ Not only Jessie but also Nadia wonder if the speaker is lying.

서답형

14 우리말과 일치하도록 (1)과 (2)에 공통으로 알맞은 접속사를 추가하여, 주어진 단어들을 바르게 배열하시오.

(1) 내가 샤워를 하는 동안에 전화가 울렸다.

(a shower, was, I, taking), the phone rang.

➡ _____

(2) 그녀는 지하철을 타고 출근하는 것을 선호하는 반면에, 나는 버스를 타는 것을 좋아한다.

(the subway, take, work, prefers, to, to, she), I like taking the bus.

➡ _____

01 다음 우리말과 일치하도록 괄호 안에 주어진 단어들을 바르게 배열하여 빈칸을 채우시오.

(1) 따뜻한 차가 감기에 걸린 사람들에게 좋을 뿐 아니라 건강한 사람들에게도 디저트로서 인기가 있다. (for, with, only, also, popular, good, but, not, people, colds)

➡ Warm tea is _____

_____ as a dessert

for healthy people.

(2) 고골모골은 달걀뿐만 아니라 꿀을 가지고도 만들어진다. (with, eggs, but, only, honey, not, made, also)

➡ *Gogol-mogol* is _____

_____.

(3) 당신뿐만 아니라 그들도 나에게 모두 친절했다. (they, you, but, not, were, only, also)

➡ _____

all kind to me.

(4) 민주와 예나 둘 다 그 문제에 책임이 있다. (Minju, Yena, responsible, and, are, for, both)

➡ _____

the problem.

02 다음은 고골모골을 만드는 방법이다. 각 빈칸에 아래 〈보기〉의 단어들 중에서 알맞은 것을 넣으시오.

┌─ 보기 ┐
while   until   as   and   how

• (1)_____ to Make *Gogol-mogol*

1. Put the egg and the honey in a large cup (2)_____ mix them.
2. Pour half a cup of milk in a pan. Add the butter. Warm it (3)_____ the butter melts.
3. Pour the hot milk and butter into the cup with the egg and the honey. Stir (4)_____ you pour.
4. Drink (5)_____ it is hot.

[03~05] 다음에 소개하는 각각의 음료를 주어로 하여, 'not only ~ but also 구문'을 포함하는 완전한 한 문장을 영작하시오. (단, 소개에 나오는 and를 제외한 모든 단어를 사용할 것.)

03
> A chicken soup: great for a sore throat and a stuffy nose

➡ _____

_____

04
> Samgyetang: warms your body and helps reduce the pain in your throat

➡ _____

_____

05
> The onion milk: a drink that is boiled with milk and chopped onion

➡ _____

_____

[06~09] 다음 두 문장을 접속사 While로 시작하는 완전한 하나의 문장으로 쓰시오.

06
> • Steve was born into a super rich family.
> • Bob's parents were very poor.

➡ _____

_____

07

- Linda left my room to watch TV.
- I was doing my homework at that time.

➡ _____

_____

(1) _____

_____

(2) _____

_____

(3) _____

_____

(4) _____

_____

08

- Marco sets the alarm to wake up early in the morning.
- Marco's wife doesn't use the alarm.

➡ _____

_____

09

- I could hear so many kinds of birds singing in the woods.
- I was taking a walk along the lake park.

➡ _____

_____

_____

11 다음 그림을 보고 괄호 안의 단어를 배열하여 빈칸을 알맞게 채우시오.

(1)

Samgyetang _____

_____ yummy.

(but, promotes, not, is, health, only, your)

10 주어진 우리말을 〈조건〉에 맞게 영작하시오.

┤ 조건 ├

1. 'not only A but also B'를 사용할 것.
2. 주어진 단어를 괄호 안의 글자 수 조건에 맞추어 어법에 맞게 활용할 것.

(1) Ms. Elena, good teacher, great artist. (12 단어, Ms. Elena는 한 단어로 간주할 것.)

(2) can, Jenny, sing well, rap fast in English (12 단어)

(3) Dahyun, pretty, very smart (9 단어)

(4) Anna, her sisters, rich (9 단어)

(2)

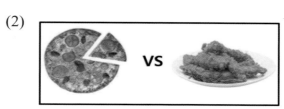

Andy enjoys pizza, _____

_____.

(the rest, love, while, members, his family, of, chicken)

Foods That Fight Colds

What do you do when you catch a cold? Of course, you want to stay
warm, so maybe you put on more clothes. Some people like to drink
hot tea. Ginger tea is something people in Korea often drink. With its
special taste, it warms your body and helps reduce the pain in your
throat. What do people drink or eat in other countries when they catch
a cold? Let's find out.

In Finland, where it is very cold in winter, people have a special
drink when they catch a cold. It is a cup of onion milk. They put
chopped onion in milk and boil it over low heat for half an hour. This
simple drink is said to be good for a cold.

While people in Korea and Finland look for drinks when sick, many
people in America want a bowl of chicken soup. It is usually made
with chicken and vegetables, but the recipe is different from one family
to another. Salt and pepper can be added before eating. People in
America believe that a bowl of warm chicken soup is great for a sore
throat and a stuffy nose.

ginger 생강
taste 맛
reduce 줄이다
pain 아픔, 통증
throat 목구멍, 목
catch a cold 감기에 걸리다
find out 알아내다, 발견하다
chop 다지다, 잘게 썰다
boil 끓다, 끓이다
recipe 요리법, 조리법
pepper 후추
sore 아픈, 따가운
stuffy (코가) 막힌

📎 **확인문제**

● 다음 문장이 본문의 내용과 일치하면 T, 일치하지 않으면 F를 쓰시오.

1 Ginger tea is what people in Korea often drink. ☐

2 Ginger tea warms your body and helps reduce a fever. ☐

3 In Finland, people have a cup of onion milk when they catch a cold. ☐

4 To make onion milk, you need to put chopped onion in milk and boil it over high heat for an hour. ☐

5 Many people in America want a bowl of chicken soup when sick. ☐

6 The recipe for chicken soup is alike everywhere. ☐

In Russia and in Eastern Europe, when people get sick, they eat a dessert called *gogol-mogol*. It is made with eggs and honey.
고골모골이라고 불리는 후식. a dessert 다음에 'which is'가 생략

Some people add chocolate, butter, lemon juice, or milk to make it taste better. It looks like thick yogurt. People often drink a cup of warm *gogol-mogol* when they have a sore throat. *Gogol-mogol* is not only good for people with a cold but also popular as a dessert for healthy people. When served as a dessert, it is usually served cold or at room temperature.

to make: 부사적 용법(목적). make(사역동사)+목적어+동사원형
taste+형용사: ~한 맛이 나다
not only A but also B = B as well as A: A뿐만 아니라 B도

Why not try making one of the foods you have found out about? It will be fun and good for your health.
제안하는 표현, '~하는 게 어때?'

How to Make *Gogol-mogol* (Serves one)
~하는 방법　　　　　　　(음식의 양이) 돌아가다

You need: 1 egg, 1/2 cup of milk, honey (5 g), butter (15 g)

1. Put the egg and the honey in a large cup and mix them.

2. Pour half a cup of milk in a pan. Add the butter. Warm it until the butter melts.

3. Pour the hot milk and butter into the cup with the egg and the honey. Stir as you pour.
~하는 동안에(접속사)

4. Drink while it is hot.

Glossary (right column):
- eastern 동쪽의
- honey 꿀
- thick 진한, 걸쭉한
- yogurt 요구르트
- serve 제공하다
- temperature 온도, 체온
- mix 섞다
- pour 붓다
- melt 녹다
- stir 젓다

 확인문제

● 다음 문장이 본문의 내용과 일치하면 T, 일치하지 <u>않으면</u> F를 쓰시오.

1　In Russia and in Eastern Europe, people eat a dessert called *gogol-mogol* when they get sick. ☐

2　*Gogol-mogol* is made with mainly chocolate, butter, lemon juice, or milk. ☐

3　*Gogol-mogol* is popular as a dessert for healthy people as well as good for people with a cold. ☐

4　When served as a dessert, *gogol-mogol* is usually served hot or at room temperature. ☐

5　To make one portion of *gogol-mogol*, 1/2 cup of milk is needed. ☐

6　When you make *gogol-mogol*, pepper is added to the milk before warming it. ☐

● 우리말을 참고하여 빈칸에 알맞은 말을 쓰시오.

1 Foods That _____ _____

2 What do you do when you _____ _____ _____?

3 Of course, you want to _____ _____, so maybe you put on more clothes.

4 Some people like _____ _____ _____ _____.

5 Ginger tea is _____ people in Korea _____ _____.

6 With its special taste, it warms your body and _____ _____ _____ _____ in your throat.

7 _____ _____ _____ _____ _____ in other countries when they catch a cold?

8 Let's _____ _____.

9 In Finland, where it is very cold in winter, people _____ _____ _____ _____ when they catch a cold.

10 It is _____ _____ _____ _____ _____.

11 They put _____ _____ in milk and boil it _____ _____ _____ for half an hour.

12 This simple drink _____ _____ _____ _____ for a cold.

13 _____ people in Korea and Finland look for drinks when sick, many people in America want _____ _____ _____ _____ _____.

14 It is usually made with chicken and vegetables, but the recipe is different _____ _____ _____ _____.

15 Salt and pepper _____ _____ _____ before eating.

16 People in America believe that a bowl of warm chicken soup is _____ _____ _____ _____ _____ _____.

1 감기와 싸우는 음식들

2 여러분은 감기에 걸리면 어떻게 하는가?

3 당연히, 따뜻함을 유지하고자 할 것이고, 아마도 옷을 더 입을 것이다.

4 몇몇 사람들은 따뜻한 차를 마시는 것을 좋아한다.

5 생강차는 한국인들이 자주 마시는 것이다.

6 특별한 맛과 함께, 그것은 여러분의 몸을 따뜻하게 하고 목 통증을 완화하는 데 도움을 준다.

7 다른 나라에서는 사람들이 감기에 걸렸을 때 무엇을 마시거나 먹을까?

8 함께 알아보자.

9 겨울이 매우 추운 핀란드에서는 사람들이 감기에 걸리면 특별한 음료를 마신다.

10 그것은 양파 우유이다.

11 그들은 우유에 잘게 썬 양파를 넣고 30분 동안 약한 불에서 끓인다.

12 이 단순한 음료는 감기에 좋다고 한다.

13 한국 사람들과 핀란드 사람들이 아플 때 음료를 찾는 반면, 미국의 많은 사람들은 닭고기 수프를 원한다.

14 그것은 보통 닭고기와 야채로 만들어지는데, 요리법은 가정마다 다르다.

15 소금과 후추를 먹기 전에 넣기도 한다.

16 미국인들은 따뜻한 닭고기 수프 한 그릇이 부은 목과 막힌 코에 좋다고 믿는다.

17 In Russia and in Eastern Europe, when people get sick, they eat a dessert _____ gogol-mogol.

18 It _____ _____ _____ eggs and honey.

19 Some people add chocolate, butter, lemon juice, or milk _____ _____ _____ _____ _____ .

20 It _____ _____ thick yogurt.

21 People often drink a cup of warm *gogol-mogol* when they _____ _____ _____ _____ .

22 *Gogol-mogol* is _____ _____ good for people with a cold _____ _____ popular as a dessert for healthy people.

23 When _____ as a dessert, it is usually served cold or _____ _____ _____ .

24 _____ _____ try making one of the foods you have found out _____ ?

25 It will be fun and _____ _____ your health.

26 _____ _____ _____ *Gogol-mogol* (Serves one)

27 _____ _____ : 1 egg, 1/2 cup of milk, honey (5 g), butter (15 g)

28 1. Put the egg and the honey in a large cup and _____ _____ .

29 2. _____ half a cup of milk in a pan.

30 _____ the butter.

31 _____ it until the butter _____ .

32 3. _____ the hot milk and butter _____ the cup _____ the egg and the honey.

33 _____ _____ you pour.

34 4. Drink _____ it is hot.

17 러시아와 동유럽에서는 사람들이 아플 때, 고골모골이라는 후식을 먹는다.

18 그것은 달걀과 꿀로 만든다.

19 어떤 사람들은 그것을 더 맛있게 하기 위해 초콜릿, 버터, 레몬주스, 또는 우유를 첨가한다.

20 그것은 진한 요구르트처럼 보인다.

21 사람들은 목이 아플 때 종종 따뜻한 고골모골 한 잔을 마신다.

22 고골모골은 감기에 걸린 사람들에게 좋을 뿐만 아니라 건강한 사람들의 후식으로도 인기가 있다.

23 후식으로 제공될 때에는 보통 차갑게 또는 실온으로 제공된다.

24 여러분이 알아본 음식들 중 하나를 만들어 보는 것은 어떨까?

25 그것은 재미있고 여러분의 건강에 좋을 것이다.

26 고골모골 만드는 방법 (1인분)

27 필요한 것: 달걀 1개, 우유 1/2 컵, 꿀 5g, 버터 15g

28 1. 달걀과 꿀을 큰 컵에 넣고 섞는다.

29 2. 우유 반 컵을 팬에 붓는다.

30 버터를 추가한다.

31 버터가 녹을 때까지 데운다.

32 3. 뜨거운 우유와 버터를 달걀과 꿀이 있는 컵에 붓는다.

33 부으면서 젓는다.

34 4. 뜨거울 때 마신다.

● 우리말을 참고하여 본문을 영작하시오.

1 감기와 싸우는 음식들
➡ _____

2 여러분은 감기에 걸리면 어떻게 하는가?
➡ _____

3 당연히, 따뜻함을 유지하고자 할 것이고, 아마도 옷을 더 입을 것이다.
➡ _____

4 몇몇 사람들은 따뜻한 차를 마시는 것을 좋아한다.
➡ _____

5 생강차는 한국인들이 자주 마시는 것이다.
➡ _____

6 특별한 맛과 함께, 그것은 여러분의 몸을 따뜻하게 하고 목 통증을 완화하는 데 도움을 준다.
➡ _____

7 다른 나라에서는 사람들이 감기에 걸렸을 때 무엇을 마시거나 먹을까?
➡ _____

8 함께 알아보자.
➡ _____

9 겨울이 매우 추운 핀란드에서는 사람들이 감기에 걸리면 특별한 음료를 마신다.
➡ _____

10 그것은 양파 우유이다.
➡ _____

11 그들은 우유에 잘게 썬 양파를 넣고 30분 동안 약한 불에서 끓인다.
➡ _____

12 이 단순한 음료는 감기에 좋다고 한다.
➡ _____

13 한국 사람들과 핀란드 사람들이 아플 때 음료를 찾는 반면, 미국의 많은 사람들은 닭고기 수프를 원한다.
➡ _____

14 그것은 보통 닭고기와 야채로 만들어지는데, 요리법은 가정마다 다르다.
➡ _____
_____

15 소금과 후추를 먹기 전에 넣기도 한다.
➡ _____

16 미국인들은 따뜻한 닭고기 수프 한 그릇이 부은 목과 막힌 코에 좋다고 믿는다.
➡ _____
_____

17 러시아와 동유럽에서는 사람들이 아플 때, 고골모골이라는 후식을 먹는다.

➡ _____

18 그것은 달걀과 꿀로 만든다.

➡ _____

19 어떤 사람들은 그것을 더 맛있게 하기 위해 초콜릿, 버터, 레몬주스, 또는 우유를 첨가한다.

➡ _____

20 그것은 진한 요구르트처럼 보인다.

➡ _____

21 사람들은 목이 아플 때 종종 따뜻한 고골모골 한 잔을 마신다.

➡ _____

22 고골모골은 감기에 걸린 사람들에게 좋을 뿐만 아니라 건강한 사람들의 후식으로도 인기가 있다.

➡ _____

_____

23 후식으로 제공될 때에는 보통 차갑게 또는 실온으로 제공된다.

➡ _____

24 여러분이 알아본 음식들 중 하나를 만들어 보는 것은 어떨까?

➡ _____

25 그것은 재미있고 여러분의 건강에 좋을 것이다.

➡ _____

26 고골모골 만드는 방법 (1인분)

➡ _____

27 필요한 것: 달걀 1개, 우유 1/2컵, 꿀 5g, 버터 15g

➡ _____

28 1. 달걀과 꿀을 큰 컵에 넣고 섞는다.

➡ _____

29 2. 우유 반 컵을 팬에 붓는다.

➡ _____

30 버터를 추가한다.

➡ _____

31 버터가 녹을 때까지 데운다.

➡ _____

32 3. 뜨거운 우유와 버터를 달걀과 꿀이 있는 컵에 붓는다.

➡ _____

33 부으면서 젓는다.

➡ _____

34 4. 뜨거울 때 마신다.

➡ _____

[01~03] 다음 글을 읽고 물음에 답하시오.

What do you do when you catch a cold? (①) Of course, ⓐyou want to stay warmly, so maybe you put on more clothes. (②) Some people like to drink hot tea. (③) Ginger tea is something people in Korea often drink. (④) What do people drink or eat in other countries when they catch a cold? (⑤) Let's find out.

01 위 글의 흐름으로 보아, 주어진 문장이 들어가기에 가장 적절한 곳은?

> With its special taste, it warms your body and helps reduce the pain in your throat.

①   ②   ③   ④   ⑤

서답형

02 위 글의 밑줄 친 ⓐ에서 어법상 틀린 부분을 찾아 고치시오.

_____ ➡ _____

중요

03 위 글의 뒤에 올 내용으로 가장 알맞은 것을 고르시오.

① the various ways to stay warm when people catch a cold
② the clothes people like to wear when they catch a cold
③ what people in other countries drink or eat as a dessert
④ the simple way to reduce the pain in the throat
⑤ the things people around the world drink or eat to fight colds

[04~06] 다음 글을 읽고 물음에 답하시오.

ⓐWhile people in Korea and Finland look for drinks when sick, many people in America want a bowl of chicken soup. It is usually made with chicken and vegetables, but the recipe is different from one family to another. Salt and pepper can be added before eating. People in America believe that a bowl of warm chicken soup is great for a sore throat and a stuffy nose.

04 위 글의 밑줄 친 ⓐWhile과 같은 의미로 쓰인 것을 모두 고르시오.

① Did anyone call while I was away?
② While Tom's very good at science, his brother is absolutely hopeless.
③ It took him a while to calm down.
④ Strike while the iron is hot.
⑤ The walls are green, while the ceiling is white.

서답형

05 다음 문장에서 위 글의 내용과 다른 부분을 찾아 고치시오.

> Many people in America look for drinks when sick.

➡ _____
_____
_____

서답형

06 What can be added to chicken soup before eating it? Answer in English in a full sentence. (6 words)

➡ _____

[07~09] 다음 글을 읽고 물음에 답하시오.

In Finland, where it is very cold in winter, people have a special drink when they catch a cold. ⓐIt is a cup of onion milk. They put ____ⓑ____ onion in milk and boil it (A)[above / over] low heat (B)[during / for] half an hour. This simple drink is said to be good (C)[at / for] a cold.

서답형

07 다음 빈칸에 알맞은 단어를 넣어 위 글의 밑줄 친 ⓐ이 가리키는 것을 완성하시오.

_____ people have in Finland when they catch a cold

서답형

08 위 글의 빈칸 ⓑ에 chop을 알맞은 형태로 쓰시오.

➡ _____

서답형

09 위 글의 괄호 (A)~(C)에서 문맥이나 어법상 알맞은 낱말을 골라 쓰시오.

(A) _____ (B) _____ (C) _____

[10~12] 다음 글을 읽고 물음에 답하시오.

In Russia and in Eastern Europe, when people get sick, they eat a dessert called *gogol-mogol*. (①) Some people add chocolate, butter, lemon juice, or milk to make it taste better. (②) It looks like thick yogurt. (③) People often drink a cup of warm *gogol-mogol* when they have a sore throat. (④) *Gogol-mogol* is ⓐnot only good for people with a cold but also popular as a dessert for healthy people. (⑤) When served as a dessert, it is usually served cold or at room temperature.

10 위 글의 흐름으로 보아, 주어진 문장이 들어가기에 가장 적절한 곳은?

It is made with eggs and honey.

①   ②   ③   ④   ⑤

11 위 글의 밑줄 친 ⓐnot only와 바꿔 쓸 수 있는 말을 모두 고르시오.

① as well as   ② not just
③ not   ④ not simply
⑤ not merely

중요

12 Which question CANNOT be answered after reading the passage?

① In Russia and in Eastern Europe, when people get sick, what do they eat?
② What is *gogol-mogol* made with?
③ To make *gogol-mogol* taste better, what do some people add?
④ How long does it take to make *gogol-mogol*?
⑤ Do people eat *gogol-mogol* only when they're sick?

[13~15] 다음 글을 읽고 물음에 답하시오.

While people in Korea and Finland look for drinks when sick, many people in America want ⓐ chicken soup. It is usually made with chicken and vegetables, but ⓑ요리법은 가정마다 다르다. Salt and pepper can be added before eating. People in America believe that a bowl of warm chicken soup is great for a sore throat and a stuffy nose.

13 위 글의 빈칸 ⓐ에 들어갈 알맞은 말을 고르시오.

① a glass of   ② a bottle of
③ a piece of   ④ a bowl of
⑤ a plate of

서답형

14 위 글의 밑줄 친 ⓑ의 우리말에 맞게 주어진 어휘를 이용하여 9 단어로 영작하시오.

the recipe, from, another

➡ _____

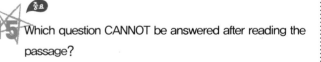

15 Which question CANNOT be answered after reading the passage?

① What do people in Korea and Finland look for when sick?
② What do many people in America want when sick?
③ How long does chicken soup have to be boiled?
④ What is chicken soup usually made with?
⑤ What do people in America believe warm chicken soup is great for?

16 주어진 문장 다음에 이어질 글의 순서로 가장 적절한 것은?

What do you do when you catch a cold?

(A) Ginger tea is something people in Korea often drink. With its special taste, it warms your body and helps reduce the pain in your throat.
(B) Of course, you want to stay warm, so maybe you put on more clothes. Some people like to drink hot tea.
(C) What do people drink or eat in other countries when they catch a cold? Let's find out.

① (A) – (C) – (B)   ② (B) – (A) – (C)
③ (B) – (C) – (A)   ④ (C) – (A) – (B)
⑤ (C) – (B) – (A)

[17~18] 다음 글을 읽고 물음에 답하시오.

In Russia and in Eastern Europe, when people get sick, they eat a dessert called ① *gogol-mogol*. It is made with eggs and honey. Some people add chocolate, butter, lemon juice, or milk to make ②it taste better. ③It looks like thick ④yogurt. People often drink a cup of warm *gogol-mogol* when they have a sore throat. *Gogol-mogol* is not only good for people with a cold but also popular as a dessert for healthy people. When served as a dessert, ⑤it is usually served cold or at room temperature.

17 밑줄 친 ①~⑤ 중에서 가리키는 대상이 나머지 넷과 다른 것은?

①   ②   ③   ④   ⑤

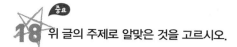 위 글의 주제로 알맞은 것을 고르시오.

① the ingredients for *gogol-mogol*, a popular dessert in Russia and in Eastern Europe

② the best way to relieve the symptoms of a cold

③ *gogol-mogol*, a popular dessert in sickness and in health in Russia and in Eastern Europe

④ the recipe for *gogol-mogol*, a popular dessert in sickness and in health

⑤ the effective therapy to treat disease

[19~20] 다음 글을 읽고 물음에 답하시오.

What do you do when you catch a cold? Of course, you want to stay warm, so maybe you put on more clothes. Some people like to drink hot tea. Ginger tea is something people in Korea often drink. With its special taste, it warms your body and helps reduce the pain in your throat. What do people drink or eat in other countries when they catch a cold? Let's find out.

19 위 글의 제목으로 알맞은 것을 고르시오.

① Put on More Clothes to Stay Warm

② The Best Hot Tea to Drink When You Feel Cold

③ What Do You Drink or Eat When You Catch a Cold?

④ The Way You Can Avoid Catching a Cold

⑤ How to Reduce the Pain in Your Throat

 According to the passage, which is NOT true?

① Some people put on more clothes when they catch a cold.

② Some people like to drink hot tea when they catch a cold.

③ Koreans often drink ginger tea when they catch a cold.

④ Ginger tea has a special smell.

⑤ Ginger tea warms your body and helps reduce the pain in your throat.

[21~22] 다음 글을 읽고 물음에 답하시오.

Why not try ⓐmake one of the foods you have found out about? It will be fun and good for your health.

_____ ⓑ _____ (Serves one)

You need: 1 egg, 1/2 cup of milk, honey (5 g), butter (15 g)

1. Put the egg and the honey in a large cup and mix them.

2. Pour half a cup of milk in a pan. Add the butter. Warm it until the butter melts.

3. Pour the hot milk and butter into the cup with the egg and the honey. Stir as you pour.

4. Drink while it is hot.

21 위 글의 밑줄 친 ⓐmake를 알맞은 형으로 고치시오.

➡ _____

22 위 글의 빈칸 ⓑ에 들어갈 제목으로 알맞은 것을 고르시오.

① What Is Good for Your Health?

② How to Make *Gogol-mogol*

③ What Is *Gogol-mogol* Made with?

④ The Reason *Gogol-mogol* Tastes Good

⑤ What Does *Gogol-mogol* Look Like?

[01~03] 다음 글을 읽고 물음에 답하시오.

What do you do when you catch a cold? Of course, ⓐyou want to stay warm, so maybe you take off more clothes. Some people like to drink hot tea. ⓑ생강차는 한국인들이 자주 마시는 것이다. With its special taste, it warms your body and helps reduce the pain in your throat. What do people drink or eat in other countries when they catch a cold? Let's find out.

01 위 글의 밑줄 친 ⓐ에서 흐름상 어색한 부분을 찾아 고치시오.

_____ ➡ _____

02 위 글의 밑줄 친 ⓑ의 우리말에 맞게 주어진 어휘를 알맞게 배열하시오.

> often / people in Korea / something / is / drink / ginger tea

➡ _____
_____

03 다음 빈칸 (A)와 (B)에 알맞은 단어를 넣어 '생강차의 효능'을 완성하시오.

> It (A)_____ your body and helps to reduce the pain in your (B)_____.

[04~06] 다음 글을 읽고 물음에 답하시오.

In Finland, ____ⓐ____ it is very cold in winter, people have a special drink when they catch a cold. It is a cup of onion milk. They put chopped onion in milk and boil ⓑit over low heat for half an hour. ⓒThis simple drink is said to be good for a cold.

04 위 글의 빈칸 ⓐ에 들어갈 알맞은 한 단어를 쓰시오.

➡ _____

05 위 글의 밑줄 친 ⓑit이 가리키는 것을 본문에서 찾아 쓰시오.

➡ _____

06 위 글의 밑줄 친 ⓒ를 다음과 같이 바꿔 쓸 때 빈칸에 들어갈 알맞은 말을 4 단어로 쓰시오.

> It is said that _____ _____ _____ good for a cold.

[07~09] 다음 글을 읽고 물음에 답하시오.

(A)While people in Korea and Finland look for drinks when sick, many people in America want a bowl of chicken soup. (B)It is usually made with chicken and vegetables, but the recipe is different from one family to another. Salt and pepper can ____ⓐ____ before eating. People in America believe that a bowl of warm chicken soup is great for a sore throat and a stuffy nose.

07 위 글의 빈칸 ⓐ에 add를 알맞은 형태로 쓰시오.

➡ _____

08 위 글의 밑줄 친 문장 (A)에 생략된 말을 넣어 문장을 다시 쓰시오.

➡ _____
_____

⭐09 위 글의 밑줄 친 (B)를 능동태로 고치시오.

➡ _____

[10~12] 다음 글을 읽고 물음에 답하시오.

> ⓐWhy not try making one of the foods you have found out about? It will be fun and good for your health.
> How to Make *Gogol-mogol* (Serves one)
> ⓑYou need: 1 egg, 1/2 cup of milk, honey (5 g), butter (15 g)
> 1. Put the egg and the honey in a large cup and mix ⓒthem.
> 2. Pour half a cup of milk in a pan. Add the butter. Warm it until the butter melts.
> 3. Pour the hot milk and butter into the cup with the egg and the honey. Stir as you pour.
> 4. Drink while it is hot.

10 위 글의 밑줄 친 ⓐ를 다음과 같이 바꿔 쓸 때 빈칸에 들어갈 알맞은 단어를 쓰시오.

(1) How about _____ making one of the foods you have found out about?

(2) _____ _____ _____ try making one of the foods you have found out about?

11 위 글의 밑줄 친 ⓑYou need와 바꿔 쓸 수 있는 한 단어를 철자 l로 시작하여 쓰시오.

➡ _____

12 위 글의 밑줄 친 ⓒthem이 가리키는 것을 본문에서 찾아 쓰시오.

➡ _____

[13~14] 다음 글을 읽고 물음에 답하시오.

> In Russia and in Eastern Europe, when people get sick, they eat a dessert called *gogol-mogol*. It is made with eggs and honey. ⓐSome people add chocolate, butter, lemon juice, or milk to make it tasting better. It looks like thick yogurt. People often drink a cup of warm *gogol-mogol* when they have a sore throat. ⓑGogol-mogol is not only good for people with a cold but also popular as a dessert for healthy people. When served as a dessert, it is usually served cold or at room temperature.

⭐13 위 글의 밑줄 친 ⓐ에서 어법상 틀린 부분을 찾아 고치시오.

_____ ➡ _____

14 위 글의 밑줄 친 ⓑ를 as well as를 사용하여 고쳐 쓰시오.

➡ _____
_____

해석

After You Read B

Look! I've made *gogol-mogol*.

Happy07: What is *gogol-mogol*?

└ Bora: It's a dessert that people in Russia and in Eastern Europe eat when
　　　　　　　　　　　　　목적격 관계대명사
they are sick.

Yumyum: It looks delicious. What is it made with?
　　　　　　　　　　　　　　　　　~으로 만들어지다
└ Bora: It's made with eggs and honey.
　　　　　　　　　with 다음에는 재료가 온다.
Yumyum: What's that you put on top of it?
　　　　　　　　　　　　　　　　　　　　↓ taste+형용사: ~한 맛이 나다
└ Bora: I put chocolate on top to make it taste better.
　　　　　　　　　　　　　　　부사적 용법(목적), 사역동사 make+목적어+동사원형.
Happy07: Do people also eat it when they're not sick?
　　　　　　　　　　　　　　gogol-mogol
└ Bora: Sure. It's a popular dessert. When served as a dessert, it's usually
　　　　　　　　　　　　　　　When과 served 사이에 it is가 생략됨.
served cold or at room temperature.

구문해설 • eastern: 동쪽의 • honey: 꿀 • serve: 제공하다 • temperature: 온도, 체온

봬! 나는 고골모골을 만들었어.

Happy07: 고골모골이 뭐야?

보라: 그것은 러시아와 동유럽에서 사람들이 아플 때 먹는 후식이야.

Yumyum: 그것은 맛있어 보여. 그것은 무엇으로 만들어지니?

보라: 그것은 달걀과 꿀로 만들어져.

Yumyum: 그것 꼭대기에 올린 것이 뭐니?

보라: 나는 그것을 더 맛있게 하기 위해 꼭대기에 초콜릿을 올렸어.

Happy07: 사람들이 아프지 않을 때도 그것을 먹니?

보라: 물론이야. 그것은 인기 있는 후식이야. 후식으로 제공될 때에는 보통 차갑게 또는 실온으로 제공돼.

Writing Workshop

While many Koreans eat Samgyetang when they are sick, many people in
'대조'의 접속사 ~인 반면에
India eat tomato soup. Here is how to make it.
　　　　　　　　　　　　유도부사(도치) 의문사+to부정사(명사구)
You need: 1 tomato, some water, black pepper, salt

First, chop one fresh tomato. Then put the chopped tomato in a pan and pour
　　　　　　　　　　　　　　　　　　　　　　　과거분사(수동)
some water over it. Next, boil the mixture for ten minutes. Then turn off the

heat and leave it to cool down. Next, blend it until it is smooth. Finally, add
　　　　　　　　　자동사: to be cooled(×)　　　　　　　'시간'의 접속사 will be(×)
some black pepper and salt. Now you can enjoy the tomato soup. This tomato

soup is not only healthy but also delicious.
　　　　　　　not only 형용사 but also 형용사

구문해설 • black pepper: 후추 • chop: (잘게) 썰다, 다지다 • blend: 섞다, 혼합하다

많은 한국인들이 아플 때 삼계탕을 먹는 반면에, 인도의 많은 사람들은 토마토 수프를 먹는다. 여기 그것을 만드는 방법이 있다.

필요한 것: 토마토 한 개, 물 약간, 후추, 소금

첫 번째로, 신선한 토마토 한 개를 다진다. 그 후, 다진 토마토를 팬 위에 놓고 그 위에 물을 조금 붓는다. 다음으로, 그 혼합물을 10분간 끓인다. 불을 끄고 식도록 둔다. 다음, 부드러워질 때까지 그것을 섞는다. 마지막으로, 후추와 소금을 약간 넣는다. 이제 토마토 수프를 즐길 수 있다. 이 토마토 수프는 건강에 좋을 뿐 아니라 맛있다.

01 다음 짝지어진 단어의 관계가 같도록 빈칸에 알맞은 말을 쓰시오.

> blend : compound = while : _____

02 다음 중 밑줄 친 부분의 뜻풀이가 바르지 <u>않은</u> 것은?

① <u>Blend</u> the flour with the milk to make a smooth paste. (혼합하다)

② The stage is covered with sand for the <u>desert</u> scenes. (후식)

③ Jasmine was <u>hurt</u> by the coldness in his voice. (아프다, 아프게 하다)

④ <u>Local</u> entertainments are listed in the newspaper. (지역의)

⑤ This <u>recipe</u> will be enough for ten servings. (요리법)

03 다음 주어진 문장의 밑줄 친 warm과 같은 의미로 쓰인 것은?

> The <u>warm</u> climate favours many types of tropical plants.

① Take a <u>warm</u> bath to soothe tense, tired muscles.

② It'll <u>warm</u> up in the day time in the spring.

③ <u>Warm</u> up before lifting heavy weights.

④ The room was decorated in <u>warm</u> shades of red and orange.

⑤ I wish it would <u>warm</u> up soon. It's been so cold.

04 다음 우리말을 주어진 단어를 이용하여 영작하시오.

> 너는 입을 통해서가 아니라, 코를 통해서 호흡해야 한다. (breathe through)

➡ _____

_____

05 다음 영영풀이에 해당하는 단어로 알맞은 것은?

> to flow, as from one container to another, or into, over, or on something

① wear   ② pour   ③ stir

④ reduce   ⑤ melt

[06~07] 다음 대화를 읽고 물음에 답하시오.

B: Alice, what's that you're eating?

G: It's *rasmalai*.

B: *Ra....* (A)Could you say that again?

G: *Ras-ma-lai*. It's like a cheesecake in a sweet cream. It's a traditional food in India.

06 위 대화의 밑줄 친 (A)와 바꿔 쓸 수 있는 표현을 두 개 이상 쓰시오.

➡ _____

07 Where is *rasmalai* from? (4 words)

➡ _____

08 다음 대화의 밑줄 친 부분과 바꿔 쓸 수 없는 것은?

> A: Have you ever tried *macaron*?
> B: Could you say that again?
> A: *Macaron*. It's a traditional dessert in France.

① Sorry?
② Pardon?
③ I beg your pardon?
④ Can you lower your voice down?
⑤ Say that again, please?

09 다음 대화의 빈칸에 들어갈 수 없는 것은?

> A: _____ a good traditional dish?
> B: Try Samgyetang. It'll give you energy.

① Can you recommend
② Could you recommend
③ Can you give me a recommendation for
④ Could you give me a recommendation for
⑤ Can I make a recommendation for

[10~12] 다음 대화를 읽고 물음에 답하시오.

> M: Good afternoon. A table for two?
> B: Yes.
> M: This way please. Here is the menu. ① I'll be back in a few minutes and take your order.
> B: Okay. Thank you.
> G: ② Could you recommend something?
> B: ③ Well, I'd recommend the Bibimbap.
> G: I'm sorry. Could you say that again, please? ④
> B: This one. Bi-bim-bap. It's made with lots of vegetables, beef and an egg over rice. It's tasty and it's also good for your health.
> G: That sounds great. ⑤ I'll try it.
> B: It's served with a spicy red pepper sauce. Is that okay?
> G: No problem. I like spicy food.

10 위 대화의 ①~⑤ 중에서 주어진 문장이 들어가기에 가장 적절한 곳은?

> I don't know much about Korean food.

①   ②   ③   ④   ⑤

11 다음 중 위 대화를 읽고 대답할 수 없는 질문은?

① What did M say to B and G?
② What kind of food did B recommend G?
③ Has G ever tried any Korean food before?
④ What is the Bibimbap made with?
⑤ What is the Bibimbap good for?

12 위 대화에 나타난 G의 심경으로 가장 적절한 것을 고르시오.

① concerned   ② bored
③ shocked   ④ scared
⑤ excited

Grammar

[13~14] 다음 중 어법상 <u>어색한</u> 문장을 <u>모두</u> 고르시오.

13 ① April not only lent me her house for a week but also offered me a job.

② Not only Karen but also Tylor had the courage to fight against the disease.

③ My mom made not only those candies but also very yummy.

④ The people were already aware of not only the event but also the rumors.

⑤ Not only Victor was good at running, but also he played soccer well.

14 ① Both the owners or the borrowers of the houses were disappointed with the government policy.

② Neither Jordan nor his basketball team members were happy with the scores.

③ Either Minsu and his friends are coming this evening.

④ Not only can the villagers imagine the story but they also guess the ending.

⑤ Not only you but also your teacher was at the meeting.

[15~16] 다음 주어진 두 문장을 같은 의미의 한 문장으로 알맞게 바꾼 것은?

15
- Sarah believed the news.
- Her daughter didn't believe it.

① Sarah believed the news as her daughter didn't.

② Since Sarah believed the news, her daughter didn't believe it.

③ Sarah believed the news before her daughter didn't.

④ Sarah believed the news while her daughter didn't.

⑤ Sarah believed the news whether her daughter didn't believe it or not.

16
- Harrison was fired from the company.
- Others had a job and could make a living.

① Because Harrison was fired from the company, others had a job and could make a living.

② While Harrison was fired from the company, others had a job and could make a living.

③ Harrison was fired from the company, and thus others had a job and could make a living.

④ If Harrison was fired from the company, others had a job and could make a living.

⑤ During Harrison was fired from the company, others had a job and could make a living.

Reading

[17~18] 다음 글을 읽고 물음에 답하시오.

In Finland, ⓐwhere it is very cold in winter, people have a special drink when they catch a cold. It is a cup of onion milk. They put chopped onion in milk and boil it over low heat for half an hour. This simple drink is said to be good for a cold.

17 위 글의 밑줄 친 ⓐwhere와 문법적 쓰임이 같은 것을 고르시오.

① Where do you live?
② This is the house where I was born.
③ Where there's a will, there's a way.
④ Where are you going?
⑤ I don't know where to go.

18 According to the passage, which is NOT true?

① In Finland, it is very cold in winter.
② In Finland, people have a cup of onion milk when they catch a cold.
③ To make the onion milk, it is necessary to put chopped onion in milk.
④ You should boil the chopped onion in milk over low heat for thirty minutes.
⑤ The onion milk is too simple to be good for a cold.

[19~20] 다음 글을 읽고 물음에 답하시오.

While people in Korea and Finland look for drinks when sick, many people in America want a bowl of chicken soup. ⓐIt is usually made with chicken and vegetables, but the recipe is different from one family to another. Salt and pepper can be added before eating. People in America believe that a bowl of warm chicken soup is great for a sore throat and a stuffy nose.

19 위 글의 밑줄 친 ⓐIt이 가리키는 것을 본문에서 찾아 쓰시오.

➡ _____

20 본문의 내용과 일치하도록 다음 빈칸에 알맞은 단어를 쓰시오.

Unlike people in Korea and Finland, many people in America look for _____ _____ _____ _____ when sick.

In Russia and in Eastern Europe, when people get sick, they eat a dessert called *gogol-mogol*. It is made ⓐ eggs and honey. Some people add chocolate, butter, lemon juice, or milk (A)그것을 더 맛있게 하기 위해. It looks like thick yogurt. People often drink a cup of warm *gogol-mogol* when they have a sore throat. *Gogol-mogol* is not only good for people with a cold but also popular ⓑ a dessert for healthy people. When ⓒ as a dessert, it is usually served cold or at room temperature.

21 위 글의 빈칸 ⓐ와 ⓑ에 들어갈 전치사가 바르게 짝지어진 것은?

	ⓐ	ⓑ			ⓐ	ⓑ
①	with	–	as	②	from	– at
③	of	–	for	④	from	– as
⑤	with	–	for			

22 위 글의 빈칸 ⓒ에 serve를 알맞은 형태로 쓰시오.

➡ _____

23 위 글의 밑줄 친 (A)의 우리말에 맞게 주어진 어휘를 이용하여 5 단어로 영작하시오.

make

➡ _____

While many Koreans eat Samgyetang when they are sick, many people in India eat tomato soup. Here is how to make it.

You need: 1 tomato, some water, black pepper, salt

First, chop one fresh tomato. Then put the chopped tomato in a pan and pour some water over it. Next, boil the mixture for ten minutes. Then turn off the heat and leave it to cool down. Next, blend it until it is smooth. Finally, add some black pepper and salt. Now you can enjoy the tomato soup. ⓐThis tomato soup is not only healthy but also delicious.

24 다음 중 인도의 토마토 수프를 만드는 재료가 아닌 것을 고르시오.

① 토마토 ② 물 ③ 쌀
④ 후추 ⑤ 소금

25 What should be mixed in a pan first? Answer in English in a full sentence.

➡ _____

_____

26 위 글의 밑줄 친 ⓐ와 같은 뜻이 아닌 문장을 고르시오.

① This tomato soup is not only healthy but delicious as well.
② This tomato soup is not just healthy but also delicious.
③ This tomato soup is delicious as well as healthy.
④ This tomato soup is not healthy but delicious.
⑤ Besides being healthy, this tomato soup is delicious.

01 다음 영영풀이가 가리키는 것을 고르시오.

> to change from a liquid to a gas as a result of heat

① boil ② chop ③ soup
④ stir ⑤ taste

02 〈보기〉에서 알맞은 단어를 골라 문장을 완성하시오.

> ┤ 보기 ├
> a bottle of / a cup of / as well as / be different from / is good for

(1) I bought _____ wine for her housewarming party.
(2) Exercising every day _____ your health.
(3) The mind _____ the body needs exercise.

[03~05] 다음 글을 읽고 물음에 답하시오.

M: Welcome to the Sydney Information Center. Sydney has many places you will want to visit. The Rocks Markets is one of (A)them. There you can buy art, clothing, books and many other things. You can also eat fresh, tasty local food. (B)저희는 the Rocks Markets에 방문하실 것을 추천합니다, and enjoying the food and the fun there.

03 위 글의 밑줄 친 (A)them이 가리키는 것을 찾아 쓰시오. (8 words)

➡ _____

04 위 글의 밑줄 친 (B)를 주어진 우리말을 이용하여 영작하시오.

➡ _____

05 위 글에서 언급된 the Rocks Markets에서 찾을 수 없는 것은?

① paintings ② clothes ③ hotels
④ books ⑤ local food

[06~08] 다음 대화를 읽고 물음에 답하시오.

B: Tomorrow is my dad's birthday. I'd like to do something special for him.
G: (A)How about cooking something for him? He would really like that.
B: That sounds great. Can you recommend something easy to cook?
G: Umm. How about Gimchijeon? (B)그건 만들기 쉽고 맛있어.
B: Oh, that's a good idea. He'll love it.

06 위 대화의 밑줄 친 (A)를 'I would'로 시작하는 문장으로 바꿔 쓰시오. (7 words)

➡ _____

07 위 대화의 밑줄 친 (B)를 영작하시오. (7 words)

➡ _____

08 위 대화를 읽고 답할 수 **없는** 질문을 고르시오.

① When is B's dad's birthday?
② What kind of birthday gift is B preparing for his dad?
③ What did G recommend B for B's dad's birthday?
④ What kind of food does B's dad like most?
⑤ What did G say about the Korean food she recommended?

[09~10] 다음 대화를 읽고 물음에 답하시오.

> **A:** Have you ever (A)tried *brigadeiro*?
> **B:** Sorry, could you say that again?
> **A:** *Brigadeiro*. It's a (B)tradition dessert in Brazil.

출제율 95%

09 다음 중 위 대화의 밑줄 친 (A)tried와 같은 의미로 쓰이지 **않은** 것은?

① This is delicious. You ought to <u>try</u> some.
② Harry isn't here. <u>Try</u> phoning his home number.
③ <u>Try</u> this new dish, created by our head chef.
④ You should <u>try</u> the shoes on before you buy them.
⑤ <u>Try</u> not to excite your baby too much before bedtime.

출제율 90%

10 위 대화의 밑줄 친 (B)를 알맞은 형으로 고치시오.

➡ _____

출제율 95%

11 다음 대화의 밑줄 친 부분의 목적으로 가장 적절한 것은?

> **B:** <u>Could you recommend a good traditional dish?</u>
> **W:** Try Samgyetang. It'll give you energy.

① to request a recommendation
② to make a recommendation
③ to request a treat
④ to give W energy
⑤ to ask to cook

[12~13] 다음 중 빈칸에 들어갈 수 **없는** 말을 고르시오.

출제율 95%

12

> Rachel of the volunteer organization was not only _____ but also generous.

① smart   ② friendly   ③ lovely
④ kind   ⑤ truly

출제율 100%

13

> *Gogol-mogol* is not only good for people with a cold but also _____.

① widely known as a cold-prevention effect for healthy people
② effective in healing people with other diseases
③ acts as a refreshing drink for the nervous people.
④ considered to be helpful in lowering body temperature
⑤ popular as a dessert for healthy people

14 다음 문장의 빈칸 (A), (B), (C)에 들어갈 말로 가장 적절하게 짝지어진 것은?

- (A)_____ she took a long walk, Sumi felt so tired.
- (B)_____ I was watching the show, I could hear something crying behind the stage.
- (C)_____ he liked to go fishing, his wife hated fishing very much.

(A)	(B)	(C)

① Since – While – While
② As – Before – While
③ Though – Until – Although
④ As – While – As
⑤ Though – Until – As

15 다음 중 밑줄 친 부분이 흐름상 어색한 것은?

① My daughter never takes off her life jacket while she is on the boat.
② While climbing the mountain, they saw a huge bear between the trees.
③ While my baby son was brushing his teeth, one of them came out.
④ While the girls were eating some snacks, they heard the news.
⑤ While you need anything at all, call me at any time.

[16~18] 다음 글을 읽고 물음에 답하시오.

What do you do when you ⓐcatch a cold? Of course, you want to stay warm, so maybe you put on more clothes. Some people like to drink hot tea. ⓑGinger tea is something people in Korea often drink. With its special taste, ⓒit warms your body and helps reduce the pain in your throat. What do people drink or eat in other countries when they catch a cold? Let's find out.

16 위 글의 밑줄 친 ⓐcatch a cold와 바꿔 쓸 수 없는 말을 고르시오.

① come down with a cold
② get a cold
③ have a cough
④ take cold
⑤ have a cold

17 위 글의 밑줄 친 문장 ⓑ에 생략된 말을 넣어 문장을 다시 쓰시오.

➡ _____

_____

18 위 글의 밑줄 친 ⓒit이 가리키는 것을 본문에서 찾아 쓰시오.

➡ _____

[19~21] 다음 글을 읽고 물음에 답하시오.

While people in Korea and Finland look for drinks when sick, many people in America want a bowl of chicken soup. It is usually made with chicken and vegetables, but the ___ⓐ___ is different from one family to another. Salt and pepper can be added before eating. People in America believe that a bowl of warm chicken soup is great for a sore throat and a stuffy nose.

✏️ 출제율 90%

19 주어진 영영풀이를 참고하여 빈칸 ⓐ에 철자 r로 시작하는 단어를 쓰시오.

> a list of ingredients and a set of instructions that tell you how to cook something

➡️ _____

✏️ 출제율 100%

20 위 글의 제목으로 알맞은 것을 고르시오.

① What Do People in Finland Look for When They Catch a Cold?

② What Do Americans Want When Sick?

③ Special Ingredients for Chicken Soup

④ The Reason Salt and Pepper Are Added Before Eating

⑤ What Is Good for a Sore Throat and a Stuffy Nose?

✏️ 출제율 95%

21 According to the passage, which is NOT true?

① People in Korea and Finland look for drinks when sick.

② Many people in America want a bowl of chicken soup when sick.

③ Chicken soup is usually made with chicken and vegetables.

④ People add salt and pepper while cooking chicken soup.

⑤ In America, a bowl of warm chicken soup is believed to be great for a sore throat and a stuffy nose.

[22~24] 다음 글을 읽고 물음에 답하시오.

In Russia and in Eastern Europe, when people get sick, they eat a dessert ____ⓐ____ *gogol-mogol*. It is made with eggs and honey. Some people add chocolate, butter, lemon juice, or milk (A)[makes / to make] it taste better. It looks like (B)[huge / thick] yogurt. People often drink a cup of warm *gogol-mogol* when they have a sore throat. *Gogol-mogol* is not only good for people with a cold but also popular as a dessert for (C)[healthful / healthy] people. When served as a dessert, ⓑ그것은 보통 차갑게 또는 실온으로 제공된다.

✏️ 출제율 95%

22 위 글의 빈칸 ⓐ에 call을 알맞은 형태로 쓰시오.

➡️ _____

✏️ 출제율 90%

23 위 글의 괄호 (A)~(C)에서 문맥이나 어법상 알맞은 낱말을 골라 쓰시오.

(A) _____ (B) _____ (C) _____

✏️ 출제율 90%

24 위 글의 밑줄 친 ⓑ의 우리말에 맞게 주어진 어휘를 알맞게 배열하시오.

> served / usually / room temperature / it / cold / at / is / or

➡️ _____

[01~02] 다음 대화를 읽고 물음에 답하시오.

> G: My favorite Korean traditional drink is Maesil-tea. What about you, Jinsu?
> B: Well, my favorite traditional drink is Sik-hye.
> G: Sik.... Can you say that again?
> B: Sik-hye. It's sweet and cool.
> G: I want to try it.

01 What is G's favorite Korean traditional drink? (7 words)

➡ _____

02 How does B describe his favorite drink? Include two features. (10 words)

➡ _____

_____

[03~04] 다음 대화를 읽고 물음에 답하시오.

> B: Have you ever tried *poke*?
> G: Sorry, could you say that again, please?
> B: *Po-ke*. It's a salad who is popular in Hawaii.
> G: What's so special about it?
> B: It's made with rice and fish. It's ___(a)___ delicious ___(b)___ very healthy.

03 위 대화에서 어법상 어색한 것을 하나 찾아 바르게 고치시오.

_____ ➡ _____

04 위 대화의 빈칸 (a)와 (b)에 들어갈 말을 각각 두 단어로 쓰시오.

(A) _____ (B) _____

05 다음 문장에서 어법상 어색한 단어를 하나씩만 찾아 바르게 고치시오.

(1) Not only Angela but also Julie believe that they have to get a perfect score on the final exam so that they can graduate.

➡ _____ ➡ _____

(2) Both your uncle and my teacher is the fan of the baseball team.

➡ _____ ➡ _____

(3) Either you or Charlie have to stay here monitoring the market situation.

➡ _____ ➡ _____

(4) The new song the composer made yesterday was not only easy to remember but also very excited.

➡ _____ ➡ _____

(5) I wonder why not only the restaurant but also the stores in my neighborhood is crowded with clients recently.

➡ _____ ➡ _____

06 다음 우리말과 같은 뜻이 되도록 접속사 while과 주어진 어구를 활용하여, 제시된 글자 수와 어법에 맞게 영작하시오.

(1) 그는 말을 많이 하는 반면에, 행동은 거의 하지 않는다. (act, talk, little, a lot, 8 단어)

➡ _____

_____

(2) Paula가 요리를 하고 있는 동안, 그녀의 삼촌이 집에 찾아오셨다. (visit, cook, uncle, 9 단어)

➡ _____

_____

What do you do when you catch a cold? Of course, you want to stay warm, so maybe you put on more (A)[cloths / clothes]. Some people like to drink hot tea. Ginger tea is something people in Korea often drink. (B)[With / Without] its special taste, it warms your body and ⓐhelps reduce the pain in your throat. What do people drink or eat in (C)[another / other] countries when they catch a cold? Let's find out.

07 위 글의 괄호 (A)~(C)에서 문맥이나 어법상 알맞은 낱말을 골라 쓰시오.

(A) _____ (B) _____ (C) _____

08 위 글의 밑줄 친 ⓐ를 다음과 같이 바꿔 쓸 때 빈칸에 들어갈 알맞은 말을 두 단어로 쓰시오.

helps _____ _____ the pain in your throat

09 본문의 내용과 일치하도록 다음 빈칸 (A)와 (B)에 알맞은 단어를 쓰시오.

When people catch a cold, some of them like to drink (A)_____ _____ like ginger tea. It has special taste, warms the body and helps (B)_____ _____ _____ in the throat.

In Russia and in Eastern Europe, when people get sick, they eat a dessert called *gogol-mogol*. It is made with eggs and honey. Some people add chocolate, butter, lemon juice, or milk to make it taste better. ⓐIt looks thick yogurt. People often drink a cup of warm *gogol-mogol* when they have a sore throat. *Gogol-mogol* is not only good for people with a cold but also popular as a dessert for healthy people. ⓑWhen served as a dessert, it is usually served cold or at room temperature.

10 위 글의 밑줄 친 ⓐ에서 어법상 틀린 부분을 찾아 고치시오.

_____ ➡ _____

11 위 글의 밑줄 친 ⓑ를 능동태로 고칠 때 다음 빈칸 (A)와 (B)에 공통으로 들어갈 알맞은 단어를 쓰시오.

When people (A)_____ it as a dessert, they usually (B)_____ it cold or at room temperature.

➡ _____

12 In Russia and in Eastern Europe, what do people often drink when they have a sore throat? Answer in English in a full sentence. (8 words)

➡ _____
_____

창의사고력 서술형 문제

01 다음 그림과 표를 보고, 〈보기〉와 같이 접속사 while을 사용하여 Hana와 Duna의 대조적인 특징을 나타내는 문장을 자유롭게 3문장 이상 영작하시오.

	Hana	Duna
hair	short	long
clothes	jeans	skirt
glasses	yes	no
favorite food	ice cream	waffle
math test result	A	C
like	singing	dancing
pet	no	yes

보기

While Duna has a pet, Hana doesn't.

(1) _____

(2) _____

(3) _____

02 다음 내용을 바탕으로 인도식 토마토 수프 요리법을 완성하시오.

1. Chop one fresh tomato.
2. Put the chopped tomato in a pan and pour some water over it.
3. Boil for ten minutes.
4. Leave it to cool down.
5. Blend it until it is smooth.
6. Add some black pepper and salt.

   While many Koreans eat Samgyetang when they are sick, many people in India eat tomato soup. Here is how to make it.
You need: 1 tomato, some water, black pepper, salt
   First, (A)_____ one fresh tomato. Then put the chopped tomato in a pan and (B)_____ over it. Next, boil the mixture (C)_____. Then turn off the heat and leave it (D)_____. Next, (E)_____ until it is smooth. Finally, add (F)_____. Now you can enjoy the tomato soup. This tomato soup is not only healthy but also delicious.

단원별 모의고사

01 다음 영영풀이가 가리키는 것은?

> a measure of the warmth of an object with reference to a standard scale

① weather
② medicine
③ temperature
④ taste
⑤ climate

02 다음 빈칸에 알맞은 단어를 고르시오.

> Thieves had broken in _____ we were away.

① while
② even though
③ as if
④ despite
⑤ where

03 다음 우리말에 맞게 빈칸에 알맞은 말을 쓰시오.

(1) 계산서에는 10프로의 서비스 비용이 추가되었다.
➡ A service charge of 10% was _____ on to the bill.

(2) 그 공동체 회의는 커뮤니티 센터에서 열릴 것이다.
➡ The community meeting will be _____ in the community center.

(3) 우리는 실험을 통해 기름과 물이 섞이지 않을 것이라는 것을 배울 수 있다.
➡ We can learn by experiment that oil and water will not _____.

[04~05] 다음 대화를 읽고 물음에 답하시오.

> B: Hi, Grace. Those are pretty. What are they called?
> G: They're called *dango*.
> B: I'm sorry. (A)Could you say that again?
> G: *Dan-go*. (B)그것들은 달콤하고 쌀가루로 만들어져. They're from Japan.

04 위 대화의 밑줄 친 (A)의 목적으로 가장 적절한 것은?

① to ask how to pronounce it
② to ask what she is eating
③ to ask what it's from
④ to ask about the dessert
⑤ to ask G to repeat what she said

05 위 대화의 밑줄 친 (B)를 주어진 우리말을 이용하여 영작하시오. (make, powder) (8 words)

➡ _____

[06~08] 다음 대화를 읽고 물음에 답하시오.

> M: Good afternoon. A table for two?
> B: Yes.
> M: This way please. Here is the menu. I'll be back in a few minutes and take your order.
> B: Okay. Thank you.
> G: I don't know much about Korean food. (A)무언가 추천해 주겠니?
> B: Well, I'd recommend the Bibimbap.
> G: I'm sorry. Could you say that again, please?
> B: This one. Bi-bim-bap. (B)그건 밥 위에 많은 야채들과 소고기, 그리고 계란을 얹어 만들어진다. (vegetables / beef and an egg / lots of / made with / over rice / it's) It's tasty and it's also good for your health.

G: That sounds great. I'll try it.

B: It's served with a spicy red pepper sauce. Is that okay?

G: No problem. I like spicy food.

06 위 대화의 밑줄 친 (A)를 주어진 단어를 이용해 영작하시오.
(could, something) (4 words)

➡ _____

07 위 대화의 밑줄 친 (B)의 우리말에 맞게 주어진 어구를 나열하시오.

➡ _____
   _____

08 위 대화의 내용과 일치하지 <u>않는</u> 것은? (2개)

① G does not know much about Korean food.
② G asks B to try Korean food.
③ The Bibimbap is good for your health.
④ The Bibimbap is served with spicy sauce.
⑤ G does not like spicy food.

09 다음 대화가 자연스럽게 이어지도록 순서대로 배열하시오.

(A) *Rasmalai*. It's a traditional dessert in India.
(B) Sorry, could you say that again?
(C) Have you ever tried *rasmalai*?

➡ _____

[10~11] 다음 대화를 읽고 물음에 답하시오.

B: Tomorrow is my birthday.

G: I know. Are you going to have a birthday party, Alex? ①

B: Yes. Can you recommend a good place to have the party? ②

G: I'd recommend the Happy Snack House. The food is really good and it'll be large enough. ③

B: What dish would you recommend? ④

G: I'd recommend the onion rings. ⑤

B: Oh, just thinking about them makes my mouth water.

10 위 대화의 ①~⑤ 중에서 주어진 문장이 들어가기에 가장 적절한 곳은?

They're fantastic!

①   ②   ③   ④   ⑤

11 위 대화를 읽고 대답할 수 <u>없는</u> 질문을 고르시오.

① Who is going to throw a birthday party?
② Who is going to be invited to the party?
③ Where is the party going to take place?
④ What kind of food does G recommend?
⑤ Does B like the onion rings?

12 다음 중 짝지어진 대화가 <u>어색한</u> 것을 고르시오.

① A: Could you recommend a good book for my little sister?
   B: I'd recommend this one. The story is touching.
② A: Could you recommend a cell phone for my grandmother?
   B: How about this phone? It's easy to use.

③ A: Could you recommend a guitar for beginners?

　　B: Try this one. Many beginners play it.

④ A: Could you recommend a good book for my sister?

　　B: Pardon me? The story is touching.

⑤ A: Could you recommend a snack for my dog?

　　B: Sure. How about this? Dogs really like it.

[13~14] 다음 주어진 우리말을 영작한 것으로 옳은 것을 고르면?

13
해피 분식집의 음식은 정말 맛있을 뿐 아니라, 혼자 먹기에 양도 너무 많다.

① The food at Happy Snack is not only delicious, but also too much to eat alone.

② The food at Happy Snack not only is delicious, but also eats too much alone.

③ Not only the food at Happy Snack is delicious, but also much to eat alone.

④ Not only is the food at Happy Snack delicious, but also too much is to eat alone.

⑤ The food at Happy Snack is not only too delicious, but also much to eat alone.

14
Henry는 바이올린을 연주할 수 있을 뿐만 아니라, 퍼즐도 빠르게 풀 수 있다.

① Henry can not only play the violin, but also solves puzzles quickly.

② Henry can play not only the violin, but also solve puzzles quickly.

③ Not only can Henry play the violin, but also solve puzzles quickly.

④ Not only Henry can play the violin, but also can he solve puzzles quickly.

⑤ Not only can Henry play the violin, but also he solve puzzles quickly.

[15~16] 다음 중 밑줄 친 while의 의미가 나머지와 다른 것은?

15
① Dave likes playing soccer while his brother likes playing the computer soccer game.

② While Elisabeth is good at music, her boyfriend is poor at it.

③ Minju wants to go out while her brother insists staying home.

④ Someone named Ryan called you while you were walking the dogs along the park.

⑤ While the girl has short hair, Tom, the only son of the family, has long hair.

16
① While Sarah was waiting for the bus, she saw a lady coming to her.

② While you are in Busan, try Busan fish cake and the soup of pork and rice.

③ You had better prepare the sauce while you are cooking the chicken salad.

④ While his girl friend Celine likes the Korean history very much, Walter doesn't like it.

⑤ Those who started late arrived while we were having dinner.

17 다음 그림의 내용에 알맞게, 주어진 어구를 배열하여 빈칸을 채우시오.

(1)

> but, made, broke, the speed limit, also, an, illegal

➡ The car not only _____
_____ lane change.

(2)

> while, in, I, a guitar, interested, was

➡ She tried to sell me _____
_____ other instruments.

[18~19] 다음 글을 읽고 물음에 답하시오.

In Finland, where it is very cold in winter, people have a special drink when they catch a cold. It is a cup of onion milk. They put chopped onion in milk and boil it over low heat for half an hour. ⓐThis simple drink is said to be good for a cold.

18 위 글의 밑줄 친 ⓐThis simple drink가 가리키는 것을 본문에서 찾아 쓰시오.

➡ _____

19 위 글을 읽고 알 수 없는 것을 고르시오.

① How is the weather in Finland in winter?
② What do people in Finland drink when they catch a cold?
③ What ingredients do you need to make the onion milk?
④ What's the recipe for the onion milk?
⑤ Why is the onion milk good for a cold?

[20~21] 다음 글을 읽고 물음에 답하시오.

____ⓐ____ people in Korea and Finland look for drinks when sick, many people in America want a bowl of chicken soup. It is usually made with chicken and vegetables, but the recipe is different from one family to another. ⓑSalt and pepper can be added before eating. People in America believe that a bowl of warm chicken soup is great for a sore throat and a stuffy nose.

20 위 글의 빈칸 ⓐ에 알맞은 말을 고르시오.

① However   ② While
③ Otherwise   ④ Unless
⑤ As long as

21 위 글의 밑줄 친 ⓑ를 능동태로 고치시오.

➡ _____

[22~23] 다음 글을 읽고 물음에 답하시오.

In Russia and in Eastern Europe, when people get sick, they eat a dessert called *gogol-mogol*. It is made with eggs and honey. Some people add chocolate, butter, lemon juice, or milk @to make it taste better. It looks like thick yogurt. People often drink a cup of warm *gogol-mogol* when they have a sore throat. *Gogol-mogol* is not only good for people with a cold but also popular as a dessert for healthy people. When served as a dessert, it is usually served cold or at room temperature.

22 아래 〈보기〉에서 위 글의 밑줄 친 @to make와 to부정사의 용법이 같은 것의 개수를 고르시오.

┌─── 보기 ───┐
① He was glad to make it taste better.
② My dream is to make it taste better.
③ Tell me the way to make it taste better.
④ She tried to make it taste better.
⑤ It was hard to make it taste better.
└──────────┘

① 1개 ② 2개 ③ 3개 ④ 4개 ⑤ 5개

23 According to the passage, which is NOT true?

① In Russia and in Eastern Europe, people eat *gogol-mogol* when sick.
② *Gogol-mogol* is made with eggs and honey.
③ Chocolate, butter, lemon juice, or milk can make *gogol-mogol* taste better.
④ *Gogol-mogol* looks like thick yogurt.
⑤ In Russia and in Eastern Europe, people eat *gogol-mogol* only when they're sick.

[24~25] 다음 글을 읽고 물음에 답하시오.

Why not try making one of the foods you have found out ___@___? It will be fun and good for your health.

How to Make *Gogol-mogol* ((A)Serves one)
You need: 1 egg, 1/2 cup of milk, honey (5 g), butter (15 g)
1. Put the egg and the honey in a large cup and mix them.
2. Pour half a cup of milk in a pan. Add the butter. Warm it until the butter melts.
3. Pour the hot milk and butter ___ⓑ___ the cup with the egg and the honey. Stir as you pour.
4. Drink while it is hot.

24 위 글의 빈칸 @와 ⓑ에 들어갈 전치사가 바르게 짝지어진 것은?

    @   ⓑ   @   ⓑ
① for – into   ② for – on
③ on – for   ④ about – into
⑤ about – on

25 위 글의 밑줄 친 (A)Serves와 같은 의미로 쓰인 것을 고르시오.

① The sofa serves as a bed for a night or two.
② He serves God.
③ This dish serves four hungry people.
④ She serves in the medical corps.
⑤ He serves behind a counter.

MEMO

Lesson

Special

A Christmas Miracle

Words & Expressions

Key Words

- **actually** [ǽktʃuəli] 부 사실은
- **address** [ədrés] 명 주소
- **aim** [eim] 명 목표
- **along** [əlɔ́:ŋ] 전 ~를 따라
- **although** [ɔ:lðóu] 접 비록 ~이긴 하지만
- **baseball** [béisbɔ̀l] 명 야구
- **begin** [bigín] 동 시작하다
- **boldly** [bóuldli] 부 대담하게
- **carol** [kǽrəl] 명 캐럴
- **either** [í:ðər] 부 ~도, ~ 또한
- **enemy** [énəmi] 명 적군, 적
- **English** [íŋgliʃ] 형 영국의 명 영어
- **entire** [intáiər] 형 전체의
- **example** [igzǽmpl] 명 예시, 본보기
- **exchange** [ikstʃéindʒ] 동 교환하다
- **expect** [ikspékt] 동 예상하다
- **face** [feis] 동 마주하다
- **familiar** [fəmíljər] 형 익숙한, 친숙한
- **few** [fju:] 형 많지 않은
- **fight** [fait] 동 싸우다
- **follow** [fálou] 동 따라가다
- **front line** 최전선, 최전방
- **German** [dʒə́:rmən] 형 독일의
- **greeting** [grí:tiŋ] 명 인사, 안부의 말
- **happen** [hǽpən] 동 일어나다
- **human** [hjú:mən] 명 인간, 사람
- **keep** [ki:p] 동 유지하다, 계속 있다
- **lantern** [lǽntərn] 명 조명
- **learn** [lə:rn] 동 ~을 알게 되다
- **light** [lait] 동 빛나다, 비추다
- **might** [mait] 조 ~일지도 모른다
- **mind** [maind] 명 마음, 정신
- **miracle** [mírəkl] 명 기적
- **miss** [mis] 동 그리워하다
- **month** [mʌnθ] 명 달, 월, 개월
- **move** [mu:v] 동 움직이다
- **peace** [pi:s] 명 평화
- **race** [reis] 명 경주, 시합
- **several** [sévərəl] 형 몇의, 수개의
- **share** [ʃɛər] 동 공유하다, 나누다
- **sheep** [ʃi:p] 명 양
- **shoot** [ʃu:t] 동 쏘다
- **shout** [ʃaut] 명 외침, 고함
- **sight** [sait] 명 광경
- **silent** [sáilənt] 형 고요한
- **soldier** [sóuldʒər] 명 군인, 병사
- **suddenly** [sʌ́dnli] 부 갑자기
- **surprise** [sərpráiz] 동 놀라게 하다
- **tired** [taiərd] 형 피곤한
- **trench** [trentʃ] 명 참호
- **trick** [trik] 명 속임수
- **truly** [trú:li] 부 정말로, 진심으로
- **unbelievable** [ʌnbəlívəbəl] 형 믿기 힘든
- **weapon** [wépən] 명 무기
- **wet** [wet] 형 젖은
- **World War I** 1차 세계 대전

Key Expressions

- **all the more** 더욱 더
- **at war** 전쟁 중인
- **be able to** ~할 수 있다
- **by ~ing** ~함으로써
- **come from** ~에서 오다
- **come out** 나오다
- **each other** 서로
- **follow one's example** ~의 사례를 따르다, 모범으로 삼다
- **for the first time** 처음으로
- **go on** (일, 상황이) 돌아가다
- **have a talk** 이야기하다
- **in peace** 평화 속에서
- **look out of** ~ 밖을 내다보다
- **no man's land** 황무지, 중간 지대
- **one after another** 잇따라서
- **one by one** 차례로
- **on the front line** 최전선에
- **pass away** 사망하다
- **put down** 내려놓다
- **shake hands** 악수하다
- **such as** ~와 같은

Word Power

※ 서로 비슷한 뜻을 가진 어휘

- ☐ **actually** 사실은 – **in fact** 사실은
- ☐ **aim** 목표 – **purpose** 목적, 의도
- ☐ **begin** 시작하다 – **initiate** 시작하다
- ☐ **entire** 전체의 – **whole** 전체의, 모든
- ☐ **expect** 예상하다 – **predict** 예측하다

- ☐ **happen** 일어나다 – **occur** 일어나다, 발생하다
- ☐ **silent** 고요한 – **quiet** 조용한, 고요한
- ☐ **suddenly** 갑자기 – **unexpectedly** 예상 외로, 갑자기
- ☐ **truly** 정말로, 진심으로 – **really** 정말로

※ 서로 반대의 뜻을 가진 어휘

- ☐ **begin** 시작하다 ↔ **end** 끝나다
- ☐ **face** 마주하다 ↔ **avoid** 피하다
- ☐ **familiar** 익숙한, 친숙한 ↔ **unfamiliar** 익숙치 못한
- ☐ **keep** 유지하다 ↔ **lose** 잃다, 상실하다
- ☐ **peace** 평화 ↔ **war** 전쟁, 무력 충돌

- ☐ **silent** 고요한 ↔ **noisy** 떠들썩한, 시끄러운
- ☐ **truly** 정말로, 진심으로 ↔ **falsely** 거짓으로, 속여서
- ☐ **unbelievable** 믿기 힘든 ↔ **credible** 믿을 수 있는
- ☐ **wet** 젖은 ↔ **dry** 마른, 물기 없는

※ 접두사 un-+ 형용사

- ☐ **un + believable → unbelievable** 믿기 힘든
- ☐ **un + known → unknown** 알려지지 않은
- ☐ **un + grateful → ungrateful** 감사할 줄 모르는
- ☐ **un + healthy → unhealthy** 건강하지 못한
- ☐ **un + necessary → unnecessary** 불필요한

- ☐ **un + clean → unclean** 더러운
- ☐ **un + fortunate → unfortunate** 운이 없는, 불운한
- ☐ **un + happy → unhappy** 불행한
- ☐ **un + important → unimportant** 중요하지 않은
- ☐ **un + usual → unusual** 특이한

English Dictionary

- ☐ **boldly** 대담하게
  → in a brave and confident way, without showing any fear
  용기 있고 자신감 있는 방식으로, 어떠한 두려움도 보이지 않고

- ☐ **carol** 캐럴
  → Christmas song or hymn
  크리스마스 노래 또는 찬송가

- ☐ **exchange** 교환하다
  → to give and receive reciprocally; interchange
  상호적으로 주고 받다; 교환하다

- ☐ **greeting** 인사, 안부의 말
  → an act or words of welcoming
  환영의 행위 또는 말

- ☐ **peace** 평화
  → freedom from war; absence of fighting between nations
  전쟁이 없는 상태; 국가 간 충돌의 부재

- ☐ **race** 경주, 시합
  → a contest of speed, such as running, riding, driving or sailing
  달리기, 라이딩, 운전 혹은 항해와 같은 속도 경쟁

- ☐ **share** 공유하다, 나누다
  → to divide and distribute something in shares
  무언가를 나누거나 분배하다

- ☐ **shoot** 쏘다
  → to hit with a bullet, shell, or other missile fired from a weapon
  총알, 포탄 혹은 무기에서 발사된 미사일로 타격하다

- ☐ **shout** 외침, 고함
  → a loud call or cry
  큰 소리로 부르거나 외침

- ☐ **sight** 광경
  → something seen or worth seeing
  보이는 어떤 것이나 볼 가치가 있는 것

- ☐ **soldier** 군인, 병사
  → a person who is in an army and wears its uniform, especially someone who fights when there is a war
  군대에 있어서 제복을 입는 사람, 특히 전쟁에서 싸우는 사람

- ☐ **surprise** 놀라게 하다
  → to strike with a sudden feeling of wonder or astonishment especially by being unexpected
  놀라움이나 깜짝 놀라는 감정, 특히 예상하지 못한 감정에 치이다

- ☐ **trick** 속임수
  → a sneaky scheme to deceive or cheat
  속이거나 사기를 치려는 교활한 계획

A Christmas Miracle

It was Christmas Eve in 1914, the first year of World War I. English
소비인칭 주어로 시간, 날씨, 요일, 날짜, 무게 등을 나타낸다.

soldiers were facing German soldiers from their trenches <u>as</u> they <u>had</u>
~처럼, ~와 같이(접속사)

<u>done</u> for the last few months. The trenches were cold and wet. The
과거에 일어났던 일보다 더 앞서 일어난 일에 대해 언급하기 위해서 과거완료를 사용

soldiers were tired and missed their home, <u>all the more</u> so because it
더욱 더

was Christmas.

Suddenly, a familiar song <u>was heard</u> coming from the German
주어가 동작을 받는 대상이므로 동사가 'was heard'라는 수동태로 쓰였음.

trenches. It was a Christmas carol! What's going on? It <u>might</u> be a trick
확실하지 않은 일을 추측할 때 사용

to <u>make</u> them come out of the trenches. A few English soldiers boldly
명사 'trick'을 수식하는 to부정사의 형용사적 용법

looked out of their trenches. <u>One by one</u>, other soldiers followed their
차례차례, 하나씩 하나씩

example.

along: ~을 따라(전치사)

<u>What</u> they saw was <u>a sight they</u> never expected. <u>Along</u> the German
선행사를 포함하고 있는 관계대명사   'a sight'와 'they' 사이에 목적격 관계대명사 'which[that]'가 생략

trenches, Christmas trees were standing <u>lit with lanterns</u>! The German
수동형 분사구문

soldiers sang one Christmas song after another. The English soldiers

began to answer by also singing Christmas songs. The warm lights and

the Christmas carols <u>made them forget</u> they were on the front line.
사역동사 make+목적어+목적격 보어(동사원형)

soldier 군인, 병사
face 마주하다
trench 참호
wet 젖은
all the more 더욱 더
carol 캐럴 (전통적으로 크리스마스 기간
에 불리는 노래)
trick 속임수, 마술
boldly 용감하게
sight 광경

✔ 확인문제

● 다음 문장이 본문의 내용과 일치하면 T, 일치하지 <u>않으면</u> F를 쓰시오.

1 On Christmas Eve in 1914, the first year of World War I, English soldiers were facing German soldiers from their trenches as they had done for the last few months. ☐

2 Suddenly, a familiar song was heard coming from the English trenches. ☐

3 Along the German trenches, Christmas trees were standing lit with lanterns. ☐

4 Even the warm lights and the Christmas carols couldn't make them forget they were on the front line. ☐

Then a shout came out from the German side: "Happy Christmas! You no shoot, we no shoot!" Soon, soldiers whose aim had been to kill
소유격 관계대명사, 사람 또는 사물을 선행사로 취하며 생략할 수 없다.
each other just a few hours before began to exchange greetings. For the first time in several months, the soldiers were able to spend a night in
가능의 의미를 가진 조동사 'could'로 바꿔 쓸 수 있다.
peace. It truly was a silent night.

Christmas morning came. Soldiers on both sides put down their
주어   V1
weapons and came out of their trenches. They met in the no man's
V2
land between their trenches and shook hands. They exchanged small
악수했다
gifts such as wine and cake. They sang carols together. Some even
~와 같은, 예를 들어(예를 들 때 사용)   몇몇, 어떤 사람들(부정대명사)
exchanged addresses and played football.
V1   V2
This unbelievable Christmas Day was written about in letters English
'letters'와 'English soldiers' 사이에 목적격 관계대명사 'which[that]'가 생략
soldiers sent home. One soldier wrote, "On Christmas Day, English and German soldiers met between the two lines and had talks. We also had bike races." Another wrote, "We didn't think that we were at
현재분사구로 앞의 명사 'enemy'를 수식
war. Here we were, enemy talking to enemy. They were like us, with
장소나 방향을 뜻하는 부사가 문장 앞으로 올 때 주어가 대명사인 경우 주어와 동사를 도치하지 않는다.   ~와 같은, ~처럼(전치사)
mothers, with friends, with wives who were waiting to welcome their
'who were'는 '주격 관계대명사+be동사'로 생략 가능
men home again."

aim 목적, 목표
exchange 교환하다
peace 평화
silent 고요한
weapon 무기
address 주소
put down 내려놓다
enemy 적군, 적

확인문제

● 다음 문장이 본문의 내용과 일치하면 T, 일치하지 않으면 F를 쓰시오.

1 For the first time in several months, the soldiers were able to spend a night peacefully. ☐

2 Soldiers met in their trenches and shook hands. ☐

3 Soldiers exchanged small gifts such as wine and cake. ☐

4 Soldiers even exchanged addresses and played basketball. ☐

5 This unbelievable Christmas Day was written about in letters English soldiers sent home. ☐

6 On Christmas Day, English and German soldiers met between the two lines and fought with each other. ☐

● 우리말을 참고하여 빈칸에 알맞은 말을 쓰시오.

1 A Christmas _____

2 It was Christmas Eve in 1914, _____ _____ _____ of World War I.

3 English soldiers _____ _____ German soldiers from their trenches as they _____ _____ for the last few months.

4 The trenches were _____ _____ _____.

5 The soldiers were tired and missed their home, _____ _____ _____ _____ because it was Christmas.

6 Suddenly, a familiar song _____ _____ _____ from the German trenches.

7 It was a Christmas _____!

8 What's _____ _____?

9 It _____ _____ _____ _____ to make them come out of the trenches.

10 A few English soldiers _____ _____ _____ _____ their trenches.

11 _____ _____ _____, other soldiers followed their example.

12 _____ they saw was a sight they never expected.

13 Along the German trenches, Christmas trees were standing _____ _____ _____!

14 The German soldiers sang _____ _____ _____ _____ _____.

15 The English soldiers began to answer _____ _____ _____ Christmas songs.

16 The warm lights and the Christmas carols _____ _____ they were on the front line.

17 Then a shout _____ _____ _____ the German side: "Happy Christmas! You no shoot, we no shoot!"

18 Soon, soldiers _____ _____ had been to kill each other just a few hours before began to _____ _____.

19 For the first time _____ _____ _____, the soldiers were able to spend a night in peace.

20 _____ _____ _____ a silent night.

21 Christmas morning _____.

22 Soldiers _____ _____ _____ put down their weapons and came out of their trenches.

23 They met _____ _____ _____ _____ _____ between their trenches and shook hands.

24 They exchanged small gifts _____ _____ wine and cake.

25 They _____ _____ together.

26 Some even _____ _____ and played football.

27 This _____ Christmas Day was written _____ in letters English soldiers sent home.

28 One soldier wrote, "On Christmas Day, English and German soldiers met _____ _____ _____ _____ and had talks.

29 We also _____ _____ _____."

30 Another wrote, "We didn't think that we _____ _____ _____.

31 _____ _____ _____, enemy talking to enemy.

32 They were _____ _____, with mothers, with friends, with wives who were _____ _____ their men home again."

17 그리고 독일 군인들 쪽에서 고함이 터져 나왔습니다. "행복한 크리스마스예요! 당신들이 쏘지 않는다면, 우리도 쏘지 않을게요!"

18 곧, 단지 몇 시간 전까지만 해도 서로를 죽이는 것이 목적이었던 군인들은 인사를 나누기 시작했습니다.

19 몇 달 만에 처음으로, 군인들은 평화롭게 밤을 지낼 수 있었어요.

20 그날은 정말로 조용한 밤이었습니다.

21 크리스마스 아침이 밝았습니다.

22 양편의 군인들은 자신들의 무기를 내려놓고 참호 밖으로 나왔어요.

23 그들은 무인 지대에서 만났고 악수를 했습니다.

24 그들은 와인과 케이크 같은 작은 선물도 교환했어요.

25 그들은 캐럴을 함께 불렀습니다.

26 몇몇은 심지어 주소를 교환하기도 했고 함께 축구를 했습니다.

27 이 믿을 수 없는 크리스마스는 영국 군인들이 집으로 보낸 편지에 적혀 있었습니다.

28 한 군인은 "크리스마스에 영국 군인들과 독일 군인들은 두 경계선 사이에서 만났고 대화를 나눴어.

29 우리는 자전거 시합도 했어."라고 적었어요.

30 다른 군인은 "우리는 전쟁 중이라는 생각이 들지 않았어.

31 여기서 우리는 적대 관계인 서로와 대화를 나누고 있는 상황이었어.

32 그들은 우리와 마찬가지로, 그들의 남자들이 집으로 다시 돌아오기를 고대하는 어머니와, 친구들, 부인이 있는 사람들이었어."라고 썼습니다.

● 우리말을 참고하여 본문을 영작하시오.

1 크리스마스의 기적

➡ _____

2 제일차 세계 대전의 첫해였던 1914년의 크리스마스이브였습니다.

➡ _____

3 영국 군인들은 지난 몇 달 동안 그래왔듯이 그들의 참호에서 독일 군인들과 대치하고 있었어요.

➡ _____

_____

4 참호는 춥고 축축했습니다.

➡ _____

5 군인들은 지쳤고 자신들의 집을 그리워했는데, 크리스마스라는 이유로 더욱 더 그랬습니다.

➡ _____

6 갑자기 익숙한 노래가 독일 군인들의 참호로부터 들려왔습니다.

➡ _____

7 그것은 크리스마스 캐럴이었어요!

➡ _____

8 무슨 일이 벌어지고 있는 걸까요?

➡ _____

9 어쩌면 그들을 참호 밖으로 유인하고자 하는 속임수일지도 모릅니다.

➡ _____

10 몇몇 영국 군인들이 용감하게 자신들의 참호 밖을 내다보았어요.

➡ _____

11 차례차례 다른 군인들도 앞사람을 따랐습니다.

➡ _____

12 영국 군인들이 본 것은 그들이 절대 예상하지 못한 광경이었어요.

➡ _____

13 독일 군인들의 참호를 따라, 크리스마스트리들이 랜턴으로 밝혀진 채 있었습니다!

➡ _____

14 독일 군인들은 크리스마스 캐럴을 연이어 불렀어요.

➡ _____

15 영국 군인들도 크리스마스 캐럴을 부르며 화답하기 시작했습니다.

➡ _____

16 따뜻한 불빛과 크리스마스 캐럴은 그들이 최전선에 있다는 것을 잊게 만들었어요.

➡ _____

17 그리고 독일 군인들 쪽에서 고함이 터져 나왔습니다. "행복한 크리스마스예요! 당신들이 쏘지 않는다면, 우리도 쏘지 않을게요!"

➡ _____

18 곧, 단지 몇 시간 전까지만 해도 서로를 죽이는 것이 목적이었던 군인들은 인사를 나누기 시작했습니다.

➡ _____

_____

19 몇 달 만에 처음으로, 군인들은 평화롭게 밤을 지낼 수 있었어요.

➡ _____

20 그날은 정말로 조용한 밤이었습니다.

➡ _____

21 크리스마스 아침이 밝았습니다.

➡ _____

22 양편의 군인들은 자신들의 무기를 내려놓고 참호 밖으로 나왔어요.

➡ _____

23 그들은 무인 지대에서 만났고 악수를 했습니다.

➡ _____

24 그들은 와인과 케이크 같은 작은 선물도 교환했어요.

➡ _____

25 그들은 캐럴을 함께 불렀습니다.

➡ _____

26 몇몇은 심지어 주소를 교환하기도 했고 함께 축구를 했습니다.

➡ _____

27 이 믿을 수 없는 크리스마스는 영국 군인들이 집으로 보낸 편지에 적혀 있었습니다.

➡ _____

28 한 군인은 "크리스마스에 영국 군인들과 독일 군인들은 두 경계선 사이에서 만났고 대화를 나눴어.

➡ _____

_____

29 우리는 자전거 시합도 했어."라고 적었어요.

➡ _____

30 다른 군인은 "우리는 전쟁 중이라는 생각이 들지 않았어.

➡ _____

31 여기서 우리는 적대 관계인 서로와 대화를 나누고 있는 상황이었어.

➡ _____

32 그들은 우리와 마찬가지로, 그들의 남자들이 집으로 다시 돌아오기를 고대하는 어머니와, 친구들, 부인이 있는 사람들이었어."라고 썼습니다.

➡ _____

_____

서술형 실전문제

01 다음 짝지어진 단어의 관계가 같도록 빈칸에 알맞은 말을 쓰시오.

> begin : end = familiar : _____

02 다음 빈칸에 알맞은 말을 쓰시오.

> 난 처음으로 유럽에 갈 것이다.
> ➡ I will go to Europe _____.

03 다음 문장의 빈칸에 들어갈 말을 〈보기〉에서 골라 쓰시오.

> ┤ 보기 ├
> come from / have a talk / for the first
> time / one by one / come out

(1) Will the colors _____ if I wash it?

(2) We solved the problems _____.

(3) My parents and I _____ every evening.

04 우리말과 일치하도록 주어진 어구를 배열하여 영작하시오.

(1) 그들은 선생님을 지나가기 위해 속임수를 생각해내야 했다. (get past / they / a trick / to / think of / the teacher / had to)

➡ _____

(2) 이른 아침의 길거리는 고요했다. (morning / the / street / silent / was / early)

➡ _____

(3) Lana는 다른 세 명의 다른 학생들과 집을 함께 쓴다. (three / shares / students / Lana / with / other / a house)

➡ _____

05 다음 우리말에 맞게 주어진 어구를 이용하여 영작하시오.

(1) 그들은 서로 사랑하게 되었다.
(each other, fall in love)

➡ _____

(2) 너는 훌륭한 과학자들을 모범으로 삼아야 한다.
(have, follow the example)

➡ _____

(3) 마라톤 선수들이 결승선에 잇따라 도착했다.
(one after another, the finish line)

➡ _____

It was Christmas Eve in 1914, the first year of (A)World War I. English soldiers were facing German soldiers from their trenches as they ____ⓐ____ for the last few months. The trenches were cold and wet. The soldiers were tired and missed their home, all the more so because it was Christmas.

06 위 글의 밑줄 친 (A)World War I을 영어로 읽는 법을 쓰시오.

➡ _____

07 위 글의 빈칸 ⓐ에 do를 알맞은 형태로 쓰시오.

➡ _____

08 Why were the soldiers tired and missed their home all the more? Answer in English beginning with "Because". (4 words)

➡ _____

What they saw was a sight they never expected. Along the German trenches, Christmas trees were standing lit with lanterns! The German soldiers sang one Christmas song after another. The English soldiers began to answer by also singing Christmas songs. (A)The warm lights and the Christmas carols made them forgetting they were on the front line. Then a shout came out from the German side: "Happy Christmas! You no shoot, we no shoot!" Soon, soldiers ____ⓐ____ aim had been to kill each other just a few hours before began to exchange greetings. For the first time in several months, the soldiers were able to spend a night in peace. It truly was a silent night.

09 위 글의 밑줄 친 (A)에서 어법상 틀린 부분을 찾아 고치시오.

_____ ➡ _____

10 위 글의 빈칸 ⓐ에 들어갈 알맞은 관계대명사를 쓰시오.

➡ _____

11 본문의 내용과 일치하도록 다음 빈칸 (A)와 (B)에 알맞은 단어를 쓰시오.

When the German soldiers sang one Christmas song after another, the English soldiers began to answer by also (A)_____ _____ _____. For the first time in several months, the soldiers were able to spend a night (B)_____.

01 출제율 90%

다음 짝지어진 단어의 관계가 같도록 빈칸에 알맞은 말을 쓰시오.

> entire : whole = silent : _____

02 출제율 95%

다음 중 밑줄 친 부분의 뜻풀이가 바르지 <u>않은</u> 것은?

① <u>Follow</u> the path through the woods. (따라가다)

② We huddled together to <u>keep</u> warm. (유지하다, 계속 있다)

③ The book is <u>aimed</u> at very young children. (목표)

④ We will <u>miss</u> her when she leaves. (그리워하다)

⑤ He has a lot of <u>enemies</u> in the company. (적군들, 적들)

03 출제율 95%

다음 우리말을 주어진 단어를 이용하여 영작하시오.

> 그 부엌은 비록 작지만, 설계가 잘 되어 있다.
> (Although)

➡ _____

04 출제율 90%

다음 주어진 문장의 밑줄 친 light와 같은 의미로 쓰인 것은?

> Ann wanted to <u>light</u> the candles.

① Flashes of <u>light</u> were followed by an explosion.

② He was about to <u>light</u> a cigarette.

③ A solitary <u>light</u> burned dimly in the hall.

④ <u>Light</u> refreshments will be served during the break.

⑤ After the accident he was moved to <u>light</u> work.

05 출제율 95%

다음 빈칸에 공통으로 들어갈 단어로 알맞은 것을 쓰시오.

> • I like tropical fruits _____ bananas and pineapples.
> • People need essential services _____ gas, water and electricity.

06 출제율 90%

다음 영영 풀이에 해당하는 단어로 알맞은 것은?

> something seen or worth seeing

① soldier   ② peace

③ miracle   ④ trick

⑤ sight

It was Christmas Eve in 1914, the first year of World War I. English soldiers were facing German soldiers from ⓐtheir trenches as they ⓑhad done for the last few months. The trenches were cold and wet. The soldiers were tired and missed their home, all the more so because it was Christmas.

출제율 90%

07 위 글의 밑줄 친 ⓐtheir가 가리키는 것을 본문에서 찾아 쓰시오.

➡ _____

출제율 95%

08 위 글의 밑줄 친 ⓑhad done과 과거완료의 용법이 같은 것을 모두 고르시오.

① I <u>had</u> never <u>seen</u> such a strange animal before.

② How long <u>had</u> he <u>worked</u> here before he quit?

③ When I reached the station, the train <u>had</u> already <u>started</u>.

④ He <u>had been</u> sick for days before he went to the hospital.

⑤ I knew him well, for I <u>had</u> often <u>met</u> him before.

출제율 95%

09 On Christmas Eve in 1914, whom were the English soldiers facing from their trenches? Answer in English in a full sentence. (6 words)

➡ _____

출제율 95%

10 주어진 글 다음에 이어질 글의 순서로 가장 적절한 것은?

Christmas morning came. Soldiers on both sides put down their weapons and came out of their trenches.

(A) They exchanged small gifts such as wine and cake. They sang carols together.

(B) They met in the no man's land between their trenches and shook hands.

(C) Some even exchanged addresses and played football.

① (A)–(C)–(B)　　② (B)–(A)–(C)
③ (B)–(C)–(A)　　④ (C)–(A)–(B)
⑤ (C)–(B)–(A)

[11~14] 다음 글을 읽고 물음에 답하시오.

_____ ⓐ _____ they saw was a sight they never expected. (①) Along the German trenches, Christmas trees were standing lit with lanterns! (②) The German soldiers sang one Christmas song after another. (③) The warm lights and the Christmas carols made them forget they were on the front line. (④) Then a shout came out from the German side: "Happy Christmas! (⑤) You no shoot, we no shoot!" Soon, ⓑ단지 몇 시간 전까지만 해도 서로를 죽이는 것이 목적이었던 군인들은 인사를 나누기 시작했습니다. For the first time in several months, the soldiers were able to spend a night in peace. It truly was a silent night.

11 위 글의 빈칸 ⓐ에 들어갈 알맞은 말을 고르시오.

① Which
② That
③ What
④ Who
⑤ Where

12 위 글의 흐름으로 보아, 주어진 문장이 들어가기에 가장 적절한 곳은?

> The English soldiers began to answer by also singing Christmas songs.

①　　②　　③　　④　　⑤

13 위 글의 밑줄 친 ⓑ의 우리말에 맞게 주어진 어휘를 알맞게 배열하시오.

> had been / aim / each other / greetings / soldiers / before / to exchange / whose / to kill / just a few hours / began

➡ _____

_____

_____

14 According to the passage, which is NOT true?

① Christmas trees were standing lit with lanterns along the German trenches.
② The German soldiers sang one Christmas song after another.
③ The English soldiers began to answer by also singing Christmas songs.
④ Thanks to the warm lights and the Christmas carols, the soldiers forgot they were on the front line.
⑤ For several months, the soldiers were able to spend a night in peace.

[15~16] 다음 글을 읽고 물음에 답하시오.

> Christmas morning came. Soldiers on both sides put down their weapons and came out of their trenches. They met in the no man's land between their trenches and shook hands. They exchanged small gifts such as wine and cake. They sang carols together. ⓐSome even changed addresses and played football.

15 위 글의 밑줄 친 ⓐ에서 흐름상 어색한 부분을 찾아 고치시오.

_____ ➡ _____

16 Which question CANNOT be answered after reading the passage?

① When did the English and German soldiers meet?
② What did the English and German soldiers do?
③ Where did the English and German soldiers meet?
④ What did the English and German soldiers exchange?
⑤ How long did the English and German soldiers play football?

[17~19] 다음 글을 읽고 물음에 답하시오.

This (A)[believable / unbelievable] Christmas Day was written about in letters English soldiers sent home. One soldier wrote, " ⓐ Christmas Day, English and German soldiers met (B)[among / between] the two lines and had talks. We also had bike races." Another wrote, "We didn't think that we were ⓑ war. Here we were, enemy talking to enemy. They were (C)[alike / like] us, with mothers, with friends, with wives who were waiting to welcome their men home again."

17 위 글의 빈칸 ⓐ와 ⓑ에 들어갈 전치사가 바르게 짝지어진 것은?

    ⓐ   ⓑ   ⓐ   ⓑ
① For – in   ② On – at
③ In – at   ④ For – on
⑤ On – in

18 위 글의 괄호 (A)~(C)에서 문맥이나 어법상 알맞은 낱말을 골라 쓰시오.

(A) _____ (B) _____ (C) _____

19 위 글을 읽고 알 수 <u>없는</u> 것을 고르시오.

① How did people know about this story?
② According to the letters, where did the English and German soldiers meet?
③ What did the English and German soldiers do when they met between the two lines?
④ How did the English and German soldiers feel when they fought again after Christmas Day?
⑤ What did the English soldiers think of the German soldiers?

[20~22] 다음 글을 읽고 물음에 답하시오.

Suddenly, ⓐa familiar song was heard coming from the German trenches. It was a Christmas carol! What's going on? It might be a trick to make ⓑthem come out of the trenches. A few English soldiers boldly looked out of their trenches. ⓒOne by one, other soldiers followed their example.

20 위 글의 밑줄 친 ⓐ를 English soldiers를 주어로 하여 능동태로 고치시오.

➡ _____

_____

21 위 글의 밑줄 친 ⓑthem이 가리키는 것을 본문에서 찾아 쓰시오.

➡ _____

22 다음 빈칸에 알맞은 단어를 넣어 위 글의 밑줄 친 ⓒ가 의미하는 것을 완성하시오. (5 단어)

One after another, other soldiers _____
_____ _____ _____ _____, too.

MEMO

INSIGHT
on the textbook
교과서 파헤치기

※ 다음 영어를 우리말로 쓰시오.

01 careful _____

02 pane _____

03 surprisingly _____

04 crispy _____

05 perhaps _____

06 swallow _____

07 result _____

08 twist _____

09 prevent _____

10 fantastic _____

11 repair _____

12 pressure _____

13 notice _____

14 steam _____

15 boil _____

16 carefully _____

17 death _____

18 emergency _____

19 amount _____

20 roof _____

21 balance _____

22 breathing _____

23 especially _____

24 couch _____

25 necessary _____

26 recently _____

27 shaped _____

28 hide _____

29 lid _____

30 fog _____

31 company _____

32 cause _____

33 product _____

34 helpful _____

35 build up _____

36 prevent A from -ing _____

37 boil over _____

38 fog up _____

39 let out _____

40 look around _____

41 be made up of _____

42 the result of ~ _____

43 pass through _____

※ 다음 우리말을 영어로 쓰시오.

01	놀랍게도	
02	비틀다, 돌리다	
03	숨기다, 숨다	
04	바삭한	
05	알아채다, 의식하다	
06	판유리	
07	숨겨져 있는	
08	호흡, 숨	
09	삼키다	
10	소파, 긴 의자	
11	유용한, 도움이 되는	
12	수리하다	
13	죽음	
14	최근에	
15	~ 모양의	
16	생산물, 상품	
17	비상사태	
18	양, 총계	
19	압력	
20	뚜껑	
21	주의 깊게, 조심스럽게	

22	끓기; 끓이다	
23	특히	
24	막다	
25	균형; 균형을 잡다	
26	안개; 수증기가 서리다	
27	주의 깊은, 조심스러운	
28	필수적인	
29	표현하다	
30	아마, 어쩌면	
31	~을 야기하다; 원인	
32	회사, 동료	
33	지붕	
34	수증기, 김	
35	끓어 넘치다	
36	내보내다	
37	~의 결과	
38	밖을 내다보다	
39	거쳐 지나가다, 통과하다	
40	주위를 둘러보다	
41	A가 ~하는 것을 막다	
42	~로 구성되다	
43	비상 상황에서	

※ 다음 영영풀이에 알맞은 단어를 <보기>에서 골라 쓴 후, 우리말 뜻을 쓰시오.

1 _____ : not long ago: _____

2 _____ : to make food go down the throat: _____

3 _____ : willing to help, or useful: _____

4 _____ : to become aware of: _____

5 _____ : in the usual or expected way: _____

6 _____ : an unexpected and dangerous situation: _____

7 _____ : needed in order to achieve a particular result: _____

8 _____ : a long comfortable seat for two or more people to sit on: _____

9 _____ : to put something damaged back into good condition: _____

10 _____ : the structure that covers or forms the top of a building or vehicle: _____

11 _____ : the process to take air into the lungs and let it out again: _____

12 _____ : very much; more than usual or more than other people or things: _____

13 _____ : to stop something from happening or someone from doing something:
_____

14 _____ : the degree to which something is a lot or a little; how much something
is: _____

15 _____ : something that is made to be sold, usually something that is produced by
an industrial process: _____

16 _____ : to be in a position where you will stand without falling to either side, or
to put something in this position: _____

보기			
amount	emergency	prevent	couch
roof	notice	repair	swallow
balance	necessary	product	normally
especially	recently	breathing	helpful

※ 다음 우리말과 일치하도록 빈칸에 알맞은 말을 쓰시오.

Listen & Speak 1 Listen

1. **G:** Look at this _____. I wonder who _____ men are.
   B: They're the Wright brothers. They _____ the airplane.
2. **G:** I wonder _____ they are standing in _____ of the bicycle shop.
   B: They had a bicycle shop. They _____ and _____ bicycles.
3. **G:** I wonder _____ the first plane _____ like.
   B: Look! There is a model. It _____ _____ a big bird.
4. **G:** I _____ where they first _____ to fly their airplane.
   B: They _____ their airplane on a hill in North Carolina.

Listen & Speak 1 A-1

B: Look at this _____. It can help us _____ _____ _____.
G: Is that _____? I wonder _____ _____ _____.
B: It uses _____ to cook food.
G: Wow. That would be really _____ when you go camping.

Listen & Speak 1 A-2

B: Hi, class. _____ you ever _____ about the Moai? They are tall, human-_____ stones in Chile. _____ of the stones are four meters _____, but the tallest one is 20 meters tall. I was _____ _____ _____ _____ them long ago. So I _____ the Internet and _____ that they used _____. Isn't that _____?

Listen & Speak 1 B-1

A: I wonder _____ those men are.
B: They're the Wright brothers. They _____ the airplane.

Listen & Speak 1 B-2

A: I wonder what the first plane _____ _____.
B: Look! There is a _____. It looked _____ a big bird.

Listen & Speak 1 B-3

A: I _____ what _____ they're _____.
B: They're _____ the U.S.

해석

1. **G:** 이 사진을 봐. 나는 그 남자들이 누구인지 궁금해.
   B: 그들은 라이트 형제야. 그들은 비행기를 발명했어.
2. **G:** 나는 그들이 왜 자전거 가게 앞에 서 있는지 궁금해.
   B: 그들은 자전거 가게를 가지고 있었어. 그들은 자전거를 팔고 수리했어.
3. **G:** 나는 최초의 비행기가 어떻게 생겼는지 궁금해.
   B: 봐! 저기 모형이 있어. 그것은 큰 새처럼 생겼네.
4. **G:** 나는 그들이 어디에서 처음으로 비행을 시도했는지 궁금해.
   B: 그들은 노스캐롤라이나주의 한 언덕에서 그들의 비행기를 시험했어.

B: 이 발명품들을 봐. 이것은 우리가 전기 없이도 요리할 수 있도록 도와줘.
G: 그게 가능해? 나는 그것이 어떻게 작용하는지 궁금해.
B: 이것은 음식을 조리하기 위해 태양광을 사용해.
G: 와. 그것은 캠핑을 갈 때 정말 유용할 것 같아.

B: 안녕하세요, 여러분. 여러분은 모아이에 대해 들어 본 적이 있나요? 그것들은 칠레에 있는 크고 사람 모양을 한 돌입니다. 대부분의 돌들은 높이가 4미터이지만, 가장 큰 것은 높이가 20미터입니다. 저는 오래 전에 사람들이 어떻게 그것들을 옮겼는지 궁금했습니다. 그래서 저는 인터넷을 검색했고 그들이 밧줄을 이용했다는 것을 알게 되었습니다. 그 사실이 놀랍지 않나요?

A: 나는 그 남자들의 누구인지 궁금해.
B: 그들은 라이트 형제야. 그들은 비행기를 발명했어.

A: 나는 최초의 비행기가 어떻게 생겼는지 궁금해.
B: 봐! 저기 모형이 있어. 그것은 큰 새처럼 생겼네.

A: 나는 그들이 어느 나라 출신인지 궁금해.
B: 그들은 미국 출신이야.

1. **G:** _____ can we do _____ these VR glasses?

   B: _____ me see.... _____ we can play soccer.

2. **B:** _____ does the ball _____ in the air?

   G: Let me see.... I think air _____ the ball _____.

3. **G:** How does this train start to _____?

   B: Let me _____.... I think you can move it _____ a smartphone app.

4. **B:** What can we do _____ this drone?

   G: Well, let me see.... Maybe we can take _____ from the sky.

Listen & Speak 2 A-1

G: _____ at the number. It's _____ _____ _____.

B: When people _____ by, the number _____.

G: Oh, you're right. What does the number _____?

B: _____ me see.... Oh, when people _____ on the floor, energy is _____. It shows the _____ of energy that is made.

G: Wow, that's _____!

Listen & Speak 2 A- 2

G: We're going on a _____ trip tomorrow to the _____ Museum.

B: I've heard that it has a lot of _____ _____.

G: That's why I'm so _____. How about _____ the tour before we go?

B: _____ idea. _____ me see.... I have the school letter and a map of the _____.

G: Perfect. _____ get _____.

Listen & Speak 2 B-1

A: _____ can we do _____ this VR glasses?

B: _____ me _____ ... We can _____ soccer.

Listen & Speak 2 B-2

A: What can we do _____ this drone?

B: Let me _____ ... We can take pictures _____ the sky.

---

1. **G:** 우리가 이 VR 안경으로 무엇을 할 수 있을까?

   B: 어디 보자.... 아마 우리는 축구를 할 수 있을 거야.

2. **G:** 어떻게 그 공이 공중에 뜰까?

   B: 어디 보자.... 내 생각에는 공기가 공을 위로 밀어 올리는 것 같아.

3. **G:** 이 기차는 어떻게 움직이기 시작할까?

   B: 어디 보자.... 내 생각에는 네가 스마트폰 앱으로 그것을 움직일 수 있을 것 같아.

4. **G:** 우리가 이 드론으로 무엇을 할 수 있을까?

   B: 음, 어디 보자.... 아마 우리는 하늘에서 사진을 찍을 수 있을 거야.

G: 저 숫자를 봐. 빠르게 올라가고 있어.

B: 사람들이 지나갈 때, 그 숫자가 증가해.

G: 오, 네 말이 맞아. 그 숫자는 무엇을 의미할까?

B: 어디 보자.... 오, 사람들이 바닥을 밟을 때 에너지가 만들어져. 그것은 만들어지는 에너지의 양을 보여 줘.

G: 와, 놀라워!

G: 우리는 내일 '발명 박물관'으로 현장학습을 가.

B: 나는 그곳에 창의적인 발명품들이 많이 있다고 들었어.

G: 그것이 내가 들른 이유야. 우리 가기 전에 관람 계획을 짜는 것은 어때?

B: 좋은 생각이야. 어디 보자.... 나는 학교에서 받은 안내서와 박물관 지도가 있어.

G: 완벽해. 시작하자.

A: 우리가 이 VR 안경으로 무엇을 할 수 있을까?

B: 어디 보자.... 우리는 축구를 할 수 있어.

A: 우리가 이 드론으로 무엇을 할 수 있을까?

B: 어디 보자.... 우리는 하늘에서 사진을 찍을 수 있어.

Listen & Speak 2 B-3

A: _____ can we do _____ the smart watch?

B: Let me see… We can _____ _____ _____.

A: 우리가 이 스마트워치로 무엇을 할 수 있을까?

B: 어디 보자…. 우리는 문자 메시지를 보낼 수 있어.

Real-Life Zone

G: I like _____ crackers. They're really good.

B: Yeah, me, too. I wonder _____ crackers have these _____ _____ in them.

G: I don't know. Let me _____…. Um … well … _____ it's because the holes _____ the crackers _____ _____.

B: That's _____, but there _____ be some other _____.

G: Let's _____ up crackers on the Internet and see _____ it says.

B: Okay. Oh, look at this.

G: It _____ _____ baking, steam comes out _____ the holes and that makes the crackers _____.

B: It also says that the holes _____ the crackers _____.

G: Wow! So that's _____ they have holes!

G: 난 이 크래커가 좋아. 정말 맛있어.

B: 응, 나도 좋아해. 나는 크래커에 왜 이 작은 구멍들이 있는지 궁금해.

G: 잘 모르겠어. 생각해 보자…. 음… 아마 그 구멍들이 크래커를 더욱 맛있게 보이도록 해 주기 때문이 아닐까.

B: 그럴 수도 있겠네. 하지만 다른 이유들이 있을 거야.

G: 크래커에 관해 인터넷에 찾아보고 뭐라고 하는지 알아보자.

B: 좋아. 오, 이것 봐.

G: 굽는 동안, 그 구멍들을 통해 수증기가 빠져나와서 크래커를 얇게 만드는 거래.

B: 또한 구멍들은 크래커를 바삭하게 만드는 거래.

G: 와! 크래커에 구멍들이 있는 거구나!

Wrap Up 1~2

B: Hi, Kate. Today's Saturday, so _____ about _____ to the Einstein Science Park today?

G: That _____ like a good idea. I heard _____ they have special programs on _____. I wonder _____ _____ _____.

B: Let me see…. I saw an _____ in the newspaper. _____ it is.

G: What does it _____?

B: It _____ that today they have two shows: the Smart Design Show and the International Drone Show in Einstein Hall 101.

G: They _____ sound _____.

B: I'll _____ them and ask _____ time they start.

B: 안녕, 케이트. 오늘은 토요일이야. 그래서 말인데, 오늘 아인슈타인 과학 공원에 가는 건 어때?

G: 좋은 생각이야. 나는 토요일마다 특별한 프로그램들이 있다고 들었어. 나는 그것들이 무엇인지 궁금해.

B: 어디 보자…. 내가 신문에서 광고를 봤어. 여기 있어.

G: 뭐라고 쓰여 있니?

B: 여기에 따르면 오늘 두 가지 공연이 있대. 아인슈타인 홀 101호에서 있는 스마트 디자인 쇼과 국제 드론 쇼야.

G: 둘 다 환상적일 것 같아.

B: 내가 전화해서 그것들이 몇 시에 시작하는지 물어볼게.

Wrap Up 3~4

G: John, look. The school is having an _____ _____.

B: Really? That _____ interesting.

G: Yeah. You should _____ that. You always have great _____.

B: Does it say _____ the _____ _____?

G: Let me see…. It says it's November 11. That's two weeks _____ today.

B: I _____ what I _____ to do to enter the competition.

G: It says here you should _____ to Mr. Harrison, the _____ teacher.

G: 존, 봐. 학교에서 발명대회가 열린대.

B: 정말? 흥미로울 것 같아.

G: 응. 너는 참가해야 해. 너는 항상 아이디어가 훌륭하잖아.

B: 대회가 언제인지 나와 있니?

G: 어디 보자…. 11월 11일이래. 오늘로부터 2주 뒤야.

B: 대회에 참가하기 위해 내가 무엇을 해야 하는지 궁금해.

G: 여기에 따르면 너는 과학 선생님이신 해리슨 선생님께 말씀드려야 해.

※ 다음 우리말에 맞도록 대화를 영어로 쓰시오.

 해석

Listen & Speak 1 Listen

1. G: _____
   B: _____

2. G: _____
   B: _____

3. G: _____
   B: _____

4. G: _____
   B: _____

1. G: 이 사진을 봐. 나는 그 남자들이 누구인지 궁금해.
   B: 그들은 라이트 형제야. 그들은 비행기를 발명했어.
2. G: 나는 그들이 왜 자전거 가게 앞에 서 있는지 궁금해.
   B: 그들은 자전거 가게를 가지고 있었어. 그들은 자전거를 팔고 수리했어.
3. G: 나는 최초의 비행기가 어떻게 생겼는지 궁금해.
   B: 봐 저기 모형이 있어. 그것은 큰 새처럼 생겼었네.
4. G: 나는 그들이 어디에서 처음으로 비행을 시도했는지 궁금해.
   B: 그들은 노스캐롤라이나주의 한 언덕에서 그들의 비행기를 시험했어.

Listen & Speak 1 A-1

B: _____
G: _____
B: _____
G: _____

B: 이 발명품들을 봐. 이것은 우리가 전기 없이도 요리할 수 있도록 도와줘.
G: 그게 가능해? 나는 그것이 어떻게 작용하는지 궁금해.
B: 이것은 음식을 조리하기 위해 태양광을 사용해.
G: 와, 그것은 캠핑을 갈 때 정말 유용할 것 같아.

Listen & Speak 1 A-2

B: _____
   _____
   _____
   _____

B: 안녕하세요, 여러분. 여러분은 모아이에 대해 들어 본 적이 있나요? 그것들은 칠레에 있는 크고 사람 모양을 한 돌입니다. 대부분의 돌들은 높이가 4미터이지만, 가장 큰 것은 높이가 20미터입니다. 저는 오래 전에 사람들이 어떻게 그것들을 옮겼는지 궁금했습니다. 그래서 저는 인터넷을 검색했고 그들이 밧줄을 이용했다는 것을 알게 되었습니다. 그 사실이 놀랍지 않나요?

Listen & Speak 1 B-1

A: _____
B: _____

A: 나는 그 남자들의 누구인지 궁금해.
B: 그들은 라이트 형제야. 그들은 비행기를 발명했어.

Listen & Speak 1 B-2

A: _____
B: _____

A: 나는 최조의 비행기가 어떻게 생겼는지 궁금해.
B: 봐! 저기 모형이 있어. 그것은 큰 새처럼 생겼었네.

Listen & Speak 1 B-3

A: _____
B: _____

A: 나는 그들이 어느 나라 출신인지 궁금해.
B: 그들은 미국 출신이야.

Listen & Speak 2 Listen

1. G: _____

   B: _____

2. B: _____

   G: _____

3. G: _____

   B: _____

4. B: _____

   G: _____

Listen & Speak 2 A-1

G: _____

B: _____

G: _____

B: _____

G: _____

Listen & Speak 2 A- 2

G: _____

B: _____

G: _____

B: _____

G: _____

Listen & Speak 2 B-1

A: _____

B: _____

Listen & Speak 2 B-2

A: _____

B: _____

1. G: 우리가 이 VR 안경으로 무엇을 할 수 있을까?

   B: 어디 보자…. 아마 우리는 축구를 할 수 있을 거야.

2. G: 어떻게 그 공이 공중에 뜰까?

   B: 어디 보자…. 내 생각에는 공기가 공을 위로 밀어 올리는 것 같아.

3. G: 이 기차는 어떻게 움직이기 시작할까?

   B: 어디 보자…. 내 생각에는 네가 스마트폰 앱으로 그것을 움직일 수 있을 것 같아.

4. G: 우리가 이 드론으로 무엇을 할 수 있을까?

   B: 음, 어디 보자…. 아마 우리는 하늘에서 사진을 찍을 수 있을 거야.

G: 저 숫자를 봐. 빠르게 올라가고 있어.

B: 사람들이 지나갈 때, 그 숫자가 증가해.

G: 오, 네 말이 맞아. 그 숫자는 무엇을 의미할까?

B: 어디 보자…. 오, 사람들이 바닥을 밟을 때 에너지가 만들어져. 그것은 만들어지는 에너지의 양을 보여 줘.

G: 와, 놀라워!

G: 우리는 내일 '발명 박물관'으로 현장학습을 가.

B: 나는 그곳에 창의적인 발명품들이 많이 있다고 들었어.

G: 그것이 내가 들뜬 이유야. 우리 가기 전에 관람 계획을 짜는 것은 어때?

B: 좋은 생각이야. 어디 보자…. 나는 학교에서 받은 안내서와 박물관 지도가 있어.

G: 완벽해. 시작하자.

A: 우리가 이 VR 안경으로 무엇을 할 수 있을까?

B: 어디 보자…. 우리는 축구를 할 수 있어.

A: 우리가 이 드론으로 무엇을 할 수 있을까?

B: 어디 보자…. 우리는 하늘에서 사진을 찍을 수 있어.

Listen & Speak 2 B-3

A: _____

B: _____

Real-Life Zone

G: _____

B: _____

G: _____

_____

B: _____

G: _____

B: _____

G: _____

B: _____

G: _____

Wrap Up 1~2

B: _____

_____

G: _____

_____

B: _____

G: _____

B: _____

_____

G: _____

B: _____

Wrap Up 3~4

G: _____

B: _____

G: _____

B: _____

G: _____

B: _____

G: _____

A: 우리가 이 스마트워치로 무엇을 할 수 있을까?
B: 어디 보자.... 우리는 문자 메시지를 보낼 수 있어.

G: 난 이 크래커가 좋아. 정말 맛있어.
B: 응, 나도 좋아해. 나는 크래커에 왜 이 작은 구멍들이 있는지 궁금해.
G: 잘 모르겠어. 생각해 보자.... 음... 아마 그 구멍들이 크래커를 더욱 맛있게 보이도록 해 주기 때문이 아닐까.
B: 그럴 수도 있겠네, 하지만 다른 이유들이 있을 거야.
G: 크래커에 관해 인터넷에 찾아보고 뭐라고 하는지 알아보자.
B: 좋아. 오, 이것 봐.
G: 굽는 동안, 그 구멍들을 통해 수증기가 빠져나와서 크래커를 얇게 만드는 거래.
B: 또한 구멍들은 크래커를 바삭하게 만드는 거래.
G: 와! 크래커에 구멍들이 있는 거구나!

B: 안녕, 케이트. 오늘은 토요일이야. 그래서 말인데, 오늘 아인슈타인 과학 공원에 가는 건 어때?
G: 좋은 생각이야. 나는 토요일마다 특별한 프로그램들이 있다고 들었어. 나는 그것들이 무엇인지 궁금해.
B: 어디 보자.... 내가 신문에서 광고를 봤어. 여기 있어.
G: 뭐라고 쓰여 있니?
B: 여기에 따르면 오늘 두 가지 공연이 있대. 아인슈타인 홀 101호에서 있는 스마트 디자인 쇼와 국제 드론 쇼야.
G: 둘 다 환상적일 것 같아.
B: 내가 전화해서 그것들이 몇 시에 시작하는지 물어볼게.

G: 존, 봐. 학교에서 발명대회가 열린대.
B: 정말? 흥미로울 것 같아.
G: 응. 너는 참가해야 해. 너는 항상 아이디어가 훌륭하잖아.
B: 대회가 언제인지 나와 있니?
G: 어디 보자.... 11월 11일이래. 오늘로부터 2주 뒤야.
B: 대회에 참가하기 위해 내가 무엇을 해야 하는지 궁금해.
G: 여기에 따르면 너는 과학 선생님이신 해리슨 선생님께 말씀드려야 해.

※ 다음 우리말과 일치하도록 빈칸에 알맞은 것을 골라 쓰시오.

1 _____ _____
   A. Holes   B. Hidden

2 _____ about a _____ that you have _____ _____ .
   A. hole   B. seen   C. think   D. recently

3 _____ it a _____ hole _____ a _____ hole?
   A. bad   B. or   C. good   D. was

4 _____ it was a _____ in your _____ , it was _____ .
   A. sock   B. if   C. bad   D. hole

5 If it was a _____ in your shirt _____ a _____ , it was _____ .
   A. button   B. for   C. hole   D. good

6 _____ are _____ _____ .
   A. everywhere   B. there   C. holes

7 Some are _____ small you _____ not _____ _____ them.
   A. even   B. so   C. notice   D. may

8 They are well _____ , but many of these small holes are very important and _____ your _____ _____ .
   A. make   B. hidden   C. safe   D. life

9 _____ a _____ .
   A. pen   B. take

10 _____ _____ it _____ .
   A. at   B. look   C. carefully

11 Do you see a _____ _____ in the _____ ?
   A. hole   B. small   C. cap

12 Do you know _____ _____ _____ _____ ?
   A. it   B. there   C. is   D. why

13 The _____ in a pen cap can _____ _____ _____ .
   A. help   B. hole   C. lives   D. save

14 People, _____ children, often _____ small things _____ pen caps _____ their mouths.
   A. like   B. especially   C. in   D. put

15 _____ they _____ _____ them.
   A. even   B. sometimes   C. swallow

16 This can _____ their _____ and _____ _____ .
   A. breathing   B. stop   C. death   D. cause

17 A _____ pen _____ started _____ a small _____ in their pen caps.
   A. company   B. hole   C. famous   D. putting

18 The hole in the cap _____ air _____ _____ and has saved _____ .
   A. pass   B. lives   C. lets   D. through

1 숨겨진 구멍들

2 여러분이 최근에 본 구멍에 대해 생각해 보라.

3 그것은 좋은 구멍이었는가, 아니면 나쁜 구멍이었는가?

4 만약 그것이 여러분의 양말에 있는 구멍이었다면, 그것은 좋지 않은 것이었다.

5 만약 그것이 단추를 위해 셔츠에 있는 구멍이었다면, 그것은 좋은 것이었다.

6 구멍은 어디에나 있다.

7 어떤 것들은 너무 작아서 인지하지 못할 수도 있다.

8 그것들은 잘 숨겨져 있지만, 이 작은 구멍들 중 많은 것들이 매우 중요하고 여러분의 삶을 안전하게 해 준다.

9 펜을 꺼내라.

10 그것을 자세히 관찰해 보라.

11 뚜껑에 작은 구멍이 보이는가?

12 여러분은 왜 거기에 구멍이 있는지 아는가?

13 펜 뚜껑에 있는 구멍이 생명을 구하는 데 도움을 줄 수 있기 때문이다.

14 사람들, 특히 아이들은 종종 펜 뚜껑 같은 작은 것들을 그들의 입에 넣는다.

15 때때로 그들은 심지어 그것들을 삼키기도 한다.

16 이것은 그들의 호흡을 막고 죽음을 초래할 수도 있다.

17 유명한 펜 회사가 자사의 펜 뚜껑에 작은 구멍을 넣기 시작했다.

18 뚜껑에 있는 그 구멍은 공기를 통하게 해 주고 생명들을 구했다.

19 If you _____ _____, you will see other holes that play a _____ _____ in your life.

 A. around   B. role   C. look   D. helpful

20 If you have ever cooked anything in a pot _____ a _____, _____ you _____ a small hole in the lid.

 A. perhaps   B. with   C. noticed   D. lid

21 This _____, _____, is there for _____.

 A. safety   B. too   C. hole

22 When _____ something in a pot with a lid, the _____ inside the pot _____ _____.

 A. pressure   B. up   C. cooking   D. builds

23 The water _____ would quickly _____ _____ if the lid did not have that _____.

 A. hole   B. boil   C. inside   D. over

24 The hole lets steam _____ and _____ the water _____ out.

 A. from   B. out   C. coming   D. keeps

25 _____ you _____ _____ _____ an airplane?

 A. ever   B. have   C. on   D. been

26 _____ _____ _____ to look out the window and see the world _____?

 A. exciting   B. it   C. below   D. wasn't

27 _____, _____ _____ a small hole _____ your window.

 A. was   B. surprisingly   C. in   D. there

28 Airplane windows _____ _____ _____ _____ three panes.

 A. made   B. of   C. are   D. up

29 There is a hole _____ _____ _____ _____.

 A. the   B. pane   C. in   D. middle

30 It _____ the _____ _____.

 A. air   B. balances   C. pressure

31 _____ this _____ hole, airplane windows might _____ in an _____.

 A. little   B. emergency   C. without   D. break

32 The hole also _____ the window _____ so that you can enjoy that fantastic view.

 A. from   B. up   C. prevents   D. fogging

33 There are many _____ _____ that have small _____ _____.

 A. hidden   B. products   C. more   D. holes

34 In the future, when you see a little hole in something, ask yourself _____ _____ _____ _____.

 A. is   B. why   C. there   D. it

35 Maybe it is the _____ of a _____ design to make your _____.

 A. careful   B. safer   C. result   D. life

---

19 여러분이 주위를 둘러본다면, 여러분의 생활에 도움을 주는 다른 구멍들을 보게 될 것이다.

20 만약 여러분이 뚜껑 있는 냄비에 어떤 것을 요리해 본 적이 있다면, 아마도 여러분은 뚜껑에 작은 구멍이 있다는 것을 알아챘을 수도 있다.

21 이 구멍 역시 안전을 위해 존재한다.

22 뚜껑이 있는 냄비에 무언가를 요리할 때, 냄비 안쪽의 압력이 상승한다.

23 만약 뚜껑에 그 구멍이 없다면, 그 안의 물은 금방 끓어 넘칠 것이다.

24 그 구멍이 수증기를 나가게 해 주고 물이 밖으로 넘치는 것을 막아 준다.

25 비행기를 타 본 적이 있는가?

26 창밖을 내다보고 아래에 있는 세상을 보는 것이 신나지 않았는가?

27 놀랍게도, 여러분의 창문에는 작은 구멍이 하나 있었다.

28 비행기 창문은 세 개의 유리판으로 구성되어 있다.

29 그 중간 유리판에 구멍이 있다.

30 그것은 기압의 균형을 맞춰 준다.

31 이 작은 구멍이 없다면, 비행기 창문은 비상시에 깨질 수 있다.

32 그 구멍은 또한, 멋진 경치를 즐길 수 있도록 창문에 김이 서리는 것을 막아 준다.

33 숨겨진 작은 구멍들이 있는 더 많은 제품들이 있다.

34 앞으로, 여러분이 어떤 물건에서 작은 구멍을 본다면, 왜 그것이 거기에 있는지 자신에게 물어보라.

35 아마도 그것은 여러분의 삶을 더 안전하게 만들려는 사려 깊은 디자인의 결과일 것이다.

Step2

※ 다음 우리말과 일치하도록 빈칸에 알맞은 것을 골라 쓰시오.

1 _____ Holes

2 Think about a hole that you _____ _____ _____.

3 Was it a _____ hole or a _____ hole?

4 If it was a hole _____ _____ _____, it was bad.

5 If it was a hole in your shirt _____ _____ _____, it was good.

6 _____ are holes _____.

7 Some are _____ _____ you may not even _____ them.

8 They are _____ _____, but many of these small holes are very important and _____ _____ _____ _____.

9 _____ a pen.

10 _____ _____ it _____.

11 Do you see _____ _____ _____ in the cap?

12 Do you know _____ _____ _____ _____ _____?

13 The hole in a pen cap can _____ _____ _____.

14 People, especially children, often _____ small things _____ pen caps _____ their mouths.

15 _____ they even _____ _____.

16 This can _____ _____ _____ and _____ _____.

17 A famous pen company started _____ _____ _____ in their pen caps.

18 The hole in the cap _____ air _____ _____ and has _____ _____.

1 숨겨진 구멍들

2 여러분이 최근에 본 구멍에 대해 생각해 보라.

3 그것은 좋은 구멍이었는가, 아니면 나쁜 구멍이었는가?

4 만약 그것이 여러분의 양말에 있는 구멍이었다면, 그것은 좋지 않은 것이었다.

5 만약 그것이 단추를 위해 셔츠에 있는 구멍이었다면, 그것은 좋은 것이었다.

6 구멍은 어디에나 있다.

7 어떤 것들은 너무 작아서 인지하지 못할 수도 있다.

8 그것들은 잘 숨겨져 있지만, 이 작은 구멍들 중 많은 것들이 매우 중요하고 여러분의 삶을 안전하게 해 준다.

9 펜을 꺼내라.

10 그것을 자세히 관찰해 보라.

11 뚜껑에 작은 구멍이 보이는가?

12 여러분은 왜 거기에 구멍이 있는지 아는가?

13 펜 뚜껑에 있는 구멍이 생명을 구하는 데 도움을 줄 수 있기 때문이다.

14 사람들, 특히 아이들은 종종 펜 뚜껑 같은 작은 것들을 그들의 입에 넣는다.

15 때때로 그들은 심지어 그것들을 삼키기도 한다.

16 이것은 그들의 호흡을 막고 죽음을 초래할 수도 있다.

17 유명한 펜 회사가 자사의 펜 뚜껑에 작은 구멍을 넣기 시작했다.

18 뚜껑에 있는 그 구멍은 공기를 통하게 해 주고 생명들을 구했다.

19 If you _____ _____, you will see other holes that _____ _____ _____ _____ in your life.

20 If you have ever cooked anything in a pot _____ _____ _____, perhaps you _____ a small hole in the _____.

21 This hole, too, is there _____ _____.

22 _____ _____ something in a pot with a lid, the _____ inside the pot _____ _____.

23 The water inside would quickly _____ _____ if the lid did not have that hole.

24 The hole lets _____ _____ and _____ the water _____ _____ out.

25 _____ you ever _____ on an airplane?

26 _____ _____ _____ to _____ _____ the window and see the world below?

27 _____, there was a small hole in your window.

28 Airplane windows _____ _____ _____ _____ three panes.

29 There is a hole _____ _____ _____ _____.

30 It _____ the _____ _____.

31 _____ this _____ _____, airplane windows might break _____ _____ _____.

32 The hole also _____ the window _____ _____ _____ so that you can enjoy that _____ _____.

33 There are many more products _____ _____ small _____ _____.

34 In the future, when you see a little hole in something, ask yourself _____ _____ _____ _____.

35 Maybe it is _____ _____ of a careful design _____ _____ _____ _____ _____.

19 여러분이 주위를 둘러본다면, 여러분의 생활에 도움을 주는 다른 구멍들을 보게 될 것이다.

20 만약 여러분이 뚜껑 있는 냄비에 어떤 것을 요리해 본 적이 있다면, 아마도 여러분은 뚜껑에 작은 구멍이 있다는 것을 알아챘을 수도 있다.

21 이 구멍 역시 안전을 위해 존재한다.

22 뚜껑이 있는 냄비에 무언가를 요리할 때, 냄비 안쪽의 압력이 상승한다.

23 만약 뚜껑에 그 구멍이 없다면, 그 안의 물은 금방 끓어 넘칠 것이다.

24 그 구멍이 수증기를 나가게 해 주고 물이 밖으로 넘치는 것을 막아 준다.

25 비행기를 타 본 적이 있는가?

26 창밖을 내다보고 아래에 있는 세상을 보는 것이 신나지 않았는가?

27 놀랍게도, 여러분의 창문에는 작은 구멍이 하나 있었다.

28 비행기 창문은 세 개의 유리판으로 구성되어 있다.

29 그 중간 유리판에 구멍이 있다.

30 그것은 기압의 균형을 맞춰 준다.

31 이 작은 구멍이 없다면, 비행기 창문은 비상시에 깨질 수 있다.

32 그 구멍은 또한, 멋진 경치를 즐길 수 있도록 창문에 김이 서리는 것을 막아 준다.

33 숨겨진 작은 구멍들이 있는 더 많은 제품들이 있다.

34 앞으로, 여러분이 어떤 물건에서 작은 구멍을 본다면, 왜 그것이 거기에 있는지 자신에게 물어보라.

35 아마도 그것은 여러분의 삶을 더 안전하게 만들려는 사려 깊은 디자인의 결과일 것이다.

※ 다음 문장을 우리말로 쓰시오.

1 ▸ Hidden Holes
➡ _____

2 ▸ Think about a hole that you have seen recently.
➡ _____

3 ▸ Was it a good hole or a bad hole?
➡ _____

4 ▸ If it was a hole in your sock, it was bad.
➡ _____

5 ▸ If it was a hole in your shirt for a button, it was good.
➡ _____

6 ▸ There are holes everywhere.
➡ _____

7 ▸ Some are so small you may not even notice them.
➡ _____

8 ▸ They are well hidden, but many of these small holes are very important and make your life safe.
➡ _____

9 ▸ Take a pen.
➡ _____

10 ▸ Look at it carefully.
➡ _____

11 ▸ Do you see a small hole in the cap?
➡ _____

12 ▸ Do you know why it is there?
➡ _____

13 ▸ The hole in a pen cap can help save lives.
➡ _____

14 ▸ People, especially children, often put small things like pen caps in their mouths.
➡ _____

15 ▸ Sometimes they even swallow them.
➡ _____

16 ▸ This can stop their breathing and cause death.
➡ _____

17 ▸ A famous pen company started putting a small hole in their pen caps.
➡ _____

18 ▸ The hole in the cap lets air pass through and has saved lives.
➡ _____

19 If you look around, you will see other holes that play a helpful role in your life.

➡ _____

20 If you have ever cooked anything in a pot with a lid, perhaps you noticed a small hole in the lid.

➡ _____

_____

21 This hole, too, is there for safety.

➡ _____

22 When cooking something in a pot with a lid, the pressure inside the pot builds up.

➡ _____

23 The water inside would quickly boil over if the lid did not have that hole.

➡ _____

24 The hole lets steam out and keeps the water from coming out.

➡ _____

25 Have you ever been on an airplane?

➡ _____

26 Wasn't it exciting to look out the window and see the world below?

➡ _____

27 Surprisingly, there was a small hole in your window.

➡ _____

28 Airplane windows are made up of three panes.

➡ _____

29 There is a hole in the middle pane.

➡ _____

30 It balances the air pressure.

➡ _____

31 Without this little hole, airplane windows might break in an emergency.

➡ _____

32 The hole also prevents the window from fogging up so that you can enjoy that fantastic view.

➡ _____

33 There are many more products that have small hidden holes.

➡ _____

34 In the future, when you see a little hole in something, ask yourself why it is there.

➡ _____

35 Maybe it is the result of a careful design to make your life safer.

➡ _____

※ 다음 괄호 안의 단어들을 우리말에 맞도록 바르게 배열하시오.

1 (Holes / Hidden)
➡ _____

2 (about / think / hole / a / you / that / seen / have / recently.)
➡ _____

3 (it / was / good / a / hole / or / bad / a / hole?)
➡ _____

4 (it / if / a / was / hole / your / in / sock, / was / it / bad.)
➡ _____

5 (it / if / was / hole / a / your / in / shirt / for / button, / a / was / it / good.)
➡ _____

6 (are / there / everywhere. / holes)
➡ _____

7 (are / some / small / so / may / you / even / not / them. / notice)
➡ _____

8 (are / they / hidden, / well / many / but / these / of / holes / small / are / important / very / and / your / make / safe. / life)
➡ _____

9 (a / pen. / take)
➡ _____

10 (at / look / carefully. / it)
➡ _____

11 (you / do / a / see / hole / small / the / in / cap?)
➡ _____

12 (you / do / why / know / is / it / there?)
➡ _____

13 (hole / the / a / in / cap / pen / help / can / lives. / save)
➡ _____

14 (especially / people, / often / children, / put / things / small / pen / like / in / caps / mouths. / their)
➡ _____

15 (they / sometimes / swallow / even / them.)
➡ _____

16 (can / this / their / stop / and / breathing / death. / cause)
➡ _____

17 (famous / a / company / pen / putting / started / small / a / hole / their / in / caps. / pen)
➡ _____

18 (hole / the / the / in / lets / cap / pass / air / and / through / saved / has / lives.)
➡ _____

1 숨겨진 구멍들

2 여러분이 최근에 본 구멍에 대해 생각해 보라.

3 그것은 좋은 구멍이었는가, 아니면 나쁜 구멍이었는가?

4 만약 그것이 여러분의 양말에 있는 구멍이었다면, 그것은 좋지 않은 것이었다.

5 만약 그것이 단추를 위해 셔츠에 있는 구멍이었다면, 그것은 좋은 것이었다.

6 구멍은 어디에나 있다.

7 어떤 것들은 너무 작아서 인지하지 못할 수도 있다.

8 그것들은 잘 숨겨져 있지만, 이 작은 구멍들 중 많은 것들이 매우 중요하고 여러분의 삶을 안전하게 해 준다.

9 펜을 꺼내라.

10 그것을 자세히 관찰해 보라.

11 뚜껑에 작은 구멍이 보이는가?

12 여러분은 왜 거기에 구멍이 있는지 아는가?

13 펜 뚜껑에 있는 구멍이 생명을 구하는 데 도움을 줄 수 있기 때문이다.

14 사람들, 특히 아이들은 종종 펜 뚜껑 같은 작은 것들을 그들의 입에 넣는다.

15 때때로 그들은 심지어 그것들을 삼키기도 한다.

16 이것은 그들의 호흡을 막고 죽음을 초래할 수도 있다.

17 유명한 펜 회사가 자사의 펜 뚜껑에 작은 구멍을 넣기 시작했다.

18 뚜껑에 있는 그 구멍은 공기를 통하게 해 주고 생명들을 구했다.

19 (you / if / around, / look / will / you / see / holes / other / play / that / role / a / helpful / in / life. / your)
➡

20 (you / if / ever / have / anything / cooked / in / pot / a / with / lid, / a / perhaps / noticed / you / hole / a / small / the / in / lid.)
➡

21 (hole, / this / is / too, / for / there / safety.)
➡

22 (cooking / when / something / a / in / with / pot / lid, / a / the / inside / pressure / the / up. / builds)
➡

23 (water / the / would / inside / boil / quickly / if / over / lid / the / did / have / not / hole. / that)
➡

24 (hole / the / steam / lets / out / and / the / keeps / from / water / out. / coming)
➡

25 (you / have / been / ever / an / on / airplane?)
➡

26 (it / wasn't / exciting / look / to / out / window / the / and / the / see / below? / world)
➡

27 (there / surprisingly, / was / small / a / hole / your / in / window.)
➡

28 (windows / airplane / made / are / of / up / panes. / three)
➡

29 (is / there / hole / a / the / in / pane. / middle)
➡

30 (balances / it / air / the / pressure.)
➡

31 (this / without / hole, / little / windows / airplane / break / might / an / in / emergency.)
➡

32 (hole / the / prevents / also / window / the / fogging / from / so / up / that / can / you / that / enjoy / view. / fantastic)
➡

33 (are / there / more / many / that / products / have / hidden / small / holes.)
➡

34 (the / in / when / future, / see / you / little / a / hole / something, / in / yourself / ask / it / why / there. / is)
➡

35 (it / maybe / the / is / of / result / a / design / careful / make / to / life / your / safer.)
➡

19 여러분이 주위를 둘러본다면, 여러분의 생활에 도움을 주는 다른 구멍들을 보게 될 것이다.

20 만약 여러분이 뚜껑 있는 냄비에 어떤 것을 요리해 본 적이 있다면, 아마도 여러분은 뚜껑에 작은 구멍이 있다는 것을 알아챘을 수도 있다.

21 이 구멍 역시 안전을 위해 존재한다.

22 뚜껑이 있는 냄비에 무언가를 요리할 때, 냄비 안쪽의 압력이 상승한다.

23 만약 뚜껑에 그 구멍이 없다면, 그 안의 물은 금방 끓어 넘칠 것이다.

24 그 구멍이 수증기를 나가게 해 주고 물이 밖으로 넘치는 것을 막아 준다.

25 비행기를 타 본 적이 있는가?

26 창밖을 내다보고 아래에 있는 세상을 보는 것이 신나지 않았는가?

27 놀랍게도, 여러분의 창문에는 작은 구멍이 하나 있었다.

28 비행기 창문은 세 개의 유리판으로 구성되어 있다.

29 그 중간 유리판에 구멍이 있다.

30 그것은 기압의 균형을 맞춰 준다.

31 이 작은 구멍이 없다면, 비행기 창문은 비상시에 깨질 수 있다.

32 그 구멍은 또한, 멋진 경치를 즐길 수 있도록 창문에 김이 서리는 것을 막아 준다.

33 숨겨진 작은 구멍들이 있는 더 많은 제품들이 있다.

34 앞으로, 여러분이 어떤 물건에서 작은 구멍을 본다면, 왜 그것이 거기에 있는지 자신에게 물어보라.

35 아마도 그것은 여러분의 삶을 더 안전하게 만들려는 사려 깊은 디자인의 결과일 것이다.

※ 다음 우리말을 영어로 쓰시오.

1 숨겨진 구멍들

➡ _____

2 여러분이 최근에 본 구멍에 대해 생각해 보라.

➡ _____

3 그것은 좋은 구멍이었는가, 아니면 나쁜 구멍이었는가?

➡ _____

4 만약 그것이 여러분의 양말에 있는 구멍이었다면, 그것은 좋지 않은 것이었다.

➡ _____

5 만약 그것이 단추를 위해 셔츠에 있는 구멍이었다면, 그것은 좋은 것이었다.

➡ _____

6 구멍은 어디에나 있다.

➡ _____

7 어떤 것들은 너무 작아서 인지하지 못할 수도 있다.

➡ _____

8 그것들은 잘 숨겨져 있지만, 이 작은 구멍들 중 많은 것들이 매우 중요하고 여러분의 삶을 안전하게 해 준다.

➡ _____

9 펜을 꺼내라.

➡ _____

10 그것을 자세히 관찰해 보라.

➡ _____

11 뚜껑에 작은 구멍이 보이는가?

➡ _____

12 여러분은 왜 거기에 구멍이 있는지 아는가?

➡ _____

13 펜 뚜껑에 있는 구멍이 생명을 구하는 데 도움을 줄 수 있기 때문이다.

➡ _____

14 사람들, 특히 아이들은 종종 펜 뚜껑 같은 작은 것들을 그들의 입에 넣는다.

➡ _____

15 때때로 그들은 심지어 그것들을 삼키기도 한다.

➡ _____

16 이것은 그들의 호흡을 막고 죽음을 초래할 수도 있다.

➡ _____

17 유명한 펜 회사가 자사의 펜 뚜껑에 작은 구멍을 넣기 시작했다.

➡ _____

18 뚜껑에 있는 그 구멍은 공기를 통하게 해 주고 생명들을 구했다.

➡ _____

19 여러분이 주위를 둘러본다면, 여러분의 생활에 도움을 주는 다른 구멍들을 보게 될 것이다.

➡ _____

20 만약 여러분이 뚜껑 있는 냄비에 어떤 것을 요리해 본 적이 있다면, 아마도 여러분은 뚜껑에 작은 구멍이 있다는 것을 알아챘을 수도 있다.

➡ _____

21 이 구멍 역시 안전을 위해 존재한다.

➡ _____

22 뚜껑이 있는 냄비에 무언가를 요리할 때, 냄비 안쪽의 압력이 상승한다.

➡ _____

23 만약 뚜껑에 그 구멍이 없다면, 그 안의 물은 금방 끓어 넘칠 것이다.

➡ _____

24 그 구멍이 수증기를 나가게 해 주고 물이 밖으로 넘치는 것을 막아 준다.

➡ _____

25 비행기를 타 본 적이 있는가?

➡ _____

26 창밖을 내다보고 아래에 있는 세상을 보는 것이 신나지 않았는가?

➡ _____

27 놀랍게도, 여러분의 창문에는 작은 구멍이 하나 있었다.

➡ _____

28 비행기 창문은 세 개의 유리판으로 구성되어 있다.

➡ _____

29 그 중간 유리판에 구멍이 있다.

➡ _____

30 그것은 기압의 균형을 맞춰 준다.

➡ _____

31 이 작은 구멍이 없다면, 비행기 창문은 비상시에 깨질 수 있다.

➡ _____

32 그 구멍은 또한, 멋진 경치를 즐길 수 있도록 창문에 김이 서리는 것을 막아 준다.

➡ _____

33 숨겨진 작은 구멍들이 있는 더 많은 제품들이 있다.

➡ _____

34 앞으로, 여러분이 어떤 물건에서 작은 구멍을 본다면, 왜 그것이 거기에 있는지 자신에게 물어보라.

➡ _____

35 아마도 그것은 여러분의 삶을 더 안전하게 만들려는 사려 깊은 디자인의 결과일 것이다.

➡ _____

※ 다음 우리말과 일치하도록 빈칸에 알맞은 말을 쓰시오.

After You Read B

1. It _____ _____ _____ _____ _____ even when people _____ the pen cap.

2. It _____ _____ _____ _____.

3. It _____ _____ _____ and _____ the water in the pot _____ _____ _____.

1. 사람들이 펜 뚜껑을 삼킬 때도 그것은 공기를 통하게 해준다.
2. 그것은 기압의 균형을 맞춰 준다.
3. 그것은 수증기를 나가게 해 주고 냄비의 물이 끓어 넘치는 것을 막아 준다.

Work Together

1. _____ _____ Helmet

2. This invention _____ _____ _____ _____ _____ _____ _____.

3. If you use the Sweet Dream Helmet, you will _____ _____ _____ _____ _____ _____.

4. You can even _____ _____ _____ _____ _____ you want to dream _____ _____ you can have different experiences _____ _____ _____ _____.

1. 단 잠 헬멧
2. 이 발명품은 사람들이 단 잠을 잘 수 있도록 돕는다..
3. 만약 단 잠 헬멧을 사용한다면, 당신은 매일 밤 행복한 꿈을 꿀 것입니다.
4. 당신이 잠든 동안 다양한 경험을 할 수 있기 위해 당신은 심지어 당신이 꿈꾸고 싶은 꿈의 형태를 고를 수 있습니다.

Writing Workshop

1. A _____

2. _____ you _____ _____ a refrigerator?

3. We use it every day _____ _____ we can _____ _____ _____ and _____.

4. In 1755, William Cullen _____ the first _____ _____ _____ _____.

5. After that, it _____ _____ the years and _____ _____ _____ _____ _____ _____ _____.

6. _____ we _____ _____ _____ refrigerators in today's world, we _____ _____ _____ _____ _____ _____ ice cream on hot summer days.

1. 냉장고
2. 여러분은 냉장고가 없는 세상을 상상할 수 있나요?
3. 우리는 음식을 차갑고 신선하게 보관하기 위해 이것을 매일 사용합니다.
4. 1755년, 윌리엄 컬런이 초기 형태의 냉장고를 발명했습니다.
5. 그 이후, 이것을 수년 동안 발전했고, 현대의 생활에서 필수적인 부분이 되었습니다.
6. 만약 우리에게 오늘날 냉장고가 없다면, 더운 여름날 아이스크림을 즐겨 먹을 수 없을 것입니다.

구석구석 지문 Test

※ 다음 우리말을 영어로 쓰시오.

After You Read B

1. 사람들이 펜 뚜껑을 삼킬 때도 그것은 공기를 통하게 해준다.
   ➡ _____

2. 그것은 기압의 균형을 맞춰 준다.
   ➡ _____

3. 그것은 수증기를 나가게 해 주고 냄비의 물이 끓어 넘치는 것을 막아 준다.
   ➡ _____

Work Together

1. 단 잠 헬멧
   ➡ _____

2. 이 발명품은 사람들이 단 잠을 잘 수 있도록 돕는다.
   ➡ _____

3. 만약 단 잠 헬멧을 사용한다면, 당신은 매일 밤 행복한 꿈을 꿀 것입니다.
   ➡ _____

4. 당신이 잠든 동안 다양한 경험을 할 수 있기 위해 당신은 심지어 당신이 꿈꾸고 싶은 꿈의 형태를 고를 수 있습니다.
   ➡ _____
   _____

Writing Workshop

1. 냉장고
   ➡ _____

2. 여러분은 냉장고가 없는 세상을 상상할 수 있나요?
   ➡ _____

3. 우리는 음식을 차갑고 신선하게 보관하기 위해 이것을 매일 사용합니다.
   ➡ _____

4. 1755년, 윌리엄 컬런이 초기 형태의 냉장고를 발명했습니다.
   ➡ _____

5. 그 이후, 이것을 수년 동안 발전했고, 현대의 생활에서 필수적인 부분이 되었습니다.
   ➡ _____

6. 만약 우리에게 오늘날 냉장고가 없다면, 더운 여름날 아이스크림을 즐겨 먹을 수 없을 것입니다.
   ➡ _____
   _____

Step1

※ 다음 영어를 우리말로 쓰시오.

01	boil
02	touching
03	warm
04	chop
05	while
06	serve
07	add
08	blend
09	ginger
10	cool
11	treasure
12	taste
13	pain
14	smooth
15	hold
16	throat
17	pepper
18	temperature
19	reduce
20	melt
21	local

22	stuffy
23	thick
24	low
25	stay
26	medicine
27	seafood
28	recommend
29	stir
30	mixture
31	sore
32	pour
33	mix
34	recipe
35	such as A
36	be made with
37	find out
38	a bowl of
39	as well as
40	be different from
41	show A around B
42	be good for
43	not only A but also B

※ 다음 우리말을 영어로 쓰시오.

01 붓다, 따르다

02 요리법

03 식히다

04 열다, 개최하다

05 더하다, 첨가하다

06 섞다

07 추천하다

08 잘게 썰다

09 끓다, 끓이다

10 약

11 고루 잘 섞인

12 동쪽에 위치한

13 생강

14 혼합물

15 제공하다

16 코가 막힌, 답답한

17 맛

18 반면에, ~하는 동안에

19 아픔, 통증

20 녹다

21 후추, 고추

22 온도, 기온

23 두꺼운, 걸쭉한

24 목구멍, 목

25 휘젓다

26 줄이다

27 감동적인

28 보물

29 해산물

30 지역의, 현지의

31 섞다

32 양고기

33 그대로 있다

34 아픈, 따가운

35 ~와 다르다

36 ~ 한 접시

37 ~에 더하여, 게다가

38 알아내다, 발견하다

39 몸에 걸치다

40 처음으로

41 A와 같은

42 A뿐만 아니라 B도

43 ~로 만들어지다

※ 다음 영영풀이에 알맞은 단어를 <보기>에서 골라 쓴 후, 우리말 뜻을 쓰시오.

1 _____ : physical suffering: _____

2 _____ : causing strong emotion: _____

3 _____ : to cut into smaller pieces: _____

4 _____ : anything or person greatly valued: _____

5 _____ : having a great distance from one surface to the opposite: _____

6 _____ : to make something smaller in size, amount, number, etc.: _____

7 _____ : to change from a liquid to a gas as a result of heat: _____

8 _____ : something made by combining two or more ingredients: _____

9 _____ : to urge or suggest as proper, useful or beneficial: _____

10 _____ : to flow, as from once container to another, or into, over, or on something: _____

11 _____ : to remain over a length of time, as in a place or situation: _____

12 _____ : to move a liquid or substance around, using a spoon or something similar: _____

13 _____ : a measure of the warmth of an object with reference to a standard scale: _____

14 _____ : to change or to cause something to change from a solid to a liquid usually because of heat: _____

15 _____ : relating to a city, town or small district rather than an entire state or country: _____

16 _____ : a reed-like plant originally from Southeast Asia but now grown in most warm countries, having a strong-smelling and spicy root used in cookery and medicine: _____

보기			
pour	temperature	chop	thick
stir	local	mixture	treasure
recommend	stay	touching	pain
melt	ginger	reduce	boil

※ 다음 우리말과 일치하도록 빈칸에 알맞은 말을 쓰시오.

Listen & Speak 1 Listen 1

B: Hi, Grace. Those are pretty. What are _____ _____?

G: They're _____ *dango*.

B: I'm sorry. _____ you say that _____?

G: *Dan-go*. They're sweet and _____ _____ rice cake powder. They're _____ Japan.

B: Grace, 안녕. 그거 예쁘다. 그거 뭐라고 불리니?
G: 당고라고 불러.
B: 미안, 다시 말해 줄래?
G: 당–고. 달고 쌀가루로 만들어진 거야. 일본에서 온 거야.

Listen & Speak 1 Listen 2

B: Alice, what's that you're _____?

G: It's *rasmalai*.

B: *Ra*.... Could you _____ that _____?

G: *Ras-ma-lai*. It's _____ a cheesecake in a sweet cream. It's a _____ _____ in India.

B: Alice, 네가 먹고 있는 것은 무엇이니?
G: 라스말라이야.
B: 라… 다시 한 번 말해 줄래?
G: 라스–마–라이. 달콤한 크림 안에 있는 치즈 케이크 같은 거야. 인도의 전통 음식이지.

Listen & Speak 1 Listen 3

G: What's _____ you're _____, David? It _____ _____ a chocolate ball.

B: It's *brigadeiro*.

G: _____? Could you say that _____?

B: B*ri-ga-dei-ro*. It's sweet and _____. It's _____ in Brazil.

G: David, 뭐 먹고 있니? 그거 초콜릿 볼처럼 생겼다.
B: 브리가데이로야.
G: 뭐라고? 다시 한 번 말해 줄래?
B: 브리–가–데이–로. 달고 맛있어. 브라질에서 인기 많아.

Listen & Speak 1 A-1

G: My _____ Korean traditional drink is Maesil-tea. _____ about you, Jinsu?

B: Well, my favorite _____ _____ is Sikhye.

G: Sik.... Can you _____ that _____?

B: Sik-hye. It's _____ and cool.

G: I want to _____ it.

G: 내가 제일 좋아하는 한국 전통 음료는 매실차야. 진수, 너는 뭐니?
B: 음, 내가 제일 좋아하는 음료는 식혜야.
G: 식… 다시 말해 줄래?
B: 식–혜. 달고 시원해.
G: 먹어 보고 싶다.

Listen & Speak 1 A-2

B: Have you ever _____ *poke*?

G: Sorry, _____ you say that again, please?

B: *Po-ke*. It's a _____ that is _____ in Hawaii.

G: What's so _____ about it?

B: It's made _____ _____ and _____. It's not _____ delicious _____ also very _____.

Listen & Speak 1 B

1. **A:** _____ you ever _____ *rasmalai*?

   B: _____, could you say that again?

   A: *Rasmalai*. It's a _____ _____ in India.

2. **A:** Have you ever _____ *brigadeiro*?

   B: Sorry, could you say that again?

   A: *Brigadeiro*. It's a _____ dessert in Brazil.

3. **A:** Have you _____ _____ *macaron*?

   B: Sorry, could you say _____ again?

   A: *Macaron*. It's a traditional dessert _____ France.

Listen & Speak 2 Listen

1. **B:** Could you _____ a good _____ dish?

   W: _____ Samgyetang. It'll give you energy.

2. **G:** _____ you recommend a good book _____ my little sister?

   M: I recommend this one. The story is _____.

3. **B:** Could you _____ a guitar for _____?

   W: How _____ this one? Many beginners play it.

4. **G:** Could you recommend a _____ for my dog?

   M: Sure. _____ about this? Dogs really like it.

Listen & Speak 2 A-1

B: Tomorrow is my dad's birthday. I'd like to do _____ _____ for him.

G: _____ about _____ something for him? He _____ really like that.

B: That sounds great. Can you _____ something _____ to cook?

G: Umm. How _____ Gimchijeon? It's _____ to make and it's _____.

B: Oh, that's a good _____. He'll love it.

B: 너 포케 먹어 본 적 있니?

G: 미안, 다시 한 번 말해 줄래?

G: 포-케. 하와이에서 인기 많은 샐러드야.

G: 그게 뭐가 그렇게 특별한데?

G: 쌀이랑 생선으로 만들어. 맛도 있고 매우 건강한 음식이야.

1. **A:** 너 라스말라이 먹어 본 적 있니?
   B: 미안, 다시 말해 줄래?
   A: 라스말라이. 그건 인도의 전통 디저트야.
2. **A:** 너 브리가데이로 먹어 본 적 있니?
   B: 미안, 다시 말해 줄래?
   A: 브리가데이로. 그건 브라질의 전통 디저트야.
3. **A:** 너 마카롱 먹어 본 적 있니?
   B: 미안, 다시 말해 줄래?
   A: 마카롱. 그건 프랑스 전통 디저트야.

1. **B:** 좋은 전통 음식 추천해 줄 수 있니?
   W: 삼계탕을 먹어봐. 너에게 에너지를 줄 거야.
2. **G:** 내 여동생에게 좋은 책을 추천해 줄 수 있니?
   M: 이것을 추천해. 이야기가 감동적이야.
3. **B:** 초보자를 위한 기타를 추천해 줄 수 있니?
   W: 이거 어때? 많은 초보자들이 그걸 연주해.
4. **G:** 내 개를 위한 간식을 추천해 줄래?
   M: 물론, 이거 어때? 개들이 그걸 정말 좋아해.

B: 내일은 우리 아빠의 생신이야. 난 아빠를 위해 좀 특별한 것을 하고 싶어.

G: 아버지를 위해 무언가를 요리하는 건 어때? 정말 좋아하실 거야.

B: 그거 좋겠다. 요리하기 쉬운 것을 추천해 줄래?

G: 음, 김치전 어때? 만들기 쉽고 맛있어.

B: 오, 좋은 생각이다. 아빠가 좋아하실 거야.

Listen & Speak 2 B-2

M: _____ to the Sydney Information Center. Sydney has _____ places you will want to _____. The Rocks Markets is one of them. _____ you can buy art, _____, books and many _____ things. You can also eat fresh, _____ _____ food. We _____ _____ the Rocks Markets and _____ the food and the fun there.

M: 시드니 여행 정보 센터에 오신 걸 환영합니다. 시드니는 여러분께서 방문하시고 싶으실 만한 장소들이 많습니다. Rocks Markets은 그 중의 하나죠. 그곳에선 예술 작품과 의류, 책 그리고 다른 많은 것들을 사실 수 있습니다. 또한 신선하고 맛있는 지역 음식도 드실 수 있습니다. 저희는 Rocks Markets에 가시는 것을 추천해 드리며 그곳에서 음식과 재미를 즐기시기를 추천합니다.

Real-Life Zone

M: Good afternoon. A table _____ two?

B: Yes.

M: This way please. _____ is the menu. I'll be _____ in a few minutes and _____ your order.

B: Okay. Thank you.

G: I don't know _____ about Korean food. Could you _____ something?

B: Well, I'd _____ the Bibimbap.

G: I'm sorry. _____ you say that again, please?

B: This one. Bi-bim-bap. It's _____ with lots of vegetables, beef and an egg _____ rice. It's tasty and it's also _____ for your _____.

G: That sounds great. I'll _____ it.

B: It's _____ with a _____ red _____ sauce. Is that _____?

G: No _____. I like spicy food.

M: 안녕하세요. 두 분이신가요?
B: 네.
M: 이쪽으로 오십시오. 메뉴는 여기 있습니다. 잠시 후에 와서 주문 받겠습니다.
B: 알겠습니다. 감사합니다.
G: 나 한국 음식에 대해서 잘 알지 못해. 네가 추천해 줄래?
B: 음, 나는 비빔밥을 추천할게.
G: 미안, 다시 한 번 말해 줄래?
B: 이거. 비-빔-밥. 그것은 밥 위에 많은 야채들과 소고기, 그리고 계란을 얹어 만들어. 맛있고 건강에도 좋아.
G: 굉장한데. 난 그거 먹어 볼래.
B: 매운 고추장 양념이랑 같이 나오는 거야. 괜찮겠니?
G: 문제 없어. 나 매운 음식을 좋아해.

Wrap Up 1-2

B: Tomorrow is my birthday.

G: I know. _____ you going to _____ a birthday party, Alex?

B: Yes. _____ you recommend a good _____ to have the party?

G: I'd _____ the Happy Snack House. The food is really good and it'll be large _____.

B: What dish _____ you _____?

G: I'd recommend the onion rings. They're _____!

B: Oh, just _____ about them _____ my mouth _____.

B: 내일은 내 생일이야.
G: 알고 있어. Alex, 생일 파티할 거니?
B: 응. 파티 열기에 좋은 장소 추천해 줄래?
G: 나는 Happy Snack House를 추천할게. 음식이 정말 맛있고 장소도 충분히 넓어.
B: 넌 무슨 음식을 추천해 줄래?
G: 나는 양파 튀김을 추천할게. 정말 환상적이야!
B: 오, 그거 생각하는 것만으로도 침이 고인다.

Step2

※ 다음 우리말에 맞도록 대화를 영어로 쓰시오.

해석

Listen & Speak 1 Listen 1

B: _____

G: _____

B: _____

G: _____

B: Grace, 안녕. 그거 예쁘다. 그거 뭐라고 불리니?
G: 당고라고 불러.
B: 미안, 다시 말해 줄래?
G: 당-고. 달고 쌀가루로 만들어진 거야. 일본에서 온 거야.

Listen & Speak 1 Listen 2

B: _____

G: _____

B: _____

G: _____

B: Alice, 네가 먹고 있는 것은 무엇이니?
G: 라스말라이야.
B: 라… 다시 한 번 말해 줄래?
G: 라스-마-라이. 달콤한 크림 안에 있는 치즈 케이크 같은 거야. 인도의 전통 음식이지.

Listen & Speak 1 Listen 3

G: _____

B: _____

G: _____

B: _____

G: David, 뭐 먹고 있니? 그거 초콜릿 볼처럼 생겼다.
B: 브리가데이로야.
G: 뭐라고? 다시 한 번 말해 줄래?
B: 브리-가-데이-로. 달고 맛있어. 브라질에서 인기 많아.

Listen & Speak 1 A-1

G: _____

B: _____

G: _____

B: _____

G: _____

G: 내가 제일 좋아하는 한국 전통 음료는 매실차야. 진수, 너는 뭐니?
B: 음, 내가 제일 좋아하는 음료는 식혜야.
G: 식… 다시 말해 줄래?
B: 식-혜. 달고 시원해.
G: 먹어 보고 싶다.

Listen & Speak 1 A-2

B: _____

G: _____

B: _____

G: _____

B: _____

B: 너 포케 먹어 본 적 있니?

G: 미안, 다시 한 번 말해 줄래?

G: 포-케. 하와이에서 인기 많은 샐러드야.

G: 그게 뭐가 그렇게 특별한데?

G: 쌀이랑 생선으로 만들어. 맛도 있고 매우 건강한 음식이야.

Listen & Speak 1 B

1. A: _____

   B: _____

   A: _____

2. A: _____

   B: _____

   A: _____

3. A: _____

   B: _____

   A: _____

1. A: 너 라스말라이 먹어 본 적 있니?
   B: 미안, 다시 말해 줄래?
   A: 라스말라이. 그건 인도의 전통 디저트야.
2. A: 너 브리가데이로 먹어 본 적 있니?
   B: 미안, 다시 말해 줄래?
   A: 브리가데이로. 그건 브라질의 전통 디저트야.
3. A: 너 마카롱 먹어 본 적 있니?
   B: 미안, 다시 말해 줄래?
   A: 마카롱. 그건 프랑스 전통 디저트야.

Listen & Speak 2 Listen

1. B: _____

   W: _____

2. G: _____

   M: _____

3. B: _____

   W: _____

4. G: _____

   M: _____

1. B: 좋은 전통 음식 추천해 줄 수 있니?
   W: 삼계탕을 먹어봐. 너에게 에너지를 줄 거야.
2. G: 내 여동생에게 좋은 책을 추천해 줄 수 있니?
   M: 이것을 추천해. 이야기가 감동적이야.
3. B: 초보자를 위한 기타를 추천해 줄 수 있니?
   W: 이거 어때? 많은 초보자들이 그걸 연주해.
4. G: 내 개를 위한 간식을 추천해 줄래?
   M: 물론, 이거 어때? 개들이 그걸 정말 좋아해.

Listen & Speak 2 A-1

B: _____

G: _____

B: _____

G: _____

B: _____

B: 내일은 우리 아빠의 생신이야. 난 아빠를 위해 좀 특별한 것을 하고 싶어.

G: 아버지를 위해 무언가를 요리하는 건 어때? 정말 좋아하실 거야.

B: 그거 좋겠다. 요리하기 쉬운 것을 추천해 줄래?

G: 음, 김치전 어때? 만들기 쉽고 맛있어.

B: 오, 좋은 생각이다. 아빠가 좋아하실 거야.

Listen & Speak 2 B-2

M: _____
_____
_____
_____
_____

Real-Life Zone

M: _____
B: _____
M: _____
_____
B: _____
G: _____
B: _____
G: _____
B: _____
_____
G: _____
B: _____
G: _____

Wrap Up 1-2

B: _____
G: _____
B: _____
G: _____
_____
B: _____
G: _____
B: _____

M: 시드니 여행 정보 센터에 오신 걸 환영합니다. 시드니는 여러분께서 방문하시고 싶으실 만한 장소들이 많습니다. Rocks Markets은 그 중의 하나죠. 그곳에선 예술 작품과 의류, 책 그리고 다른 많은 것들을 사실 수 있습니다. 또한 신선하고 맛있는 지역 음식도 드실 수 있습니다. 저희는 Rocks Markets에 가시는 것을 추천해 드리며 그곳에서 음식과 재미를 즐기시기를 추천합니다.

M: 안녕하세요. 두 분이신가요?
B: 네.
M: 이쪽으로 오십시오. 메뉴는 여기 있습니다. 잠시 후에 와서 주문 받겠습니다.
B: 알겠습니다. 감사합니다.
G: 나 한국 음식에 대해서 잘 알지 못해. 네가 추천해 줄래?
B: 음, 나는 비빔밥을 추천할게.
G: 미안, 다시 한 번 말해 줄래?
B: 이거. 비−빔−밥. 그것은 밥 위에 많은 야채들과 소고기, 그리고 계란을 얹어 만들어. 맛있고 건강에도 좋아.
G: 굉장한데. 난 그거 먹어 볼래.
B: 매운 고추장 양념이랑 같이 나오는 거야. 괜찮겠니?
G: 문제 없어. 나 매운 음식을 좋아해.

B: 내일은 내 생일이야.
G: 알고 있어. Alex, 생일 파티할 거니?
B: 응. 파티 열기에 좋은 장소 추천해 줄래?
G: 나는 Happy Snack House를 추천할게. 음식이 정말 맛있고 장소도 충분히 넓어.
B: 넌 무슨 음식을 추천해 줄래?
G: 나는 양파 튀김을 추천할게. 정말 환상적이야!
B: 오, 그거 생각하는 것만으로도 침이 고인다.

※ 다음 우리말과 일치하도록 빈칸에 알맞은 것을 골라 쓰시오.

1 _____ That _____ _____
   A. Fight   B. Foods   C. Colds

2 What do you do _____ you _____ a _____?
   A. cold   B. when   C. catch

3 Of course, you want to _____ _____, so maybe you _____ on more _____.
   A. warm   B. clothes   C. put   D. stay

4 _____ people like to _____ _____ _____.
   A. drink   B. some   C. tea   D. hot

5 Ginger tea is _____ _____ in Korea _____ _____.
   A. often   B. something   C. drink   D. people

6 With its special _____, it _____ your body and helps _____ the _____ in your throat.
   A. pain   B. taste   C. reduce   D. warms

7 _____ do people drink or eat in _____ _____ when they catch a _____?
   A. other   B. cold   C. what   D. countries

8 _____ _____ _____.
   A. out   B. let's   C. find

9 In Finland, where it is very cold in winter, people _____ a _____ _____ when they _____ a cold.
   A. special   B. catch   C. drink   D. have

10 It is a _____ of _____ _____.
   A. milk   B. cup   C. onion

11 They put _____ onion in milk and boil it _____ _____ heat for _____ an hour.
   A. low   B. chopped   C. half   D. over

12 This _____ drink is _____ to _____ _____ for a cold.
   A. said   B. simple   C. good   D. be

13 _____ people in Korea and Finland look for _____ when _____, many people in America want a _____ of chicken soup.
   A. bowl   B. while   C. sick   D. drinks

14 It is usually made with chicken and vegetables, but the _____ is different from _____ family _____ _____.
   A. recipe   B. one   C. another   D. to

15 Salt and pepper _____ _____ _____ before _____.
   A. added   B. eating   C. be   D. can

16 People in America believe that a bowl of warm chicken soup is great for a _____ _____ and a _____ _____.
   A. nose   B. sore   C. stuffy   D. throat

---

1 감기와 싸우는 음식들

2 여러분은 감기에 걸리면 어떻게 하는가?

3 당연히, 따뜻함을 유지하고자 할 것이고, 아마도 옷을 더 입을 것이다.

4 몇몇 사람들은 따뜻한 차를 마시는 것을 좋아한다.

5 생강차는 한국인들이 자주 마시는 것이다.

6 특별한 맛과 함께, 그것은 여러분의 몸을 따뜻하게 하고 목 통증을 완화하는 데 도움을 준다.

7 다른 나라에서는 사람들이 감기에 걸렸을 때 무엇을 마시거나 먹을까?

8 함께 알아보자.

9 겨울이 매우 추운 핀란드에서는 사람들이 감기에 걸리면 특별한 음료를 마신다.

10 그것은 양파 우유이다.

11 그들은 우유에 잘게 썬 양파를 넣고 30분 동안 약한 불에서 끓인다.

12 이 단순한 음료는 감기에 좋다고 한다.

13 한국 사람들과 핀란드 사람들이 아플 때 음료를 찾는 반면, 미국의 많은 사람들은 닭고기 수프를 원한다.

14 그것은 보통 닭고기와 야채로 만들어지는데, 요리법은 가정마다 다르다.

15 소금과 후추를 먹기 전에 넣기도 한다.

16 미국인들은 따뜻한 닭고기 수프 한 그릇이 부은 목과 막힌 코에 좋다고 믿는다.

17 In Russia and in _____ Europe, when people _____, they eat a dessert _____ *gogol-mogol.*
A. called   B. get   C. Eastern   D. sick

18 It _____ eggs and honey.
A. with   B. is   C. made

19 Some people add chocolate, butter, lemon juice, or milk _____ it _____ .
A. better   B. to   C. taste   D. make

20 It _____ _____ yogurt.
A. thick   B. looks   C. like

21 People often drink a cup of _____ *gogol-mogol* when they _____ a _____ .
A. warm   B. throat   C. have   D. sore

22 *Gogol-mogol* is not _____ good for people with a cold _____ also _____ as a dessert for _____ people.
A. healthy   B. only   C. popular   D. but

23 When _____ as a dessert, it is _____ served _____ or at room _____ .
A. temperature   B. served   C. cold   D. usually

24 _____ _____ try making one of the foods you have _____ out _____ ?
A. about   B. not   C. found   D. why

25 It will be _____ and _____ _____ your _____ .
A. for   B. good   C. fun   D. health

26 _____ _____ *Gogol-mogol* (Serves one)
A. Make   B. to   C. How

27 _____ _____ : 1 egg, 1/2 cup of milk, _____ (5 g), butter (15 g)
A. need   B. you   C. honey

28 1. _____ the egg and the honey _____ a large cup and _____ .
A. in   B. them   C. put   D. mix

29 2. _____ a cup of milk _____ a _____ .
A. half   B. in   C. pour   D. pan

30 _____ the _____ .
A. butter   B. add

31 _____ it _____ the butter _____ .
A. melts   B. warm   C. until

32 3. _____ the _____ milk and butter _____ the cup _____ the egg and the honey.
A. into   B. pour   C. with   D. hot

33 _____ _____ you _____ .
A. as   B. pour   C. stir

34 4. _____ _____ it is _____ .
A. while   B. hot   C. drink

17 러시아와 동유럽에서는 사람들이 아플 때, 고골모골이라는 후식을 먹는다.

18 그것은 달걀과 꿀로 만든다.

19 어떤 사람들은 그것을 더 맛있게 하기 위해 초콜릿, 버터, 레몬주스, 또는 우유를 첨가한다.

20 그것은 진한 요구르트처럼 보인다.

21 사람들은 목이 아플 때 종종 따뜻한 고골모골 한 잔을 마신다.

22 고골모골은 감기에 걸린 사람들에게 좋을 뿐만 아니라 건강한 사람들의 후식으로도 인기가 있다.

23 후식으로 제공될 때에는 보통 차갑게 또는 실온으로 제공된다.

24 여러분이 알아본 음식들 중 하나를 만들어 보는 것은 어떨까?

25 그것은 재미있고 여러분의 건강에 좋을 것이다.

26 고골모골 만드는 방법 (1인분)

27 필요한 것: 달걀 1개, 우유 1/2 컵, 꿀 5g, 버터 15g

28 1. 달걀과 꿀을 큰 컵에 넣고 섞는다.

29 2. 우유 반 컵을 팬에 붓는다.

30 버터를 추가한다.

31 버터가 녹을 때까지 데운다.

32 3. 뜨거운 우유와 버터를 달걀과 꿀이 있는 컵에 붓는다.

33 부으면서 젓는다.

34 4. 뜨거울 때 마신다.

※ 다음 우리말과 일치하도록 빈칸에 알맞은 말을 쓰시오.

1 Foods That _____ _____

2 What do you do when you _____ _____ _____?

3 Of course, you want to _____ _____, so maybe you _____ _____ more clothes.

4 Some people like _____ _____ _____ _____ .

5 Ginger tea is _____ people in Korea _____ _____ .

6 With its special taste, it warms your body and _____ _____ _____ _____ in your _____ .

7 _____ _____ _____ _____ _____ _____ _____ in other countries when they catch a cold?

8 Let's _____ _____ .

9 In Finland, where it is very cold in winter, people _____ _____ _____ _____ when they catch a cold.

10 It is _____ _____ _____ _____ _____ .

11 They put _____ _____ in milk and boil it _____ _____ for _____ _____ _____ .

12 This simple drink _____ _____ for a cold.

13 _____ people in Korea and Finland _____ _____ drinks when sick, many people in America want _____ _____ _____ _____ _____ .

14 It is usually made with chicken and vegetables, but the recipe is different _____ _____ _____ _____ _____ .

15 Salt and pepper _____ _____ _____ before _____ .

16 People in America believe that a bowl of warm chicken soup is _____ _____ _____ _____ _____ _____ _____ _____ .

1 감기와 싸우는 음식들

2 여러분은 감기에 걸리면 어떻게 하는가?

3 당연히, 따뜻함을 유지하고자 할 것이고, 아마도 옷을 더 입을 것이다.

4 몇몇 사람들은 따뜻한 차를 마시는 것을 좋아한다.

5 생강차는 한국인들이 자주 마시는 것이다.

6 특별한 맛과 함께, 그것은 여러분의 몸을 따뜻하게 하고 목 통증을 완화하는 데 도움을 준다.

7 다른 나라에서는 사람들이 감기에 걸렸을 때 무엇을 마시거나 먹을까?

8 함께 알아보자.

9 겨울이 매우 추운 핀란드에서는 사람들이 감기에 걸리면 특별한 음료를 마신다.

10 그것은 양파 우유이다.

11 그들은 우유에 잘게 썬 양파를 넣고 30분 동안 약한 불에서 끓인다.

12 이 단순한 음료는 감기에 좋다고 한다.

13 한국 사람들과 핀란드 사람들이 아플 때 음료를 찾는 반면, 미국의 많은 사람들은 닭고기 수프를 원한다.

14 그것은 보통 닭고기와 야채로 만들어지는데, 요리법은 가정마다 다르다.

15 소금과 후추를 먹기 전에 넣기도 한다.

16 미국인들은 따뜻한 닭고기 수프 한 그릇이 부은 목과 막힌 코에 좋다고 믿는다.

17 In Russia and in Eastern Europe, when people get sick, they eat a dessert _____ *gogol-mogol*.

18 It _____ _____ _____ eggs and honey.

19 Some people _____ chocolate, butter, lemon juice, or milk _____ _____ _____ _____ _____ .

20 It _____ _____ _____ yogurt.

21 People often drink a cup of warm *gogol-mogol* when they _____ _____ _____ _____ .

22 *Gogol-mogol* is _____ _____ good for people with a cold _____ _____ popular as a dessert for _____ people.

23 When _____ as a dessert, it is usually _____ cold or _____ _____ _____ .

24 _____ _____ try making one of the foods you have _____ _____ _____ ?

25 It will be fun and _____ _____ your health.

26 _____ _____ _____ *Gogol-mogol* (Serves one)

27 _____ _____ : 1 egg, 1/2 cup of milk, honey (5 g), butter (15 g)

28 1. _____ the egg and the honey _____ a large cup and _____ _____ .

29 2. _____ half a cup of milk in a pan.

30 _____ the butter.

31 _____ it _____ the butter _____ .

32 3. _____ the hot milk and butter _____ the cup _____ the egg and the honey.

33 _____ _____ you _____ .

34 4. Drink _____ it is hot.

---

17 러시아와 동유럽에서는 사람들이 아플 때, 고골모골이라는 후식을 먹는다.

18 그것은 달걀과 꿀로 만든다.

19 어떤 사람들은 그것을 더 맛있게 하기 위해 초콜릿, 버터, 레몬주스, 또는 우유를 첨가한다.

20 그것은 진한 요구르트처럼 보인다.

21 사람들은 목이 아플 때 종종 따뜻한 고골모골 한 잔을 마신다.

22 고골모골은 감기에 걸린 사람들에게 좋을 뿐만 아니라 건강한 사람들의 후식으로도 인기가 있다.

23 후식으로 제공될 때에는 보통 차갑게 또는 실온으로 제공된다.

24 여러분이 알아본 음식들 중 하나를 만들어 보는 것은 어떨까?

25 그것은 재미있고 여러분의 건강에 좋을 것이다.

26 고골모골 만드는 방법 (1인분)

27 필요한 것: 달걀 1개, 우유 1/2 컵, 꿀 5g, 버터 15g

28 1. 달걀과 꿀을 큰 컵에 넣고 섞는다.

29 2. 우유 반 컵을 팬에 붓는다.

30 버터를 추가한다.

31 버터가 녹을 때까지 데운다.

32 3. 뜨거운 우유와 버터를 달걀과 꿀이 있는 컵에 붓는다.

33 부으면서 젓는다.

34 4. 뜨거울 때 마신다.

※ 다음 문장을 우리말로 쓰시오.

1 ▶ Foods That Fight Colds

➡ _____

2 ▶ What do you do when you catch a cold?

➡ _____

3 ▶ Of course, you want to stay warm, so maybe you put on more clothes.

➡ _____

4 ▶ Some people like to drink hot tea.

➡ _____

5 ▶ Ginger tea is something people in Korea often drink.

➡ _____

6 ▶ With its special taste, it warms your body and helps reduce the pain in your throat.

➡ _____

7 ▶ What do people drink or eat in other countries when they catch a cold?

➡ _____

8 ▶ Let's find out.

➡ _____

9 ▶ In Finland, where it is very cold in winter, people have a special drink when they catch a cold.

➡ _____

10 ▶ It is a cup of onion milk.

➡ _____

11 ▶ They put chopped onion in milk and boil it over low heat for half an hour.

➡ _____

12 ▶ This simple drink is said to be good for a cold.

➡ _____

13 ▶ While people in Korea and Finland look for drinks when sick, many people in America want a bowl of chicken soup.

➡ _____

14 ▶ It is usually made with chicken and vegetables, but the recipe is different from one family to another.

➡ _____

15 ▶ Salt and pepper can be added before eating.

➡ _____

16 ▶ People in America believe that a bowl of warm chicken soup is great for a sore throat and a stuffy nose.

➡ _____

17 In Russia and in Eastern Europe, when people get sick, they eat a dessert called *gogol-mogol*.
➡ _____

18 It is made with eggs and honey.
➡ _____

19 Some people add chocolate, butter, lemon juice, or milk to make it taste better.
➡ _____

20 It looks like thick yogurt.
➡ _____

21 People often drink a cup of warm *gogol-mogol* when they have a sore throat.
➡ _____

22 *Gogol-mogol* is not only good for people with a cold but also popular as a dessert for healthy people.
➡ _____

23 When served as a dessert, it is usually served cold or at room temperature.
➡ _____

24 Why not try making one of the foods you have found out about?
➡ _____

25 It will be fun and good for your health.
➡ _____

26 How to Make *Gogol-mogol* (Serves one)
➡ _____

27 You need: 1 egg, 1/2 cup of milk, honey (5 g), butter (15 g)
➡ _____

28 1. Put the egg and the honey in a large cup and mix them.
➡ _____

29 2. Pour half a cup of milk in a pan.
➡ _____

30 Add the butter.
➡ _____

31 Warm it until the butter melts.
➡ _____

32 3. Pour the hot milk and butter into the cup with the egg and the honey.
➡ _____

33 Stir as you pour.
➡ _____

34 4. Drink while it is hot.
➡ _____

※ 다음 괄호 안의 단어들을 우리말에 맞도록 바르게 배열하시오.

1 (That / Foods / Colds / Fight)
➡ _____

2 (do / what / do / you / when / catch / you / cold? / a)
➡ _____

3 (course, / of / want / you / stay / to / warm, / maybe / so / put / you / on / clothes. / more)
➡ _____

4 (people / some / to / like / hot / drink / tea.)
➡ _____

5 (tea / ginger / something / is / people / Korea / in / drink. / often)
➡ _____

6 (its / with / taste, / special / warms / it / body / your / and / reduce / helps / pain / the / in / throat. / your)
➡ _____

7 (do / what / drink / people / or / in / eat / other / when / countries / catch / they / cold? / a)
➡ _____

8 (find / let's / out.)
➡ _____

9 (Finland, / in / it / where / is / cold / very / winter, / in / have / people / a / drink / special / they / when / catch / cold. / a)
➡ _____

10 (is / it / cup / a / onion / of / milk.)
➡ _____

11 (put / they / onion / chopped / milk / in / and / it / boil / low / over / heat / half / for / hour. / an)
➡ _____

12 (simple / this / is / drink / to / said / good / be / for / cold. / a)
➡ _____

13 (people / while / Korea / in / and / look / Finland / for / when / drinks / sick, / people / many / America / in / a / want / of / bowl / soup. / chicken)
➡ _____

14 (is / it / made / usually / chicken / with / vegetables, / and / the / but / is / recipe / from / different / one / to / family / another.)
➡ _____

15 (pepper / and / salt / be / can / before / added / eating.)
➡ _____

16 (in / people / Americia / that / believe / a / of / bowl / chicken / warm / is / soup / great / a / for / throat / sore / a / and / nose. / stuffy)
➡ _____

1 감기와 싸우는 음식들

2 여러분은 감기에 걸리면 어떻게 하는가?

3 당연히, 따뜻함을 유지하고자 할 것이고, 아마도 옷을 더 입을 것 이다.

4 몇몇 사람들은 따뜻한 차를 마 시는 것을 좋아한다.

5 생강차는 한국인들이 자주 마시 는 것이다.

6 특별한 맛과 함께, 그것은 여러 분의 몸을 따뜻하게 하고 목 통 증을 완화하는 데 도움을 준다.

7 다른 나라에서는 사람들이 감기 에 걸렸을 때 무엇을 마시거나 먹을까?

8 함께 알아보자.

9 겨울이 매우 추운 핀란드에서는 사람들이 감기에 걸리면 특별한 음료를 마신다.

10 그것은 양파 우유이다.

11 그들은 우유에 잘게 썬 양파를 넣고 30분 동안 약한 불에서 끓 인다.

12 이 단순한 음료는 감기에 좋다 고 한다.

13 한국 사람들과 핀란드 사람들이 아플 때 음료를 찾는 반면, 미국 의 많은 사람들은 닭고기 수프 를 원한다.

14 그것은 보통 닭고기와 야채로 만 들어지는데, 요리법은 가정마다 다르다.

15 소금과 후추를 먹기 전에 넣기 도 한다.

16 미국인들은 따뜻한 닭고기 수프 한 그릇이 부은 목과 막힌 코에 좋다고 믿는다.

17 (Russia / in / and / Eastern / in / when / Europe, / get / people / sick, / eat / they / dessert / a / called *gogol-mogol*.)

➡ _____

18 (is / it / with / made / hoeny. / and / eggs)

➡ _____

19 (people / some / add / butter, / chocolate, / juice, / lemon / or / to / milk / it / make / better. / taste)

➡ _____

20 (looks / it / thick / like / yogurt.)

➡ _____

21 (often / people / a / drink / cup / warm / of / when / *gogol-mogol* / have / they / sore / a / throat.)

➡ _____

22 (is / *gogol-mogol* / only / not / for / good / with / people / cold / a / also / but / as / popular / dessert / a / healthy / for / people.)

➡ _____

23 (served / when / a / as / dessert, / is / it / served / usually / cold / at / or / temperature. / room)

➡ _____

24 (not / why / making / try / of / one / foods / the / have / you / out / found / about?)

➡ _____

25 (will / it / fun / be / and / for / good / health. / your)

➡ _____

26 (to / How / *Gogol-mogol* / Make / one) / (serves)

➡ _____

27 (need: / you / egg, / 1 / cup / 1/2 / milk, / of / (5 g), / honey / (15 g) / butter)

➡ _____

28 (1. / the / put / and / egg / honey / the / a / in / large / and / cup / them. / mix)

➡ _____

29 (2. / half / pour / cup / a / of / in / milk / pan. / a)

➡ _____

30 (the / add / butter.)

➡ _____

31 (it / warm / the / until / melts. / butter)

➡ _____

32 (3. / the / pour / milk / hot / and / into / butter / cup / the / the / with / egg / the / and / honey.)

➡ _____

33 (as / stir / pour. / you)

➡ _____

34 (4. / while / drink / is / it / hot.)

➡ _____

17 러시아와 동유럽에서는 사람들이 아플 때, 고골모골이라는 후식을 먹는다.

18 그것은 달걀과 꿀로 만든다.

19 어떤 사람들은 그것을 더 맛있게 하기 위해 초콜릿, 버터, 레몬주스, 또는 우유를 첨가한다.

20 그것은 진한 요구르트처럼 보인다.

21 사람들은 목이 아플 때 종종 따뜻한 고골모골 한 잔을 마신다.

22 고골모골은 감기에 걸린 사람들에게 좋을 뿐만 아니라 건강한 사람들의 후식으로도 인기가 있다.

23 후식으로 제공될 때에는 보통 차갑게 또는 실온으로 제공된다.

24 여러분이 알아본 음식들 중 하나를 만들어 보는 것은 어떨까?

25 그것은 재미있고 여러분의 건강에 좋을 것이다.

26 고골모골 만드는 방법 (1인분)

27 필요한 것: 달걀 1개, 우유 1/2 컵, 꿀 5g, 버터 15g

28 1. 달걀과 꿀을 큰 컵에 넣고 섞는다.

29 2. 우유 반 컵을 팬에 붓는다.

30 버터를 추가한다.

31 버터가 녹을 때까지 데운다.

32 3. 뜨거운 우유와 버터를 달걀과 꿀이 있는 컵에 붓는다.

33 부으면서 젓는다.

34 4. 뜨거울 때 마신다.

※ 다음 우리말을 영어로 쓰시오.

1 감기와 싸우는 음식들

➡ _____

2 여러분은 감기에 걸리면 어떻게 하는가?

➡ _____

3 당연히, 따뜻함을 유지하고자 할 것이고, 아마도 옷을 더 입을 것이다.

➡ _____

4 몇몇 사람들은 따뜻한 차를 마시는 것을 좋아한다.

➡ _____

5 생강차는 한국인들이 자주 마시는 것이다.

➡ _____

6 특별한 맛과 함께, 그것은 여러분의 몸을 따뜻하게 하고 목 통증을 완화하는 데 도움을 준다.

➡ _____

7 다른 나라에서는 사람들이 감기에 걸렸을 때 무엇을 마시거나 먹을까?

➡ _____

8 함께 알아보자.

➡ _____

9 겨울이 매우 추운 핀란드에서는 사람들이 감기에 걸리면 특별한 음료를 마신다.

➡ _____

10 그것은 양파 우유이다.

➡ _____

11 그들은 우유에 잘게 썬 양파를 넣고 30분 동안 약한 불에서 끓인다.

➡ _____

12 이 단순한 음료는 감기에 좋다고 한다.

➡ _____

13 한국 사람들과 핀란드 사람들이 아플 때 음료를 찾는 반면, 미국의 많은 사람들은 닭고기 수프를 원한다.

➡ _____

_____

14 그것은 보통 닭고기와 야채로 만들어지는데, 요리법은 가정마다 다르다.

➡ _____

_____

15 소금과 후추를 먹기 전에 넣기도 한다.

➡ _____

16 미국인들은 따뜻한 닭고기 수프 한 그릇이 부은 목과 막힌 코에 좋다고 믿는다.

➡ _____

_____

17 러시아와 동유럽에서는 사람들이 아플 때, 고골모골이라는 후식을 먹는다.
➡ _____

18 그것은 달걀과 꿀로 만든다.
➡ _____

19 어떤 사람들은 그것을 더 맛있게 하기 위해 초콜릿, 버터, 레몬주스, 또는 우유를 첨가한다.
➡ _____

20 그것은 진한 요구르트처럼 보인다.
➡ _____

21 사람들은 목이 아플 때 종종 따뜻한 고골모골 한 잔을 마신다.
➡ _____

22 고골모골은 감기에 걸린 사람들에게 좋을 뿐만 아니라 건강한 사람들의 후식으로도 인기가 있다.
➡ _____
_____

23 후식으로 제공될 때에는 보통 차갑게 또는 실온으로 제공된다.
➡ _____

24 여러분이 알아본 음식들 중 하나를 만들어 보는 것은 어떨까?
➡ _____

25 그것은 재미있고 여러분의 건강에 좋을 것이다.
➡ _____

26 고골모골 만드는 방법 (1인분)
➡ _____

27 필요한 것: 달걀 1개, 우유 1/2컵, 꿀 5g, 버터 15g
➡ _____

28 1. 달걀과 꿀을 큰 컵에 넣고 섞는다.
➡ _____

29 2. 우유 반 컵을 팬에 붓는다.
➡ _____

30 버터를 추가한다.
➡ _____

31 버터가 녹을 때까지 데운다.
➡ _____

32 3. 뜨거운 우유와 버터를 달걀과 꿀이 있는 컵에 붓는다.
➡ _____

33 부으면서 젓는다.
➡ _____

34 4. 뜨거울 때 마신다.
➡ _____

※ 다음 우리말과 일치하도록 빈칸에 알맞은 말을 쓰시오.

After You Read B

1. Look! _____ _____ *gogol-mogol*.

2. Happy07: _____ _____ *gogol-mogol*?

3. Bora: It's a dessert _____ people in Russia and _____ _____ _____ eat _____ they _____ _____.

4. Yumyum: It _____ _____. What is it _____ _____?

5. Bora: It's _____ _____ _____ and honey.

6. Yumyum: What's that you _____ _____ _____ _____ _____?

7. Bora: I put chocolate on top _____ _____ it _____ _____.

8. Happy07: Do people also eat it _____ _____ _____ _____?

9. Bora: Sure. It's a _____ _____. _____ _____ as a dessert, it's _____ _____ cold or _____ _____ _____.

1. 봐! 나는 고골모골을 만들었어.
2. Happy07: 고골모골이 뭐야?
3. 보라: 그것은 러시아와 동유럽에서 사람들이 아플 때 먹는 후식이야.
4. Yumyum: 그것은 맛있어 보여. 그것은 무엇으로 만들어지니?
5. 보라: 그것은 달걀과 꿀로 만들어져.
6. Yumyum: 그것 꼭대기에 올린 것이 뭐니?
7. 보라: 나는 그것을 더 맛있게 하기 위해 꼭대기에 초콜릿을 올렸어.
8. Happy07: 사람들이 아프지 않을 때도 그것을 먹니?
9. 보라: 물론이야. 그것은 인기 있는 후식이야. 후식으로 제공될 때에는 보통 차갑게 또는 실온으로 제공돼.

Writing Workshop

1. _____ many Koreans eat Samgyetang _____ _____ _____ _____, _____ _____ _____ _____ eat tomato soup.

2. Here is _____ _____ _____ it.

3. _____ _____: 1 tomato, some water, _____ _____, _____

4. First, _____ one fresh tomato. Then _____ the _____ tomato _____ a pan and _____ some water _____ it.

5. Next, _____ _____ _____ for ten minutes. Then _____ _____ the heat and _____ it _____ _____ _____.

6. Next, _____ it _____ it _____ smooth. Finally, _____ some _____ _____ and _____.

7. Now you _____ _____ the tomato soup.

8. This tomato soup is _____ _____ _____ _____ _____.

1. 많은 한국인들이 아플 때 삼계탕을 먹는 반면에, 인도의 많은 사람들은 토마토 수프를 먹는다.
2. 여기 그것을 만드는 방법이 있다.
3. 필요한 것: 토마토 한 개, 물 약간, 후추, 소금
4. 첫 번째로, 신선한 토마토 한 개를 다진다. 그 후, 다진 토마토를 팬 위에 놓고 그 위에 물을 조금 붓는다.
5. 다음으로, 그 혼합물을 10분간 끓인다. 불을 끄고 식도록 둔다.
6. 다음, 부드러워질 때까지 그것을 섞는다. 마지막으로, 후추와 소금을 약간 넣는다.
7. 이제 토마토 수프를 즐길 수 있다.
8. 이 토마토 수프는 건강에 좋을 뿐 아니라 맛있다.

※ 다음 우리말을 영어로 쓰시오.

After You Read B

1. 봐! 나는 고골모골을 만들었어.
   ➡ _____

2. Happy07: 고골모골이 뭐야?
   ➡ _____

3. 보라: 그것은 러시아와 동유럽에서 사람들이 아플 때 먹는 후식이야.
   ➡ _____

4. Yumyum: 그것은 맛있어 보여. 그것은 무엇으로 만들어지니?
   ➡ _____

5. 보라: 그것은 달걀과 꿀로 만들어져.
   ➡ _____

6. Yumyum: 그것 꼭대기에 올린 것이 뭐니?
   ➡ _____

7. 보라: 나는 그것을 더 맛있게 하기 위해 꼭대기에 초콜릿을 올렸어.
   ➡ _____

8. Happy07: 사람들이 아프지 않을 때도 그것을 먹니?
   ➡ _____

9. 보라: 물론이야. 그것은 인기 있는 후식이야. 후식으로 제공될 때에는 보통 차갑게 또는 실온으로 제공돼.
   ➡ _____

Writing Workshop

1. 많은 한국인들이 아플 때 삼계탕을 먹는 반면에, 인도의 많은 사람들은 토마토 수프를 먹는다.
   ➡ _____

2. 여기 그것을 만드는 방법이 있다.
   ➡ _____

3. 필요한 것: 토마토 한 개, 물 약간, 후추, 소금
   ➡ _____

4. 첫 번째로, 신선한 토마토 한 개를 다진다. 그 후, 다진 토마토를 팬 위에 놓고 그 위에 물을 조금 붓는다.
   ➡ _____

5. 다음으로, 그 혼합물을 10분간 끓인다. 불을 끄고 식도록 둔다.
   ➡ _____

6. 다음, 부드러워질 때까지 그것을 섞는다. 마지막으로, 후추와 소금을 약간 넣는다.
   ➡ _____

7. 이제 토마토 수프를 즐길 수 있다.
   ➡ _____

8. 이 토마토 수프는 건강에 좋을 뿐 아니라 맛있다.
   ➡ _____

※ 다음 영어를 우리말로 쓰시오.

01	aim	_____
02	weapon	_____
03	along	_____
04	suddenly	_____
05	happen	_____
06	face	_____
07	human	_____
08	surprise	_____
09	miracle	_____
10	trench	_____
11	entire	_____
12	sight	_____
13	although	_____
14	wet	_____
15	might	_____
16	follow	_____
17	actually	_____
18	unbelievable	_____
19	soldier	_____
20	address	_____
21	front line	_____

22	greeting	_____
23	miss	_____
24	truly	_____
25	boldly	_____
26	exchange	_____
27	shout	_____
28	either	_____
29	enemy	_____
30	trick	_____
31	familiar	_____
32	share	_____
33	several	_____
34	keep	_____
35	look out of	_____
36	all the more	_____
37	each other	_____
38	in peace	_____
39	at war	_____
40	pass away	_____
41	such as	_____
42	put down	_____
43	one after another	_____

※ 다음 우리말을 영어로 쓰시오.

01 몇의, 수개의

02 전체의

03 속임수

04 사실은

05 그리워하다

06 ~를 따라

07 외침, 고함

08 목표

09 마주하다

10 빛나다, 비추다

11 주소

12 정말로, 진심으로

13 무기

14 군인, 병사

15 익숙한, 친숙한

16 믿기 힘든

17 기적

18 대담하게

19 광경

20 젖은

21 갑자기

22 적군, 적

23 교환하다

24 놀라게 하다

25 참호

26 인사, 안부의 말

27 인간, 사람

28 예상하다

29 조명

30 비록 ~이긴 하지만

31 일어나다

32 공유하다, 나누다

33 ~도, ~ 또한

34 따라가다

35 잇따라서

36 전쟁 중인

37 차례로

38 내려놓다

39 악수하다

40 ~와 같은

41 최전선에

42 사망하다

43 ~ 밖을 내다보다

※ 다음 영영풀이에 알맞은 단어를 <보기>에서 골라 쓴 후, 우리말 뜻을 쓰시오.

1 _____ : Christmas song or hymn: _____

2 _____ : a loud call or cry: _____

3 _____ : an act or words of welcoming: _____

4 _____ : to divide and distribute something in shares: _____

5 _____ : something seen or worth seeing: _____

6 _____ : a sneaky scheme to deceive or cheat: _____

7 _____ : something you hope to achieve by doing something: _____

8 _____ : to give and receive reciprocally; interchange: _____

9 _____ : freedom from war; absence of fighting between nations: _____

10 _____ : a contest of speed, such as running, riding, driving or sailing:

    _____

11 _____ : to hit with a bullet, shell, or other missile fired from a weapon: _____

12 _____ : in a brave and confident way, without showing any fear: _____

13 _____ : details of where someone lives or works and where letters, etc. can be sent:

    _____

14 _____ : an object such as a knife, gun, bomb, etc. that is used for fighting or

    attacking somebody: _____

15 _____ : a person who is in an army and wears its uniform, especially someone

    who fights when there is a war: _____

16 _____ : to strike with a sudden feeling of wonder or astonishment especially by

    being unexpected: _____

보기			
trick	weapon	aim	exchange
greeting	boldly	shout	address
surprise	carol	soldier	shoot
peace	sight	race	share

※ 다음 우리말과 일치하도록 빈칸에 알맞은 것을 골라 쓰시오.

1 A _____ _____
　　A. Miracle 　　　 B. Christmas

2 _____ was Christmas Eve _____ 1914, the _____ _____ of World War I.
　　A. year 　　　 B. it 　　　 C. in 　　　 D. first

3 English soldiers were _____ German soldiers from their trenches as they _____ _____ for the last _____ months.
　　A. done 　　　 B. facing 　　　 C. few 　　　 D. had

4 The _____ were _____ and _____.
　　A. wet 　　　 B. trenches 　　　 C. cold

5 The soldiers were _____ and _____ their home, all the _____ _____ because it was Christmas.
　　A. more 　　　 B. tired 　　　 C. so 　　　 D. missed

6 _____, a _____ song was _____ _____ from the German trenches.
　　A. heard 　　　 B. suddenly 　　　 C. coming 　　　 D. familiar

7 _____ was a _____ _____!
　　A. Christmas 　　　 B. it 　　　 C. carol

8 What's _____ _____?
　　A. on 　　　 B. going

9 It _____ _____ a _____ to make them come _____ of the trenches.
　　A. trick 　　　 B. might 　　　 C. out 　　　 D. be

10 A few English soldiers _____ _____ _____ their trenches.
　　A. out 　　　 B. boldly 　　　 C. of 　　　 D. looked

11 One _____ one, _____ soldiers _____ their _____.
　　A. followed 　　　 B. by 　　　 C. example 　　　 D. other

12 _____ they saw was a _____ they _____ _____.
　　A. sight 　　　 B. expected 　　　 C. never 　　　 D. what

13 _____ the German trenches, Christmas trees were _____ _____ _____ lanterns!
　　A. lit 　　　 B. along 　　　 C. with 　　　 D. standing

14 The German soldiers sang _____ Christmas _____ _____.
　　A. after 　　　 B. one 　　　 C. another 　　　 D. song

15 The English soldiers began to _____ _____ _____ _____ Christmas songs.
　　A. by 　　　 B. answer 　　　 C. singing 　　　 D. also

16 The warm _____ and the Christmas carols _____ them _____ they were on the _____ line.
　　A. forget 　　　 B. lights 　　　 C. front 　　　 D. made

1 크리스마스의 기적

2 제일차 세계 대전의 첫해였던 1914년의 크리스마스이브였습니다.

3 영국 군인들은 지난 몇 달 동안 그래왔듯이 그들의 참호에서 독일 군인들과 대치하고 있었어요.

4 참호는 춥고 축축했습니다.

5 군인들은 지쳤고 자신들의 집을 그리워했는데, 크리스마스라는 이유로 더욱 더 그랬습니다.

6 갑자기 익숙한 노래가 독일 군인들의 참호로부터 들려왔습니다.

7 그것은 크리스마스 캐럴이었어요!

8 무슨 일이 벌어지고 있는 걸까요?

9 어쩌면 그들을 참호 밖으로 유인하고자 하는 속임수일지도 모릅니다.

10 몇몇 영국 군인들이 용감하게 자신들의 참호 밖을 내다보았어요.

11 차례차례 다른 군인들도 앞사람을 따랐습니다.

12 영국 군인들이 본 것은 그들이 절대 예상하지 못한 광경이었어요.

13 독일 군인들의 참호를 따라, 크리스마스트리들이 랜턴으로 밝혀진 채 있었습니다!

14 독일 군인들은 크리스마스 캐럴을 연이어 불렀어요.

15 영국 군인들도 크리스마스 캐럴을 부르며 화답하기 시작했습니다.

16 따뜻한 불빛과 크리스마스 캐럴은 그들이 최전선에 있다는 것을 잊게 만들었어요.

17 Then a shout _____ _____ _____ the German side:
"Happy Christmas! You no _____, we no shoot!"

    A. out   B. shoot   C. came   D. from

18 Soon, soldiers _____ _____ had been to kill each other just a few hours before began to _____ _____.

    A. aim   B. greetings   C. whose   D. exchange

19 For the first time in _____ months, the soldiers were _____ to spend a night _____ _____.

    A. able   B. peace   C. several   D. in

20 It _____ was a _____ _____.

    A. night   B. truly   C. silent

21 Christmas _____ _____.

    A. came   B. morning

22 Soldiers _____ _____ _____ put _____ their weapons and came out of their trenches.

    A. down   B. on   C. sides   D. both

23 They met in the no _____ _____ _____ their trenches _____ shook hands.

    A. between   B. man's   C. and   D. land

24 They _____ small _____ _____ _____ wine and cake.

    A. such   B. exchanged   C. as   D. gifts

25 They _____ _____ _____.

    A. together   B. sang   C. carols

26 _____ _____ _____ and played football.

    A. exchanged   B. some   C. addresses   D. even

27 This _____ Christmas Day was _____ about in English _____ sent home.

    A. soldiers   B. unbelievable   C. written   D. letters

28 One soldier _____, "On Christmas Day, English and German soldiers met _____ the two _____ and had _____.

    A. lines   B. wrote   C. between   D. talks

29 We _____ _____ bike _____."

    A. had   B. races   C. also

30 _____ wrote, "We didn't _____ that we were _____ _____.

    A. at   B. another   C. war   D. think

31 _____ we _____, enemy _____ to _____.

    A. enemy   B. here   C. talking   D. were

32 They were _____ us, with mothers, with friends, with _____ who were _____ to _____ their men home again."

    A. welcome   B. like   C. waiting   D. wives

17 그리고 독일 군인들 쪽에서 고함이 터져 나왔습니다. "행복한 크리스마스예요! 당신들이 쏘지 않는다면, 우리도 쏘지 않을게요!"

18 곧, 단지 몇 시간 전까지만 해도 서로를 죽이는 것이 목적이었던 군인들은 인사를 나누기 시작했습니다.

19 몇 달 만에 처음으로, 군인들은 평화롭게 밤을 지낼 수 있었어요.

20 그날은 정말로 조용한 밤이었습니다.

21 크리스마스 아침이 밝았습니다.

22 양편의 군인들은 자신들의 무기를 내려놓고 참호 밖으로 나왔어요.

23 그들은 무인 지대에서 만났고 악수를 했습니다.

24 그들은 와인과 케이크 같은 작은 선물도 교환했어요.

25 그들은 캐럴을 함께 불렀습니다.

26 몇몇은 심지어 주소를 교환하기도 했고 함께 축구를 했습니다.

27 이 믿을 수 없는 크리스마스는 영국 군인들이 집으로 보낸 편지에 적혀 있었습니다.

28 한 군인은 "크리스마스에 영국 군인들과 독일 군인들은 두 경계선 사이에서 만났고 대화를 나눴어.

29 우리는 자전거 시합도 했어."라고 적었어요.

30 다른 군인은 "우리는 전쟁 중이라는 생각이 들지 않았어.

31 여기서 우리는 적대 관계인 서로와 대화를 나누고 있는 상황이었어.

32 그들은 우리와 마찬가지로, 그들의 남자들이 집으로 다시 돌아오기를 고대하는 어머니와, 친구들, 부인이 있는 사람들이었어."라고 썼습니다.

※ 다음 우리말과 일치하도록 빈칸에 알맞은 것을 골라 쓰시오.

1 A Christmas _____

2 It was Christmas Eve in 1914, _____ _____ _____ of World War I.

3 English soldiers _____ _____ German soldiers from their trenches as they _____ _____ for the last _____ .

4 The trenches were _____ _____ _____ .

5 The soldiers were tired and _____ their home, _____ _____ _____ _____ _____ it was Christmas.

6 _____ , a familiar song _____ _____ _____ from the German trenches.

7 It was a Christmas _____ !

8 What's _____ _____ ?

9 It _____ _____ _____ to make them come out of the _____ .

10 A few English soldiers _____ _____ _____ _____ their trenches.

11 _____ _____ _____ , other soldiers _____ their example.

12 _____ they saw was a _____ they never _____ .

13 Along the German trenches, Christmas trees were standing _____ _____ _____ !

14 The German soldiers sang _____ _____ .

15 The English soldiers began to answer _____ _____ Christmas songs.

16 The warm lights and the Christmas carols _____ _____ they were on the _____ _____ .

본문 Test 49

---

1 크리스마스의 기적

2 제일차 세계 대전의 첫해였던 1914년의 크리스마스이브였습니다.

3 영국 군인들은 지난 몇 달 동안 그래왔듯이 그들의 참호에서 독일 군인들과 대치하고 있었어요.

4 참호는 춥고 축축했습니다.

5 군인들은 지쳤고 자신들의 집을 그리워했는데, 크리스마스라는 이유로 더욱 더 그랬습니다.

6 갑자기 익숙한 노래가 독일 군인들의 참호로부터 들려왔습니다.

7 그것은 크리스마스 캐럴이었어요!

8 무슨 일이 벌어지고 있는 걸까요?

9 어쩌면 그들을 참호 밖으로 유인하고자 하는 속임수일지도 모릅니다.

10 몇몇 영국 군인들이 용감하게 자신들의 참호 밖을 내다보았어요.

11 차례차례 다른 군인들도 앞사람을 따랐습니다.

12 영국 군인들이 본 것은 그들이 절대 예상하지 못한 광경이었어요.

13 독일 군인들의 참호를 따라, 크리스마스트리들이 랜턴으로 밝혀진 채 있었습니다!

14 독일 군인들은 크리스마스 캐럴을 연이어 불렀어요.

15 영국 군인들도 크리스마스 캐럴을 부르며 화답하기 시작했습니다.

16 따뜻한 불빛과 크리스마스 캐럴은 그들이 최전선에 있다는 것을 잊게 만들었어요.

17 Then a shout _____ _____ _____ the German side: "Happy Christmas! You no _____, we no shoot!"

18 Soon, soldiers _____ _____ had been to kill _____ _____ just a few hours before began to _____ _____.

19 For the first time _____ _____ _____, the soldiers were able to spend a night _____ _____.

20 _____ _____ _____ a silent night.

21 Christmas morning _____.

22 Soldiers _____ _____ _____ put down their weapons and _____ _____ _____ their trenches.

23 They met _____ _____ _____ _____ _____ _____ between their trenches and _____ _____.

24 They exchanged small gifts _____ _____ wine and cake.

25 They _____ _____ together.

26 Some even _____ _____ and played football.

27 This _____ Christmas Day was written _____ in letters English soldiers _____ home.

28 One soldier wrote, "On Christmas Day, English and German soldiers met _____ _____ _____ _____ and had talks.

29 We also _____ _____ _____."

30 Another wrote, "We didn't think that we _____ _____ _____.

31 _____ _____ _____, enemy talking to _____.

32 They were _____ _____, with mothers, with friends, with wives who were _____ _____ _____ their men home again."

17 그리고 독일 군인들 쪽에서 고함이 터져 나왔습니다. "행복한 크리스마스예요! 당신들이 쏘지 않는다면, 우리도 쏘지 않을게요!"

18 곧, 단지 몇 시간 전까지만 해도 서로를 죽이는 것이 목적이었던 군인들은 인사를 나누기 시작했습니다.

19 몇 달 만에 처음으로, 군인들은 평화롭게 밤을 지낼 수 있었어요.

20 그날은 정말로 조용한 밤이었습니다.

21 크리스마스 아침이 밝았습니다.

22 양편의 군인들은 자신들의 무기를 내려놓고 참호 밖으로 나왔어요.

23 그들은 무인 지대에서 만났고 악수를 했습니다.

24 그들은 와인과 케이크 같은 작은 선물도 교환했어요.

25 그들은 캐럴을 함께 불렀습니다.

26 몇몇은 심지어 주소를 교환하기도 했고 함께 축구를 했습니다.

27 이 믿을 수 없는 크리스마스는 영국 군인들이 집으로 보낸 편지에 적혀 있었습니다.

28 한 군인은 "크리스마스에 영국 군인들과 독일 군인들은 두 경계선 사이에서 만났고 대화를 나눴어.

29 우리는 자전거 시합도 했어."라고 적었어요.

30 다른 군인은 "우리는 전쟁 중이라는 생각이 들지 않았어.

31 여기서 우리는 적대 관계인 서로와 대화를 나누고 있는 상황이었어.

32 그들은 우리와 마찬가지로, 그들의 남자들이 집으로 다시 돌아오기를 고대하는 어머니와, 친구들, 부인이 있는 사람들이었어."라고 썼습니다.

※ 다음 문장을 우리말로 쓰시오.

1 ▶ A Christmas Miracle

➡ _____

2 ▶ It was Christmas Eve in 1914, the first year of World War I.

➡ _____

3 ▶ English soldiers were facing German soldiers from their trenches as they had done for the last few months.

➡ _____

4 ▶ The trenches were cold and wet.

➡ _____

5 ▶ The soldiers were tired and missed their home, all the more so because it was Christmas.

➡ _____

6 ▶ Suddenly, a familiar song was heard coming from the German trenches.

➡ _____

7 ▶ It was a Christmas carol!

➡ _____

8 ▶ What's going on?

➡ _____

9 ▶ It might be a trick to make them come out of the trenches.

➡ _____

10 ▶ A few English soldiers boldly looked out of their trenches.

➡ _____

11 ▶ One by one, other soldiers followed their example.

➡ _____

12 ▶ What they saw was a sight they never expected.

➡ _____

13 ▶ Along the German trenches, Christmas trees were standing lit with lanterns!

➡ _____

14 ▶ The German soldiers sang one Christmas song after another.

➡ _____

15 ▶ The English soldiers began to answer by also singing Christmas songs.

➡ _____

16 ▶ The warm lights and the Christmas carols made them forget they were on the front line.

➡ _____

17 ▶ Then a shout came out from the German side: "Happy Christmas! You no shoot, we no shoot!"

➡ _____

18 ▶ Soon, soldiers whose aim had been to kill each other just a few hours before began to exchange greetings.

➡ _____

19 ▶ For the first time in several months, the soldiers were able to spend a night in peace.

➡ _____

20 ▶ It truly was a silent night.

➡ _____

21 ▶ Christmas morning came.

➡ _____

22 ▶ Soldiers on both sides put down their weapons and came out of their trenches.

➡ _____

23 ▶ They met in the no man's land between their trenches and shook hands.

➡ _____

24 ▶ They exchanged small gifts such as wine and cake.

➡ _____

25 ▶ They sang carols together.

➡ _____

26 ▶ Some even exchanged addresses and played football.

➡ _____

27 ▶ This unbelievable Christmas Day was written about in letters English soldiers sent home.

➡ _____

28 ▶ One soldier wrote, "On Christmas Day, English and German soldiers met between the two lines and had talks.

➡ _____

29 ▶ We also had bike races."

➡ _____

30 ▶ Another wrote, "We didn't think that we were at war.

➡ _____

31 ▶ Here we were, enemy talking to enemy.

➡ _____

32 ▶ They were like us, with mothers, with friends, with wives who were waiting to welcome their men home again."

➡ _____

※ 다음 괄호 안의 단어들을 우리말에 맞도록 바르게 배열하시오.

1 (Christmas / A / Miracle)
➡ _____

2 (was / it / Eve / Christmas / 1914, / in / first / the / of / year / War / World / I.)
➡ _____

3 soldiers / English / facing / were / soldiers / German / their / from / as / trenches / had / they / for / done / last / the / months. / few)
➡ _____

4 (trenches / the / cold / were / wet. / and)
➡ _____

5 (soldiers / the / tired / were / and / their / missed / home, / the / all / so / more / it / because / Christmas. / was)
➡ _____

6 (a / suddenly, / familiar / was / song / coming / heard / the / from / trenches. / German)
➡ _____

7 (was / it / Christmas / a / carol!)
➡ _____

8 (going / what's / on?)
➡ _____

9 (might / it / a / be / to / trick / them / make / out / come / the / of / trenches.)
➡ _____

10 (few / a / soldiers / English / looked / boldly / of / out / trenches. / their)
➡ _____

11 (by / one / other / one, / soldiers / their / followed / example.)
➡ _____

12 (they / what / was / saw / sight / a / never / they / expected.)
➡ _____

13 (the / along / trenches, / German / trees / Christmas / standing / were / with / lit / lanterns!)
➡ _____

14 (German / the / sang / soldiers / Chrtistmas / one / after / another. / song)
➡ _____

15 (English / the / began / soldiers / answer / to / also / by / Christmas / singing / songs.)
➡ _____

16 (warm / the / and / lights / Christmas / the / made / carols / forget / them / were / they / the / on / line. / front)
➡ _____
_____

1 크리스마스의 기적

2 제일차 세계 대전의 첫해였던 1914년의 크리스마스이브였습니다.

3 영국 군인들은 지난 몇 달 동안 그래왔듯이 그들의 참호에서 독일 군인들과 대치하고 있었어요.

4 참호는 춥고 축축했습니다.

5 군인들은 지쳤고 자신들의 집을 그리워했는데, 크리스마스라는 이유로 더욱 더 그랬습니다.

6 갑자기 익숙한 노래가 독일 군인들의 참호로부터 들려왔습니다.

7 그것은 크리스마스 캐럴이었어요!

8 무슨 일이 벌어지고 있는 걸까요?

9 어쩌면 그들을 참호 밖으로 유인하고자 하는 속임수일지도 모릅니다.

10 몇몇 영국 군인들이 용감하게 자신들의 참호 밖을 내다보았어요.

11 차례차례 다른 군인들도 앞사람을 따랐습니다.

12 영국 군인들이 본 것은 그들이 절대 예상하지 못한 광경이었어요.

13 독일 군인들의 참호를 따라, 크리스마스트리들이 랜턴으로 밝혀진 채 있었습니다!

14 독일 군인들은 크리스마스 캐럴을 연이어 불렀어요.

15 영국 군인들도 크리스마스 캐럴을 부르며 화답하기 시작했습니다.

16 따뜻한 불빛과 크리스마스 캐럴은 그들이 최전선에 있다는 것을 잊게 만들었어요.

17 (a / then / came / shout / out / the / from / side: / German / Christmas! / "happy // no / you / shoot, / no / we / shoot!")
  ➡ _____
  _____

18 (soldiers / soon, / whose / had / aim / to / been / each / kill / other / a / just / hours / few / began / before / exchange / to / greetings.)
  ➡ _____

19 (the / for / time / first / several / in / months, / soldiers / the / able / were / spend / to / night / a / peace. / in)
  ➡ _____

20 (truly / it / a / was / night. / silent)
  ➡ _____

21 (morning / Christmas / came.)
  ➡ _____

22 (on / soldiers / sides / both / down / put / weapons / their / and / out / came / their / of / trenches.)
  ➡ _____

23 (met / they / the / in / no / land / man's / their / between / and / trenches / hands. / shook)
  ➡ _____

24 (exchanged / they / gifts / small / as / such / cake. / and / wine)
  ➡ _____

25 (sang / they / together. / carols)
  ➡ _____

26 (even / some / addresses / exchanged / and / football. / played)
  ➡ _____

27 (unbelievable / this / Day / Christmas / written / was / about / letters / in / soldiers / English / home. / sent)
  ➡ _____

28 (soldier / one / wrote, / Christmas / "on / Day, / German / and / English / met / soldiers / the / between / lines / two / and / talks. / had)
  ➡ _____

29 (also / we / bike / had / races.")
  ➡ _____

30 (wrote, / another / didn't / "we / that / think / were / we / war. / at)
  ➡ _____

31 (we / here / were, / talking / enemy / enemy. / to)
  ➡ _____

32 (were / they / us, / like / mothers, / with / friends, / with / wives / with / were / who / waiting / welcome / to / men / their / again." / home)
  ➡ _____

17 그리고 독일 군인들 쪽에서 고함이 터져 나왔습니다. "행복한 크리스마스예요! 당신들이 쏘지 않는다면, 우리도 쏘지 않을게요!"

18 곧, 단지 몇 시간 전까지만 해도 서로를 죽이는 것이 목적이었던 군인들은 인사를 나누기 시작했습니다.

19 몇 달 만에 처음으로, 군인들은 평화롭게 밤을 지낼 수 있었어요.

20 그날은 정말로 조용한 밤이었습니다.

21 크리스마스 아침이 밝았습니다.

22 양편의 군인들은 자신들의 무기를 내려놓고 참호 밖으로 나왔어요.

23 그들은 무인 지대에서 만났고 악수를 했습니다.

24 그들은 와인과 케이크 같은 작은 선물도 교환했어요.

25 그들은 캐럴을 함께 불렀습니다.

26 몇몇은 심지어 주소를 교환하기도 했고 함께 축구를 했습니다.

27 이 믿을 수 없는 크리스마스는 영국 군인들이 집으로 보낸 편지에 적혀 있었습니다.

28 한 군인은 "크리스마스에 영국 군인들과 독일 군인들은 두 경계선 사이에서 만났고 대화를 나눴어.

29 우리는 자전거 시합도 했어."라고 적었어요.

30 다른 군인은 "우리는 전쟁 중이라는 생각이 들지 않았어.

31 여기서 우리는 적대 관계인 서로와 대화를 나누고 있는 상황이었어.

32 그들은 우리와 마찬가지로, 그들의 남자들이 집으로 다시 돌아오기를 고대하는 어머니와, 친구들, 부인이 있는 사람들이었어."라고 썼습니다.

※ 다음 우리말을 영어로 쓰시오.

1 크리스마스의 기적

➡ _____

2 제일차 세계 대전의 첫해였던 1914년의 크리스마스이브였습니다.

➡ _____

3 영국 군인들은 지난 몇 달 동안 그래왔듯이 그들의 참호에서 독일 군인들과 대치하고 있었어요.

➡ _____

_____

4 참호는 춥고 축축했습니다.

➡ _____

5 군인들은 지쳤고 자신들의 집을 그리워했는데, 크리스마스라는 이유로 더욱 더 그랬습니다.

➡ _____

6 갑자기 익숙한 노래가 독일 군인들의 참호로부터 들려왔습니다.

➡ _____

7 그것은 크리스마스 캐럴이었어요!

➡ _____

8 무슨 일이 벌어지고 있는 걸까요?

➡ _____

9 어쩌면 그들을 참호 밖으로 유인하고자 하는 속임수일지도 모릅니다.

➡ _____

10 몇몇 영국 군인들이 용감하게 자신들의 참호 밖을 내다보았어요.

➡ _____

11 차례차례 다른 군인들도 앞사람을 따랐습니다.

➡ _____

12 영국 군인들이 본 것은 그들이 절대 예상하지 못한 광경이었어요.

➡ _____

13 독일 군인들의 참호를 따라, 크리스마스트리들이 랜턴으로 밝혀진 채 있었습니다!

➡ _____

14 독일 군인들은 크리스마스 캐럴을 연이어 불렀어요.

➡ _____

15 영국 군인들도 크리스마스 캐럴을 부르며 화답하기 시작했습니다.

➡ _____

16 따뜻한 불빛과 크리스마스 캐럴은 그들이 최전선에 있다는 것을 잊게 만들었어요.

➡ _____

17 그리고 독일 군인들 쪽에서 고함이 터져 나왔습니다. "행복한 크리스마스예요! 당신들이 쏘지 않는다면, 우리도 쏘지 않을게요!"
➡️ _____

18 곧, 단지 몇 시간 전까지만 해도 서로를 죽이는 것이 목적이었던 군인들은 인사를 나누기 시작했습니다.
➡️ _____
_____

19 몇 달 만에 처음으로, 군인들은 평화롭게 밤을 지낼 수 있었어요.
➡️ _____

20 그날은 정말로 조용한 밤이었습니다.
➡️ _____

21 크리스마스 아침이 밝았습니다.
➡️ _____

22 양편의 군인들은 자신들의 무기를 내려놓고 참호 밖으로 나왔어요.
➡️ _____

23 그들은 무인 지대에서 만났고 악수를 했습니다.
➡️ _____

24 그들은 와인과 케이크 같은 작은 선물도 교환했어요.
➡️ _____

25 그들은 캐럴을 함께 불렀습니다.
➡️ _____

26 몇몇은 심지어 주소를 교환하기도 했고 함께 축구를 했습니다.
➡️ _____

27 이 믿을 수 없는 크리스마스는 영국 군인들이 집으로 보낸 편지에 적혀 있었습니다.
➡️ _____

28 한 군인은 "크리스마스에 영국 군인들과 독일 군인들은 두 경계선 사이에서 만났고 대화를 나눴어.
➡️ _____
_____

29 우리는 자전거 시합도 했어."라고 적었어요.
➡️ _____

30 다른 군인은 "우리는 전쟁 중이라는 생각이 들지 않았어.
➡️ _____

31 여기서 우리는 적대 관계인 서로와 대화를 나누고 있는 상황이었어.
➡️ _____

32 그들은 우리와 마찬가지로, 그들의 남자들이 집으로 다시 돌아오기를 고대하는 어머니와, 친구들, 부인이 있는 사람들이었어."라고 썼습니다.
➡️ _____
_____

영어 기출 문제집

적중100

2학기

정답 및 해설

시사 | 송미정

중 3

영어 기출 문제집

적중100

2학기

정답 및 해설

시사 | 송미정

중 3

Lesson 7

Small Ideas, Big Differences

시험대비 실력평가
p.08

01 useful   02 ④   03 ①   04 ⑤
05 (1) pass through   (2) cause death   (3) think about
06 ②

01 careful(주의 깊은, 조심스러운, 세심한)과 cautious(조심성 있는)는 동의어 관계이다. 따라서 helpful(유용한, 도움이 되는)과 동의어 관계에 있는 단어는 useful(도움이 되는)이다.

02 '어떤 것이 일어나는 것을 막거나 혹은 어떤 사람이 어떤 것을 하는 것을 막다'는 뜻을 가진 영영풀이가 가리키는 것은 ④ prevent(막다)이다.

03 ① repair는 '수리하다'라는 동사적 의미가 아닌 '수리'라는 명사적 의미로 사용되었다.

04 '직원들은 비상사태 절차를 충분히 알고 있어야 한다.', '그 파일럿은 어쩔 수 없이 비상 착륙을 해야 했다.'라는 문장에서 공통으로 들어갈 수 있는 단어는 ⑤ emergency(비상 상황, 비상 사태)이다.

05 (1) pass through ~을 지나가다 (2) cause death 죽음을 야기하다 (3) think about ~에 대해 생각하다

06 (A) look out 밖을 내다보다 / let out 내보내다 (B) build up 점점 커지다 / be made up of ~로 구성되다

서술형 시험대비
p.09

01 unnecessary   02 notice
03 (1) pane   (2) hill   (3) twist
04 (1) Surprisingly   (2) recently   (3) carefully
05 (1) The well-finished roof should be weatherproof for years.
   (2) How quickly can you prepare the paperwork?
   (3) He drew a circle in the sand with a stick.
06 (1) His face was reflected in the mirror.
   (2) I had a sore throat and it hurt to swallow.
   (3) Be careful not to hurt yourself with the steam.

01 death(죽음)와 birth(탄생)는 반의어 관계이다. 따라서 necessary(필수적인)와 반의어 관계에 있는 단어는 unnecessary(불필요한, 쓸데없는)이다.

02 '알게 되다'라는 영영풀이에 맞는 단어는 'notice'(알아채다, 의식하다)이다.

03 (1) pane 판유리 (2) hill 언덕, 산 (3) twist 돌리다

04 (1) surprisingly 놀랍게도 (2) recently 최근에 (3) carefully 조심스럽게

05 (1) roof 지붕 (2) quickly 빨리 (3) stick 막대기

06 (1) mirror 거울 (2) swallow 삼키다 (3) steam 수증기

교과서 Conversation

핵심 Check
p.10~11

1 I wonder what the first plane looked like.
2 ⑤

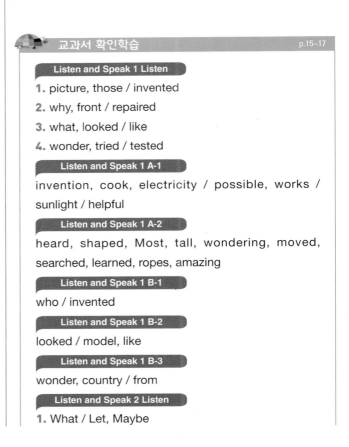

교과서 대화문 익히기

Check(√) True or False
p.12

1 T   2 T   3 F   4 T

교과서 확인학습
p.15~17

Listen and Speak 1 Listen
1. picture, those / invented
2. why, front / repaired
3. what, looked / like
4. wonder, tried / tested

Listen and Speak 1 A-1
invention, cook, electricity / possible, works / sunlight / helpful

Listen and Speak 1 A-2
heard, shaped, Most, tall, wondering, moved, searched, learned, ropes, amazing

Listen and Speak 1 B-1
who / invented

Listen and Speak 1 B-2
looked / model, like

Listen and Speak 1 B-3
wonder, country / from

Listen and Speak 2 Listen
1. What / Let, Maybe

2. How, float / pushes

3. move / see, with

4. pictures

Listen & Speak 2 A-1

Look, quickly / pass, increases / Let, step, made / amazing

Listen & Speak 2 A-2

field, Invention / creative / excited, planning / Good, museum / started

Listen & Speak 2 B-1

What / play

Listen & Speak 2 B-2

with / see, from

Listen & Speak 2 B-3

What / send

Real-Life Zone

these / why, holes / think, maybe, look / possible, must, reasons / look, what / says during, through, thin / crispy, why

Wrap Up 1-2

what, going / sounds, that, Saturdays, what / advertisement, Here / say / says / both, fantastic / what

Wrap Up 3~4

competition / sounds / enter, ideas / when / from / wonder, have / talk, science

---

 시험대비 기본평가　　　　　　　　　　p.18

01 I wonder how it works.

02 The invention　　　　　03 ⑤

04 It is made when people step on the floor.

---

01 상대방에게 궁금한 점을 물을 때 "I wonder ~." 또는 "I am wondering ~.", 'I was wondering ~.'과 같은 표현을 쓸 수 있다. 이때 '어떻게 작동하는지'라는 목적어는 의문사 how를 이용한 간접의문문을 사용해서 만든다.

02 음식을 요리하기 위해 태양광을 사용하는 건 위 대화 전반에서 이야기하고 있는 'the invention'(그 발명품)이다.

03 "Let me see."는 '잠깐만.', '어디 보자.'의 뜻으로 어떤 것을 기억해 내거나 잠시 생각을 정리할 시간이 필요할 때 사용하는 표현이다. 같은 표현인 "Let me think."를 대신 사용할 수 있다.

04 위 대화의 후반에서 사람들이 바닥을 밟으면 에너지가 만들어진다고 언급되어 있다.

시험대비 실력평가　　　　　　　　　　p.19~20

01 ⓑthinking → think	02 ①	03 steam
04 ②	05 I wonder what they are.	06 ③
07 ③	08 ②	09 ⑤	10 ②, ⑤
11 ④		

01 동사 let은 목적보어로 동사원형을 취한다. 따라서 ⓑthinking을 think로 고쳐야 한다.

02 빈칸이 포함된 문장 모두 의문사가 포함된 간접의문문이 쓰였다. 대화의 문맥상 (A) '무엇을 말하는지'(what it says)와 (B) '그것들이 구멍을 가진 이유'(why they have holes)가 들어가는 것이 적절하다.

03 '물이 끓을 때 만들어지는 뜨거운 가스'는 'steam'(수증기)을 의미한다.

04 '여기 있어.'라는 표현은 어떤 것을 상대방에게 건네줄 때, 혹은 무언가가 여기 있다고 말할 때 쓸 수 있는 표현이다. 이 대화에서는 후자의 의미로 사용되었으며 신문에 있는 광고를 찾았다고 말하는 ②에 들어가는 것이 가장 적절하다.

05 대화 상대방에게 궁금한 점을 물을 때 "I wonder ~." 또는 "I am wondering ~."과 같은 표현을 쓸 수 있다. 이때 '그 프로그램들이 무엇인지'라는 목적어는 의문사 what과 대명사 they를 이용해 what they are로 쓸 수 있다.

06 ③ '토요일마다 몇 번 씩 프로그램이 진행되는가'는 위 대화에서 언급되어 있지 않다.

07 (A) 현재완료 구문으로 과거분사가 쓰여야 한다. (B) most는 일반적인 것을, most of는 특정한 것을 가리킬 때 사용한다. (C) 문맥상 가장 큰 Moai는 높이가 20미터라는 문장이 되어야 적절하다. 따라서 비교급이 아니라 최상급이 쓰여야 한다.

08 ② '가장 큰 모아이는 높이가 20미터'라고 언급되어 있다.

09 ⑤의 대화에서 A가 최초의 비행기가 어디서 비행을 시도했는지 궁금하다고 질문했는데, 이에 B는 실험 비행을 100년 전에 했다고 대답했다. 따라서 B의 대답은 문맥상 적절하지 않다.

10 ② 누가 그들과 같이 현장 학습을 가는지는 언급되어 있지 않으며, ⑤ '현장 학습의 계획이 무엇인지'는 역시 언급되지 않았다.

11 대화 후반에 G가 가기 전에 계획을 세우자고 제안했고 B가 승낙했으므로 ④ '현장 학습 계획 세우기'를 할 것으로 추정된다.

서술형 시험대비　　　　　　　　　　p.21

01 (A) when　(B) what

02 He has to talk to Mr. Harrison.

03 (B) – (C) – (A)

04 It employs sunlight to cook food.

05 I was wondering how people moved them long ago.

06 search

07 They moved the stones by using ropes.

01 위 대화의 문맥상, (A) 대회가 언제인지(when), (B) 대회에 출전하기 위해 뭘 해야 하는지(what) 물어보는 질문이 들어가야 한다.

02 대회에 출전하기 위해 B가 무엇을 해야 하는지는 G의 마지막 말에 언급되어 있다.

03 전기를 쓰지 않고 요리를 할 수 있게 도와주는 발명품에 대해 소개하고 있는 B의 말에 상대방은 (B) 그것이 가능하냐고 묻고 어떻게 작동하는지 되묻는 것이 자연스럽다. 이에 (C) 태양광을 이용해 요리를 할 수 있게 만든다고 하자 (A) 캠핑을 갈 때 정말 유용하겠다고 하는 내용이 이어지는 것이 문맥상 가장 자연스럽다.

04 위 대화의 (C)에서 나와 있듯이, 그 발명품은 전기 없이 태양광을 이용해 음식을 요리할 수 있게 한다. employ: 사용하다, 쓰다

05 상대방에게 궁금한 점을 물을 때 "I wonder ~." 또는 "I am wondering ~.", 'I was wondering ~."과 같은 표현을 쓸 수 있다. 또한 목적어 자리에는 의문사 how를 이용한 목적어 'how people moved them long ago'라고 나열할 수 있다.

06 '무언가를 찾기 위해 주의 깊게 어느 곳을 찾다'라는 영영풀이에 맞는 단어는 search(찾다, 검색하다)이다.

07 위 글의 마지막 문장에 나와 있듯이, 모아이를 만들기 위해 밧줄을 이용했다. by -ing: ~을 함으로써

[교과서] Grammar

핵심 Check p.22~23

1 (1) got (2) would   2 (1) so (2) that

시험대비 기본평가 p.24

01 (1) has → had (2) will → would
　　(3) what → that (4) can't → can
02 (1) Jack is so tall that he can touch the ceiling.
　　(2) We worked hard so that everything would be ready in time.
　　(3) I got up early so that I could catch the first bus.
　　(4) She works so hard that she deserves a vacation.
03 (1) If I had longer arms, I could grab that apple.
　　(2) If I were[was] in the UK, I could speak English better.

01 (1) 가정법 과거. If S 동사의 과거형 ~, S would(should/could/might) 동사원형. 현재 사실과 반대되는 일이나 상황일

때 사용한다. 현재 그녀는 네 것과 같은 예쁜 드레스가 없어서 울고 있는 것을 의미한다. has를 had로 고치는 것이 적절하다. (2) 가정법 과거. 현재 나는 대통령이 아닌 상황을 묘사하고 있으며 주절의 will을 would로 고치는 것이 적절하다. (3) '~하기 위해서'라는 의미를 표현할 때 'so that S 조동사'를 사용하므로 what을 that으로 고치는 것이 적절하다. (4) 의미상 실수 없이 바이올린을 연주하기 위해 바이올린 연습을 하는 것이므로 can't를 can으로 쓰는 것이 적절하다.

02 (1)과 (4)는 'so 형/부 that S V'의 구문이다. (2)와 (3)은 'S V so that S V'로 'so that S V'는 '~하기 위해서, ~하도록'으로 해석한다.

03 가정법 과거는 현재 사실에 대한 반대를 표현할 때 사용하며 'If S 동사의 과거형 ~, S would/should/could/might 동사원형'이다. (1) If 절의 동사는 had로 쓰는 것이 적절하고 주절에는 could grab으로 쓰는 것이 적절하다. (2)의 경우 가정법 과거에서 be동사의 과거형은 were로 쓰며 구어체에서는 was도 가능하다. 그러므로 If 절의 동사는 were 또는 was로 쓰고 주절은 could speak으로 쓰는 것이 적절하다.

시험대비 실력평가 p.25~27

01 could gone → could have gone
02 As he is not rich, he does not buy that car.
03 Sit a little closer so that we can have a talk.
04 ①　　05 ②　　06 ①　　07 would
08 ③　　09 ④　　10 ②　　11 ①
12 ①
13 She folded her arms as if she was[were] cold.
14 ⑤　　15 ②, ④　　16 so as to
17 I got up early in order not to miss the first train.
18 (1) exercised (2) were (3) had　　19 ⑤

01 • 내가 시간이 있었더라면 너랑 갈 수 있었을 텐데. 가정법 과거완료로 과거 사실에 대해 반대되는 상황이나 일을 가정할 때 쓰고 'If S had p.p. ~, S would/should/could/might have p.p.'이므로 could gone을 could have gone으로 쓰는 것이 적절하다.

02 만약 그가 부자라면 그 차를 살 텐데. 보기의 문장은 현재 사실에 대한 반대를 나타내고 있다. 부자가 아니어서 그 차를 사지 않는 것이므로 As를 활용하여 현재시제로 동사를 써야 한다.

03 'so that ~ can'을 활용한 명령문으로 주절 내용은 '좀 더 가까이 앉아라.'이고 부사절은 '이야기하기 위해서'이다.

04 나는 그녀가 나에게 연락할 수 있도록 나의 전화번호를 주었다. so that ~ can은 in order that과 같은 의미로 쓸 수 있으므로 ①처럼 바꿔 쓰는 것이 적절하다.

05 ② 만일 내가 알았더라면 그 일을 하지 않았을 것이다. 가정법

과거완료이므로 would not have done이 오는 것이 적절하다. ① Peter가 Karen에게 데이트 신청하면, 그녀가 승낙할 것이다. ③ 내가 백만 달러가 있다면, 나는 헬리콥터를 살 수 있을 텐데. ④ Diane이 지금 여기 있다면, 그녀는 동의할 텐데. ⑤ 내가 아프지 않다면, 나는 파티에 갈 수 있을 텐데.

06 • 내가 그녀의 이름을 안다면, 너에게 말할 텐데. 가정법 과거 문장으로 'If 주어 동사의 과거형 ~, S would/should/could/might 동사원형 ~'으로 쓰고 현재 사실에 대한 반대되는 일이나 상황을 가정할 때 사용한다.

07 • 내가 너라면, 나는 거기에 혼자 가지 않을 텐데. 가정법 과거는 현재 사실에 대한 반대되는 사실이나 일을 가정할 때 사용하며 빈칸에는 would가 들어가는 것이 적절하다.

08 ③ 우리는 재충전을 위해 휴식이 필요하다. 5개 문장 모두 빈칸 뒤를 '~하기 위해'로 해석한다. 하지만 ③은 to나 in order[so as] to가 들어가고 나머지 4개 문장은 so that이 들어가는 것이 적절하므로 답은 ③이다. ① 다음 학기에 전액 장학금 받으려면 열심히 공부해야 해, ② 내가 볼 수 있도록 그것을 돌려주세요. ④ 자세히 좀 보게 그를 앞으로 데려와 주세요. ⑤ 그는 그들이 그것을 할 수 있도록 새로운 계획을 세웠다.

09 날씨가 좋다면 소풍을 갈 텐데. 가정법 과거 문장으로 'If 주어 동사의 과거형 ~, S would/should/could/might 동사원형 ~'으로 쓰고 현재 사실에 대한 반대되는 일이나 상황을 가정할 때 사용한다. 가정법 과거에 맞춰 ④처럼 쓰는 것이 적절하다.

10 • 그는 가족을 부양하기 위해 열심히 일한다. '~하기 위해'라는 의미를 나타내는 'in order to, in order that'을 쓸 수 있다. ③은 빈칸에 that이 오면 빈칸 뒤에 'S+V'가 나와야 하므로 ②번이 들어가는 것이 적절하다.

11 '내가 지나가도록 옆으로 비켜주겠습니까?'의 의미로 'so that I can pass'는 '~하기 위해서'라고 해석하고 빈칸에 so that ~ can이 들어가는 것이 적절하다.

12 가정법 과거 문장으로 'If 주어 동사의 과거형 ~, S would/should/could/might 동사원형 ~'으로 쓰고 현재 사실에 대한 반대되는 일이나 상황을 가정할 때 사용하므로 ①처럼 쓰는 것이 적절하다.

13 as if를 활용한 가정법 과거 표현으로 주절의 시제에서 반대되는 상황이나 일을 표현할 때 쓴다. 'as if S be동사'에서 be동사는 주어가 3인칭 단수일 경우 was나 were 모두 사용 가능하므로 She folded her arms as if she was(또는 were)로 쓰는 것이 적절하다.

14 ⑤ 그녀는 마치 그녀가 날고 있는 것처럼 느꼈다. 'S V as if 가정법 과거'로 써야 하므로 'She felt as if she were flying.'으로 고치는 것이 적절하다. ① 그녀는 마치 여왕인 듯이 말했다.(as if 가정법 과거. 현재 사실과 반대되는 일이나 상황의 가정) ② 그녀는 몇 주 동안 굶었다는 듯이 다 먹어치웠다.(as if 가정법 과거. 현재 사실에 반대되는 일이나 상황의 가정) ③ 그녀는 내 생각을 읽은 것처럼 말했다.(가정법 과거완료. 과거 사실에 반

대되는 일이나 상황의 가정) ④ 그녀는 마치 유령이라도 봤던 것처럼 보인다.(as if 가정법 과거완료. 과거 사실에 대해 반대되는 일이나 상황의 가정)

15 • 그는 다음날 일찍 일어나기 위해 평소보다 더 일찍 잤다. 'S V so that S V'는 'S V in order that S V'와 'S V in order to 부정사'와 같은 뜻을 지니므로 ②와 ④처럼 쓰는 것이 적절하다.

16 우리는 좋은 자리를 잡기 위해서 일찍 갔다. '~하기 위해'라는 표현으로 'so that S V', 'in order to 동사원형', 'so as to 동사원형' 등이 있는데 괄호에 so를 사용하라고 나와 있고 빈칸 뒤에 동사원형이 있기 때문에 'so as to'가 빈칸에 오는 것이 적절하다.

17 괄호 안에 주어진 in order to를 이용하여 '~하기 위해'를 부정할 때 to 앞에 not을 써서 표현하므로 'I got up early in order not to miss the first train.'으로 영작하는 것이 적절하다.

18 어법에 맞게 배열하면 • If he exercised harder, he would be a good athlete. • If you were me, what would you do? • If I had not been sick, I would have gone on a trip together yesterday.

19 • 그 때 그는 박사 학위를 취득하기 위해 존스 홉킨스 대학에 입학했다. • 우리는 시험에 통과하기 위해 지난밤에 공부했다. 빈칸 뒤의 내용은 '~하기 위해'로 해석 되므로 'so that S V'와 같은 의미를 지닌 'in order to', 'in order that', 'so as to' 등이 올 수 있다. 빈칸 뒤에 바로 동사원형이 오기 때문에 ⑤가 오는 것이 적절하다.

서술형 시험대비
p.28~29

01 If I knew his phone number, I would call him.

02 as if I were[was] her younger brother

03 She goes jogging every morning to stay healthy. / She goes jogging every morning so as to stay healthy. / She goes jogging every morning in order to stay healthy. / She goes jogging every morning in order that she can[may] stay healthy.

04 If she studied harder, she could pass the test.

05 If she felt well, she would visit her friend's house.

06 so as to　　07 so that

08 In order not to oversleep, I set the alarm for six o'clock.

09 They took a taxi not to waste time. / They took a taxi in order not to waste time. / They took a taxi so as not to waste time.

10 If Bob worked in the team, he wouldn't be so stressed.

11 (1) I would call for help　(2) If I had a boat
(3) it would have reached Mars
(4) If I were[was] a bird

12 If I didn't have any classes today, I would go to

an amusement park.

13 (1) in order not to overcook (2) in order to have

01 가정법 과거는 현재 사실에 대해 반대되는 상황이나 일을 가정할 때 사용하고 'If S 동사의 과거형 ~, S would/should/could/might 동사원형'으로 쓴다.

02 그녀는 마치 내가 그녀의 남동생인 것처럼 나를 도와준다. 빈칸이 속한 문장은 가정법 과거 문장으로 현재 사실에 대해 반대되는 일이나 상황을 표현할 때 쓴다. 문제에서 as if를 활용하라고 했으므로 'S V as if 가정법 과거'에 맞춰 쓰면 'as if I were her younger brother.'라고 쓰는 것이 적절하다.

03 그녀는 건강을 유지하기 위해 매일 아침 조깅을 한다. '~하기 위해서'라는 표현은 'to 동사원형', 'so as to 동사원형', 'in order to 동사원형', 'in order that S V' 등이 있다.

04 • 그녀는 더 열심히 공부한다. • 그녀는 시험에 통과할 수 있다. • 만약 그녀가 더 열심히 공부한다면 시험에 통과할 텐데. 가정법 과거는 'If S 동사의 과거형 ~, S would/should/could/might 동사원형'이고 현재 사실에 대한 반대되는 상황이나 일을 가정할 때 사용한다.

05 • 그녀는 그녀의 친구 집에 방문하고 싶지만, 그녀는 몸 상태가 좋지 않다. 주어진 문장은 친구 집에 방문하고 싶지만 현재 몸 상태가 좋지 않아 가지 않는 것이므로 'If she felt well, she would visit her friend's house.'라는 가정법 과거 문장을 쓰는 것이 적절하다.

06 나는 그가 나에게 약간의 관심이라도 가지고 있는지를 알기 위해 그에게 데이트 신청을 했다. 'in order to'는 'in order that', 'so that', 'so as to'와 같고 빈칸 뒤에 know라는 동사가 있으므로 so as to를 쓰는 것이 적절하다.

07 • 그녀를 만나기 위해 나는 한 시간 동안 기다렸다. • 나의 아기는 너무 작게 태어나서 2주 동안 인큐베이터에서 지냈다. 첫 번째 문장은 'S V ~ so that S V'로 so that 종속절 문장은 '~하기 위해서'로 해석하고, 두 번째 문장은 'so 형용사 that S V'로 '너무 ~해서 …하다'로 해석한다. 그러므로 빈칸에는 so와 that이 들어가는 것이 적절하다.

08 • 늦잠을 자지 않기 위해, 나는 6시에 알람을 맞췄다. 주절의 행동에 대한 목적의 의미를 지닌 'in order to 동사원형'은 주절에서 '내'가 알람을 설정한 이유가 늦잠을 자지 않기 위해이므로 'In order not to oversleep'으로 고쳐 쓰는 것이 적절하다.

09 '~하지 않기 위해'를 표현할 때 'to부정사', 'in order to', 'so as to' 등을 쓸 수 있고 부정을 나타내기 위하여 to부정사 앞에 not을 붙여 쓰는 것이 적절하다.

10 가정법 과거는 'If S 동사의 과거형 ~, S would/should/could/might 동사원형'으로 쓰므로 'If Bob worked in the team, he wouldn't be so stressed.'로 쓰는 것이 적절하다.

11 가정법 과거로 현재 사실에 대한 반대되는 상황이나 일을 가정할 때 쓰는 표현이다. 그러므로 (1)은 'I would call you help', (2)는 'If I had a boat', (3)은 가정법 과거완료로 과

거 사실에 대한 반대되는 상황이나 일을 가정할 때 쓰는 표현이다. 'it would have reached Mars', (4)는 'If I were(또는 was) a bird'로 쓰는 것이 적절하다.

12 가정법 과거는 현재 사실에 대해 반대되는 상황이나 일을 가정할 때 사용하며 'If S 동사의 과거형 ~, S would/should/could/might 동사원형'으로 쓰므로 괄호 안의 단어를 활용하여 'If I didn't have any classes today, I would go to an amusement park.'로 영작하는 것이 적절하다.

13 '~하기 위해서'라는 표현으로 in order to를 쓰고 부정의 경우 to 앞에 not을 붙여 'in order not to 동사원형'으로 쓰는 것이 적절하다.

Reading

확인문제 p.30

1 T 2 F 3 T 4 F 5 T 6 F

확인문제 p.31

1 T 2 F 3 T 4 F 5 T 6 F

교과서 확인학습 A p.32~33

01 Hidden
02 have seen recently
03 good, bad
04 in your sock
05 for a button
06 everywhere
07 so small
08 well hidden, make your life safe
09 Take
10 Look at
11 a small hole
12 why it is there
13 help save lives
14 put, in
15 swallow them
16 stop their breathing
17 putting a small hole
18 pass through
19 play a helpful role
20 with a lid, noticed
21 for safety
22 When cooking, builds up
23 boil over
24 keeps, from coming
25 Have, been
26 Wasn't it exciting
27 Surprisingly
28 are made up of
29 in the middle pane
30 balances
31 Without, in an emergency
32 prevents, from fogging up
33 that have
34 why it is there
35 to make your life safer

1 Hidden Holes

2 Think about a hole that you have seen recently.

3 Was it a good hole or a bad hole?

4 If it was a hole in your sock, it was bad.

5 If it was a hole in your shirt for a button, it was good.

6 There are holes everywhere.

7 Some are so small you may not even notice them.

8 They are well hidden, but many of these small holes are very important and make your life safe.

9 Take a pen.

10 Look at it carefully.

11 Do you see a small hole in the cap?

12 Do you know why it is there?

13 The hole in a pen cap can help save lives.

14 People, especially children, often put small things like pen caps in their mouths.

15 Sometimes they even swallow them.

16 This can stop their breathing and cause death.

17 A famous pen company started putting a small hole in their pen caps.

18 The hole in the cap lets air pass through and has saved lives.

19 If you look around, you will see other holes that play a helpful role in your life.

20 If you have ever cooked anything in a pot with a lid, perhaps you noticed a small hole in the lid.

21 This hole, too, is there for safety.

22 When cooking something in a pot with a lid, the pressure inside the pot builds up.

23 The water inside would quickly boil over if the lid did not have that hole.

24 The hole lets steam out and keeps the water from coming out.

25 Have you ever been on an airplane?

26 Wasn't it exciting to look out the window and see the world below?

27 Surprisingly, there was a small hole in your window.

28 Airplane windows are made up of three panes.

29 There is a hole in the middle pane.

30 It balances the air pressure.

31 Without this little hole, airplane windows might break in an emergency.

32 The hole also prevents the window from fogging up so that you can enjoy that fantastic view.

33 There are many more products that have small hidden holes.

34 In the future, when you see a little hole in something, ask yourself why it is there.

35 Maybe it is the result of a careful design to make your life safer.

01 ④	02 ②	03 ⑤	04 ⑤
05 ④	06 ②	07 safety	08 ①, ⑤
09 ②, ③	10 ④	11 ①, ②	

12 will see → see

13 (A) other (B) cooking (C) out   14 part

15 ④   16 ③

17 Some are so small you may not even notice them.

18 safely → safe   19 ⑤

20 ③   21 ③   22 ③

23 The hole in the middle pane

01 ④번 다음 문장의 Some에 주목한다. 주어진 문장의 holes 중의 어떤 것들을 가리키는 것이므로 ④번이 적절하다.

02 이 글은 '구멍은 어디에나 있고, 작고 숨겨져 있어도 많은 구멍들이 매우 중요하다'는 내용의 글이므로, 제목으로는 ②번 '숨겨진 그러나 중요한 구멍들'이 적절하다.

03 이 작은 구멍들 중 많은 것들이 매우 중요하고 '여러분의 삶을 안전하게 해 준다.'

04 ⑤는 '유명한 펜 회사'를 가리키고, 나머지는 다 '아이들'을 가리킨다.

05 sometimes = occasionally = once in a while = from time to time = (every) now and then: 가끔, ④ frequently: 자주, 흔히

06 이 글은 '사람들, 특히 아이들은 종종 펜 뚜껑 같은 작은 것들을 그들의 입에 넣고 삼키기도 하는데 이것은 그들의 호흡을 막고 죽음을 초래할 수도 있기 때문에, 펜 뚜껑에 작은 구멍을 넣었고 그 구멍은 공기를 통하게 해 주고 생명들을 구했다'는 내용의 글이므로, 주제로는 ②번 '펜 뚜껑에 있는 구멍의 역할'이 적절하다.

07 safety: 안전(함), 당신이 해나 위험으로부터 안전한 상태

08 (A)와 ①, ⑤: 관계대명사, ② 명사절을 이끄는 접속사, ③ [수량·정도를 나타내는 말을 한정하여] 그만큼, 그렇게(so), 그 정도로(부사), ④ [동격절을 이끌어] ~이라는, ~하다는(접속사)

09 keep/stop/prevent A from -ing: A가 ~하는 것을 막다, ① 보호하다, ④ 부인하다 ⑤ 손상을 주다, 피해를 입히다

10 ⓐ와 ②: 경험 용법, ①과 ③ 완료 용법, ④ 계속 용법, ⑤ 결과 용법

11 be made up of = be composed of = consist of: ~로 구성되다, consist of는 수동태로 쓸 수 없다. ③ consist in: ~에

12 '때'를 나타내는 부사절에서는 현재시제가 미래시제를 대신하기 때문에, will see를 see로 고치는 것이 적절하다.

13 (A) 'another+단수명사'이므로 other가 적절하다. (B) 'when you cook ~'에서 주어가 일반인이므로 생략하고 동사를 분사로 바꾼 분사구문이므로 cooking이 적절하다. (C) 냄비 안쪽의 압력이 상승할 때 그 구멍이 수증기를 '나가게' 해 주는 것이므로 out이 적절하다.

14 play a role = play a part: 역할을 하다

15 ⓑ 냄비 '안쪽'의 압력이 상승한다고 해야 하므로 inside가 적절하다. ⓒ 물이 밖으로 넘치는 것을 '막아 준다'고 해야 하므로 from이 적절하다. keep A from -ing: A가 ~하는 것을 막다

16 (B)의 it이 주어진 글의 a small hole in the cap을 가리키므로 제일 먼저 오고 (C)는 (B)의 예에 해당하므로 (B) 다음에 (C)가 이어지고 (A)의 첫 문장은 (C)의 마지막 문장의 결과에 해당하므로 (C) 다음에 (A)가 와야 한다. 그러므로 (B)-(C)-(A)의 순서가 적절하다.

17 so ... that: 너무 …해서 ~하다, 'you' 앞에 접속사 'that'을 생략할 수 있다.

18 make의 목적격보어에 해당하므로 형용사 'safe'로 고치는 것이 적절하다.

19 '이 세상에 몇 종류의 구멍들이 있는지'는 대답할 수 없다. ① No, it isn't. ② Yes, it is. ③ We can find holes everywhere. ④ No, they aren't.

20 ⓐ look at: ~을 보다, look for: ~을 찾다, ⓑ put A in B: A를 B에 넣다

21 (A)와 ③: 구하다, ① (나중에 쓰거나 하려고) 남겨 두다[아끼다], ② (특히 무엇을 사거나 하기 위해) (돈을) 모으다, 저축하다, ④ 절약하다, (낭비하지 않고) 아끼다, ⑤ 저장하다

22 ⓐ와 ③: 가주어, ① 가목적어, ② 비인칭 주어, ④ (이미 알고 있거나 진행 중인 사실·상황을 가리켜) 그것, ⑤ It is ~ that의 구문으로, 문장의 어떤 부분을 강조할 때 쓰는 대명사

23 '중간 유리판에 있는 구멍'을 가리킨다.

서술형 시험대비
p.40~41

01 hidden

02 the hole that you have seen recently

03 Some are so small that you may not even notice them.

04 (A) small   (B) important   (C) safe

05 you cook

06 The water inside doesn't quickly boil over as the lid has that hole.

07 (A) small hole   (B) steam out

08 the small hole

09 The hole in a pen cap can help save lives.

10 to pass

11 (A) breathing   (B) air

12 (A) see   (B) pressure   (C) emergency

13 it were[was] not for

14 (A) three panes   (B) air pressure

---

01 그것들은 잘 '숨겨져 있다'고 해야 하므로, 수동태 문장을 나타내기 위해 과거분사 'hidden'으로 쓰는 것이 적절하다.

02 '여러분이 최근에 본 구멍'을 가리킨다.

03 so ~ that...: 너무 ~해서 그 결과 …하다, 'you' 앞에 접속사 'that'이 생략되었다.

04 여러분은 어디에서나 구멍을 발견할 수 있고 그것들 중의 어떤 것들은 너무 '작아서' 인지할 수 없다. 그러나 이 작은 구멍들 중 많은 것들이 매우 '중요한' 것들이고 그것들 덕분에 여러분의 삶이 '안전해'진다.

05 'When cooking ~'은 접속사를 그대로 유지한 분사구문으로 'When you cook ~'에서 주어가 일반인이므로 생략하고 동사를 분사로 바꾼 형태이다.

06 가정법 과거(if+주어+동사(과거형), 주어+과거형 조동사+동사원형)는 직설법 현재로 고치는 것이 적절하다.

07 여러분이 뚜껑 있는 냄비에 어떤 것을 요리할 때 뚜껑에 있는 작은 구멍이 '수증기를 나가게' 해 주고 물이 밖으로 넘치는 것을 막아 주기 때문에, 냄비 안의 물은 금방 끓어 넘치지 않는다.

08 '작은 구멍'을 가리킨다.

09 in a pen cap이 The hole을 수식하도록 쓰는 것이 적절하다. help 다음에는 원형부정사를 쓸 수 있다.

10 let+목적어+원형부정사 = allow+목적어+to부정사

11 어떤 사람이 펜 뚜껑을 삼키면, 그것은 그 사람의 '호흡'을 막고 죽음을 초래할 수도 있다. 그러나 만약 펜 뚜껑에 구멍이 있으면, 그것이 '공기'를 통하게 해 주어 생명을 구할 수 있다.

12 (A) 'to look'과 병렬구문을 이루도록 '(to) see'가 적절하다. (B) '기압'의 균형을 맞춰 준다고 해야 하므로, pressure로 쓰는 것이 적절하다. air pressure: 기압, pleasure: 기쁨, 즐거움, (C) 비행기 창문은 '비상시'에 깨질 수 있다고 해야 하므로 emergency가 적절하다. emergency: 비상(사태), emergence: 출현, 발생

13 Without = If it were[was] not for = But for: ~이 없다면

14 비행기 창문은 '세 개의 유리판'으로 구성되어 있고, 그 중간 유리판에 있는 구멍이 '기압'의 균형을 맞춰 준다.

01 probably   02 ③   03 ②

04 (1) Wrap it up carefully to protect against breakage.

    (2) Some of us are often told to keep our talents well hidden.

05 ③   06 ②   07 ④

08 B will call the Einstein Science Park to ask what time they start.

09 It takes place in Einstein Hall 101.   10 ⑤

11 ④   12 ⑤   13 the Invention Museum

14 ⑤   15 I went to bed early so that

16 ②

17 If I were Robinson Crusoe, I would make a boat to go fishing.

18 She loves her dogs as if they were her kids.

19 so   20 ①, ④   21 a button   22 small

23 in the lid   24 ③   25 ④   26 ③

27 ②

28 In 1755, William Cullen invented the first form of the refrigerator.

29 will → would

---

01 repair(수리하다)와 mend(수선하다, 고치다)는 동의어 관계에 있는 단어들이다. 따라서 perhaps(아마도, 어쩌면)와 동의어 관계에 있는 단어는 probably(아마도)이다.

02 ③ look out은 '조심하다, 주의하다, 신경 쓰다'라는 뜻으로 사용되었다.

03 '팔기 위해 만든 어떤 것, 보통 산업적 과정을 통해 만들어진 어떤 것'이라는 뜻을 가진 영영풀이가 가리키는 것은 ② product(생산물, 상품)이다.

04 (1) carefully: 조심스럽게 / breakage: 파손 / wrap up: 포장하다 (2) well hidden: 잘 숨긴

05 주어진 문장에서 notice는 '알아채다, 인식하다'라는 뜻으로 사용되었다. ③ '주사 맞은 후에 붉어짐과 부풀어짐을 알아챌지도 모른다.'라는 문장에서 쓰임이 같다. ① take notice of: ~을 신경 쓰다 ② 통지 ④ 공고문 ⑤ 통지, 예고

06 주어진 문장은 '소금이 아동 비만에 역할을 할 수도 있다.'는 내용으로, ② play a role(역할을 하다)이 빈칸에 가장 적절하다.

07 (A) 전치사 about은 목적어로 명사형을 취한다. 따라서 동명사 going이 적절하다. (B) 특별한 프로그램이 과거가 아닌 현재에도 존재하는 것이므로 과거형이 아니라 현재형을 쓴다. (C) '신문에 나온 광고가 뭐라고 하니?'라는 문장이므로 현재형이 적절하다.

08 대화에서 B의 마지막 말에 언급되어 있듯이, 아인슈타인 과학 공원에 연락을 해서 몇 시에 프로그램이 시작하는지 물어볼 것이다.

09 대화에서 B의 말에서 언급되었듯이, 아인슈타인 홀 101(Einstein Hall 101)에서 진행된다고 한다.

10 ⑤ "I wonder ~." 또는 "I am wondering ~.", "I was wondering ~."과 같은 표현은 대화 상대방에게 궁금한 점을 물을 때 사용한다.

11 '좋은 생각이야.'라는 문장은 상대방이 어떤 의견을 냈을 때 동의하거나 승낙하는 표현이다. 따라서 G가 계획을 짜자고 제안한 문장 다음인 ④에 들어가는 것이 문맥상 가장 적절하다.

12 위 대화에서 내일 갈 현장 학습에 대해서 이야기하고 있고 같이 현장 학습 계획을 짜기로 했으므로, G의 심정으로 가장 적절한 것은 ⑤ excited(신난, 흥분한)이다.

13 '그것은 많은 창의적인 발명품을 갖고 있다고 들었어'라는 문장에서 그것이 가리키는 것은 앞서 언급한 'the Invention Museum'이다.

14 • 만약 현대의 최고의 록 가수가 그 혹은 그녀의 다음 곡을 인터넷상에 올리면, 그것은 2천만 객석을 갖춘 극장에서 연주되는 것처럼 연주될 수 있을 텐데. 가정법 과거는 현재 사실에 대한 반대되는 일 또는 상황을 가정할 때 사용하고 'If S 동사의 과거형 ~, S would/should/could/might 동사원형'으로 쓰므로 빈칸에는 be가 들어가는 것이 적절하다.

15 so가 들어가는 '~하기 위해서'라는 표현은 'so as to 동사원형'과 'so that S V'가 있다. 제시된 영어 문장은 'I wouldn't be tired this morning'이므로 빈칸에 so that이 나와야 하며 빈칸에 해당하는 곳에는 'I went to bed early'가 들어가는 것이 적절하다.

16 ② 나는 너무 즐거워서 잠을 잘 수 없었다. 'so that' 바로 앞에 '콤마(,)'가 있으면 보통 결과의 부사절을 이끈다. 그러므로 해석도 'S가 V해서 that절하다.'로 해석하므로 답으로 ②번이 적절하다. ① 나는 그 어린 여자애가 잘 볼 수 있도록 의자 위에 세웠다. ③ 그 범인은 아무도 그를 찾을 수 없도록 도망갔다. ④ 우리는 우리가 말하는 것보다 두 배만큼 들을 수 있기 위해서 두 개의 귀와 하나의 입을 가지고 있다. ⑤ 제인은 자신의 눈으로 무슨 일이 있었는지 보기 위해 여기에 왔다.

17 가정법 과거는 'If S 동사의 과거형 ~, S would/should/could/might 동사원형'으로 현재 사실에 반대되는 상황이나 일을 가정할 때 사용한다. 그러므로 어법에 맞게 배열하면 If I were Robinson Crusoe, I would make a boat to go fishing.으로 쓰는 것이 적절하다.

18 as if를 활용한 가정법 과거는 'S V as if S 동사의 과거형 ~'이며 주절에 쓰인 동사의 시제에 반대되는 상황이나 일을 말하고자 할 때 사용한다. She loves her dogs as if they were her kids.로 쓰는 것이 적절하다.

19 영작하면, My friend worked hard so that his mother might enjoy her old age.

20 ⓐ와 ①과 ④: 경험 용법, ②: 계속 용법, ③과 ⑤ 완료 용법

21 만약 구멍이 '단추'를 위해 셔츠에 있다면, 그것은 좋은 구멍이다.

22 어떤 구멍들은 여러분이 인지하기에는 너무 '작기' 때문이다.

23 there: 뚜껑에

24 뚜껑이 '있는' 냄비에 무언가를 요리할 때, 냄비 안쪽의 압력이 상승한다.

25 주어진 문장의 the middle pane에 주목한다. ④번 앞 문장의 three panes 중 '중간 유리판'을 가리키는 것이므로 ④번이 적절하다.

26 이 글은 '비행기 창문 중간 유리판에 있는 구멍이 기압의 균형을 맞춰 주고 그 구멍이 또한, 멋진 경치를 즐길 수 있도록 창문에 김이 서리는 것을 막아 준다'는 내용의 글이므로, 제목으로는 ③번 '가운데 유리에 있는 구멍은 무엇을 하나요?'가 적절하다.

27 '비행기 창문이 왜 세 개의 유리판으로 구성되어 있는지'는 대답할 수 없다. ① They consist of three panes. ③ It is in the middle pane. ④ No. If it were not for a small hole in the airplane windows, airplane windows might break in an emergency. ⑤ A small hole in the middle pane does.

28 'William Cullen이 1755년에 냉장고의 최초 형태를 발명한 것'을 가리킨다.

29 가정법 과거(if+주어+동사(과거형), 주어+과거형 조동사+동사원형)이므로, 'will'을 'would'로 고치는 것이 적절하다.

단원별 예상문제
p.48~51

01 ④　　　02 ⑤　　　03 ③

04 steam coming out through the holes

05 So that's why they have holes!

06 That would be really helpful when you go camping.

07 ③　　　08 ①

09 I wonder what I have to do to enter the competition.

10 ③　　　11 so that 또는 in order that

12 (1) He talks as if he were a millionaire.

　 (2) He talked as if he were a millionaire.

13 ③

14 (1) would take a picture

　 (2) If I had one unbroken vase

15 I gave her my phone number so that she could contact me.

16 ②　　　17 ①, ②, ④　　18 ④

19 The hole lets steam out and keeps the water from coming out.

20 ②　　　21 With → Without

22 (A) the hole　(B) fog up　23 ③

---

01 '공기를 폐 속으로 들여마시고 내뱉는 과정'이라는 영영풀이가 가리키는 것은 ④ breathing(호흡, 숨)이다.

02 '의사들은 허리 통증이 나쁜 자세의 결과라고 말한다.'라는 문장에 들어갈 단어는 ⑤ the result of(~의 결과)가 가장 적절하다.

03 (A)와 ③의 must는 '~임에 틀림없다'의 뜻으로 추측을 나타낸다.

04 (B)that은 앞에서 언급된 단수 명사, 구 또는 절을 가리킨다. 따라서 같은 문장 안에서 쓰인 steam coming out through the holes가 대명사 that이 가리키는 명사(구)이다.

05 의문사 why를 이용한 간접의문문을 사용해 쓸 수 있다. 이때 'that's why they have holes!'는 'that is the reason why they have holes!'의 줄임말이다.

06 helpful: 도움이 되는 / go camping: 캠핑을 가다

07 ③ ⓒthat이 가리키는 것은 앞 문장('It can help us cook without electricity.') 전체이다. 나머지는 모두 ⓐthis invention을 가리킨다.

08 (A)는 '어디 보자'라는 의미로, 의도하는 것은 ① '생각할 시간 요청하기'이다.

09 상대방에게 궁금한 점을 물을 때 "I wonder ~."를 쓰는데, 이때 wonder의 목적어로 의문사를 포함한 간접의문문을 취하기도 한다.

10 ③ '대회의 1등에게 주어지는 상은 무엇인가?'는 대화에서 언급되지 않았다.

11 • 나는 더 많은 짐을 가져가기 위해 차로 갈 것이다. • 우리는 우리가 전화했다는 것을 그가 알 수 있도록 그의 이웃에게 메시지를 남겼다. 두 문장 모두 빈칸 뒤에 목적의 의미를 나타내고, 뒤에 주어와 동사가 있으므로 절을 이끄는 so that이나 in order that을 쓰는 것이 적절하다.

12 as if를 활용한 가정법 과거는 'S V as if S 동사의 과거형 ~'이며 주절에 쓰인 동사의 시제에 반대되는 상황이나 일을 말하고자 할 때 사용한다. (1)은 우리말 해석에 현재시제로 되어 있으므로 'He talks as if he were a millionaire.'로 영작하는 것이 적절하다. (2) 우리말 해석에 과거 시제로 되어 있으므로 'He talked as if he were a millionaire.'로 영작하는 것이 적절하다.

13 ③ 집 근처에 있는 상점은 너무 사람이 많아서 나는 다른 상점에 가야 했다. 'so 형용사 that S V'는 '너무 ~해서 …하다'로 해석되므로 나머지 넷과 다른 의미를 지닌다. ① 나는 당신이 보고서를 이해할 수 있도록 정확히 썼다. ② 이들 목표를 달성하려면 팀워크가 요구된다. ④ 몸매를 가꾸기 위해 헬스 클럽에 등록했다. ⑤ 훈련이 효율적이게 되도록 하려면 체계적으로 계획을 세워야 한다.

14 가정법 과거는 현재 사실에 대한 반대되는 상황이나 일을 표현할 때 사용하고 'If S 동사의 과거형 ~, S would/should/could/

might 동사원형'이다.

15 주어진 so that을 활용하여 '~하기 위해서'라는 문장을 영작할 때 'S V so that S can/could V'로 쓴다. so that 뒤에는 목적의 내용이 나오므로 'I gave her my phone number so that she could contact me.'라고 영작하는 것이 적절하다.

16 주어진 문장의 it과 there에 주목한다. 각각 ②번 앞 문장의 a small hole과 in the cap을 받고 있으므로 ②번이 적절하다.

17 ⓐ와 ①, ②, ④: 동명사, ③, ⑤ 현재분사

18 '펜 뚜껑을 만들기 위해 사용되는 흔한 재료'는 알 수 없다. ① To help save lives. ② Small things like pen caps. ③ A famous pen company. ⑤ To let air pass through.

19 keep A from -ing: A가 ~하는 것을 막다

20 이 글은 '뚜껑이 있는 냄비에 무언가를 요리할 때 냄비 안쪽의 압력이 상승하는데, 만약 뚜껑에 구멍이 없다면 그 안의 물은 금방 끓어 넘칠 것이지만 그 구멍 덕분에 수증기는 나가고 물이 밖으로 넘치지 않는다.'는 내용의 글이므로, 주제로는 ②번 '냄비 뚜껑에 있는 작은 구멍의 역할'이 적절하다.

21 이 작은 구멍이 '없다면', 비행기 창문은 비상시에 깨질 수도 있다고 해야 하므로, With를 Without으로 고치는 것이 적절하다.

22 비행기 창문의 중간 유리판에 '구멍'이 없다면, 창문에 '김이 서려' 당신은 비행기에서 멋진 경치를 즐길 수 없을 것이다. fog up 김이 서리다(자동사 또는 타동사 둘 다로 쓰일 수 있다.)

23 비행기 창문은 세 개의 유리판으로 구성되어 있는데, 그 '중간 유리판'에 구멍이 있다.

서술형 실전문제 p.52~53

01 They are classmates.

02 B heard that it has a lot of creative inventions.

03 The tallest Moai is 20 meters tall, and is a human-shaped stone.

04 He (or She) found out by searching the Internet.

05 If I exercised every day, I could lose weight.

06 Think as if you were in their place.

07 I worked hard so that I could succeed. 또는 I worked hard so as to succeed. / I worked hard in order that I could succeed. 또는 I worked hard in order to succeed.

08 He talked as if he had seen a ghost last night.

09 Do you know why it is there?

10 a famous pen company

11 (A) pass through and   (B) save

12 (A) on   (B) a little   (C) safer

13 to enjoy

01 대화의 내용으로 미루어 볼 때 두 화자는 학급 친구이다.

02 위 대화의 내용에 따르면, B는 발명 박물관에 많은 창의적인 발명품들이 있다고 들었다고 한다.

03 위 지문에 따르면 가장 큰 모아이는 높이가 20미터이고 인간 형태의 돌이라고 한다.

04 화자가 어떻게 모아이를 옮겼는지 찾은 방법은 지문의 후반부에 언급되어 있다.

05 나는 매일 운동하면서 살을 빼고 싶다. 그러나 매일 하기는 쉽지 않다. 바람과 달리 현재 매일 운동을 해서 살을 빼기 어려운 상태의 아쉬움을 나타내고 있으므로 가정법 과거 문장으로 표현할 수 있다.

06 나는 '부자가 가난한 사람을 도와주어야 한다.'는 의견에 동의해. 그러나 내 친구 Joel은 내 생각에 동의하지 않아. 이 경우, 나는 Joel에게 '입장을 바꿔 놓고 생각해 봐.'라고 말할 수 있다.

07 • 나는 열심히 일했다. • 나는 성공할 수 있었다. 목적의 의미를 나타내면서 so와 in을 활용하여 한 문장으로 만들 때 that과 to부정사를 이용하여 쓸 수 있다. so that과 in order that을 쓸 때는 that 뒤에 목적의 의미를 나타내는 절을 써서 한 문장으로 만드는 것이 적절하고, so as to, in order to를 사용할 때는 to부정사 뒤에 목적의 의미를 나타내는 동사원형을 써서 한 문장으로 만드는 것이 적절하다.

08 • 영작하면, He talked as if he had seen a ghost last night.

09 know의 목적어 자리에 간접의문문(의문사+주어+동사)인 'why it is there'의 어순으로 쓰는 것이 적절하다.

10 '유명한 펜 회사'를 가리킨다.

11 만약 어떤 사람이 펜 뚜껑을 삼키면 구멍이 공기를 '통하게' 해 주어 생명을 '구하게' 하려고 펜 뚜껑에 작은 구멍이 있다.

12 (A) '비행기를 타 본 적이 있는가?'라고 해야 하므로 on이 적절하다. have been to: ~에 가 본 적이 있다(경험 용법), ~에 다녀왔다(완료 용법) (B) '어떤 물건에서 작은 구멍을 본다면'이라고 해야 하므로 a little이 적절하다. a few+복수 명사: 약간의 ~, (C) make의 목적격보어에 '형용사'를 써야 하므로 safer가 적절하다.

13 목적(~할 수 있도록)을 나타내는 'so that ... can'을 부사적 용법(목적)의 to부정사로 고치는 것이 적절하다.

창의사고력 서술형 문제 p.54

[모범답안]

01 We use it every day so that we can talk to people who are far away from us. / Alexander Bell invented the first practical form of the telephone. / If we did not have telephones, / we would not be able to have a chat with friends living in another city.

02 (A) cool and fresh   (B) William Cullen
   (C) a necessary part of modern life   (D) ice cream

단원별 모의고사

01 ③   02 ④

03 (1) prevent, from   (2) in the future

04 When people pass by, the number increases.

05 amount   06 ③   07 ⑤

08 It's because the little holes make the crackersthin and crispy.

09 (C) – (B) – (A)

10 an advertisement in the newspaper

11 They have the Smart Design Show and the International Drone Show.

12 ②

13 (1) 없음 (2) can't → can
   (3) such → so   (4) what → that

14 ①   15 ③

16 If you were in my situation

17 so that   18 I shut my eyes in order to see.

19 so that he could get some fresh air / so as to get some fresh air

20 (1) If Jane were(또는 was) good at singing
   (2) If an idol group came to my school

21 so that, could   22 ②, ④

23 No, they aren't. If it is a hole in your sock, it is bad[a bad hole]. 또는 If a hole is in your sock, it is bad[a bad hole]. 또는 If there is a hole in your sock, it is bad[a bad hole].

24 in the cap 25 ③   26 ②   27 ⑤

28 ask yourself why it is there   29 ①, ③

01 '어느 쪽으로도 치우치지 않는 위치에 있거나 혹은 어떤 것을 이 위치에 놓다'라는 영영풀이가 가리키는 것은 ③ balance (균형을 잡다)이다.

02 주어진 문장은 '네가 즉시 돌아온다면 아마 더 좋을 것이다.'라는 의미로, 따라서 빈칸에는 ④ perhaps(아마도)가 가장 적절하다.

03 (1) prevent A from A가 ~하는 것을 막다 (2) in the future 미래에

04 pass by: 지나가다 / increase: 증가하다

05 '어떤 것이 많은가 적은가의 정도; 어떤 것이 얼마나 있는지의 정도'라는 뜻을 가진 영영풀이가 가리키는 것은 amount(양, 총량)이다.

06 나머지는 모두 생각할 시간을 요청하는 표현이지만 ③ Let me check은 '확인해 보자'라는 뜻을 갖는 문장이다.

07 위 대화에서 B와 G는 왜 크래커에 구멍이 있는지 궁금해서 인터넷 서치를 통해 이유를 찾다가 그 이유를 알게 되었다. 따라서 ⑤ curious(궁금한) → satisfied(만족스러운)가 B와 G의 심경 변화로 가장 적절하다.

08 왜 크래커가 작은 구멍을 갖고 있는지는 B와 G의 대화 후반에 직접 언급되어 있다.

09 대화 시작에 G는 내일 발명 박물관으로 현장 학습을 간다고 말한다. 상대방은 (C)에서 박물관을 그것이라고 가리키며 많은 창의적인 발명품이 있다고 들었다고 말한다. 이어서 다시 G는 신난다고 말하면서 내일 현장 학습을 위한 계획을 세우자고 제안하고, (A)에서 제안을 받아들이는 순서로 이어지는 것이 문맥상 가장 적절하다.

10 it은 단수 명사를 대신하는 인칭대명사로, 이 대화에서는 앞선 문장에서 언급된 'an advertisement in the newspaper'를 가리킨다.

11 '아인슈타인 과학 공원이 무슨 프로그램을 운영하느냐?'는 질문에 대한 답은 B의 대답에서 찾을 수 있다.

12 ②에서 A가 '어떻게 이 기차가 움직이기 시작할까?'라고 물었고 이에 B는 '잠시만, 넌 이거 탈 수 있어.'(Just a moment… I think you can take it.)라고 말하는데 이는 문맥상 어색한 대화가 된다.

13 (1) Olivia는 건강을 유지하기 위해 매일 운동을 한다. (2) 그 프로젝트를 제시간에 끝내기 위해 Joel은 열심히 일하는 중이다. so that 뒤의 내용은 주절의 내용을 위한 목적이 나와야 의미상 적절하므로 can't가 아닌 can이 적절하다. (3) 나는 그녀가 지나갈 수 있도록 다리를 비켜 주었다. '~하기 위해서'를 나타내는 표현은 'such that'이 아닌 'so that'이므로 such를 so로 고치는 것이 적절하다. (4) 그녀는 정각에 그곳에 도착하기 위해 서둘렀다. 'so that S V'가 '~하기 위해서'라는 뜻이므로 what을 that으로 고치는 것이 적절하다.

14 그녀는 마치 그녀가 모든 사람들을 알고 있었던 것처럼 행동한다. 사실 그녀는 모두를 알진 못했다. 'as if S 가정법 과거완료'가 쓰였고 acts로 현재이므로 현재보다 이전 시제인 ①이 오는 것이 적절하다.

15 ③ 만약 내가 타이머신을 갖고 있다면 6학년 때로 돌아갈 텐데. 가정법 과거로 현재 사실에 대해 이룰 수 없는 상황에 대한 가정으로 'If S 동사의 과거형 ~, S would/should/could/might 동사원형'이므로 어법에 맞게 고치면 'If I had a time machine, I would go back to the 6th grade.'가 되는 것이 적절하다.

16 가정법 과거는 현재 사실에 대한 이룰 수 없는 상황이나 일을 나타낼 때 사용하며 'If S 동사의 과거형 ~, S would/should/could/might 동사원형'이다.

17 비록 Britney Spears는 전 세계 공연을 통해 대부분의 돈을 벌지만 그녀는 그녀의 새로 태어난 아기를 돌볼 수 있게 한 동안 여행을 그만두고 싶다고 최근 말했다. 빈칸 뒤의 내용이 목적을 나타내므로 so that을 쓰는 것이 적절하다.

18 우리말에 맞게 배열하면 'I shut my eyes in order to see.'이다.

19 괄호 안의 단어 so를 활용한 목적의 의미를 나타내는 표현은 'so that S V ~'와 'so as to 동사원형'이 있으므로 so that he could get some fresh air'와 'so as to get some fresh air'로 쓰는 것이 적절하다.

20 가정법 과거는 현재 사실에 대한 반대되는 사실이나 일을 가정할 때 쓰고 'If S 동사의 과거형 ~, S would/should/could/might 동사원형'으로 쓴다.

21 그녀는 한국 사회에 적응하려고 애쓰고 있는 탈북자를 돕기 위해 국회의원에 출마하기로 결심했다.

22 recently = lately = of late: 최근에, ① those days: 그 당시에 그때, ③ previously: 이전에, 미리, ⑤ of the other day: 저번의

23 만약 여러분의 양말에 구멍이 있다면, 그것은 좋지 않은 것이다.

24 there: 뚜껑에

25 때때로 아이들은 심지어 '펜 뚜껑 같은 작은 것들'을 삼키기도 한다.

26 주어진 문장의 This hole에 주목한다. ②번 앞 문장의 a small hole을 받고 있으므로 ②번이 적절하다.

27 그 구멍이 수증기를 나가게 하는 데 얼마나 오래 걸리는지'는 대답할 수 없다. ① It is for safety. ② The pressure inside the pot builds up. ③ The water inside would quickly boil over. ④ It lets steam out and keeps the water from coming out.

28 'yourself'를 보충하면 된다. ask의 간접목적어로는 재귀대명사 'yourself'를, 직접목적어로는 간접의문문 'why it is there'를 쓰는 것이 적절하다.

29 ⓑ와 ①, ③: 형용사적 용법, ②, ⑤: 부사적 용법, ④: 명사적 용법

Healthy Food Around the World

시험대비 실력평가   p.64

01 increase   02 ②   03 ④

04 (1) Could you recommend a hotel near your office?

   (2) Sam's restaurant serves good French cuisine.

   (3) When does the snow start to melt?

05 (1) is, different from   (2) put on   (3) got sick

06 ④

01 low(낮은)와 high(높은)는 반의어 관계에 있는 단어들이다. 따라서 reduce(줄이다)와 반의어 관계에 있는 단어는 increase(증가하다, 늘다)이다.

02 '강한 감동을 유발하는'이라는 의미를 가진 영영풀이가 의미하는 것은 ② touching(감동적인)이다.

03 ④에 쓰인 dish는 요리가 아니라 접시라는 뜻으로 사용되었다.

04 (1) recommend 추천하다 (2) serve 제공하다 (3) melt 녹다

05 (1) be different from ~와 다르다 (2) put on 입다 (3) get sick 병에 걸리다

06 A as well as B B 뿐만 아니라 A도 / such as ~ ~와 같은 / take off 이륙하다 / turn off 끄다

서술형 시험대비   p.65

01 moving   02 (1) thick   (2) treasure

03 (1) for the first time   (2) shown around

   (3) look like

04 (1) They went to the park to take a walk.

   (2) I have a runny nose and a sore throat.

05 (1) We first measured the difference in temperature.

   (2) The shell is smooth on the inside.

06 not only, but also

01 pain(아픔)과 ache(아픔)는 비슷한 의미를 가진 단어들이다. 따라서 touching(감동적인)과 동의어 관계에 있는 단어는 moving(감동시키는)이다.

02 (1) '한 표면에서 반대편까지 큰 거리가 있는', thick 두꺼운 (2) '매우 가치가 있는 것 또는 사람', treasure 보물

03 (1) for the first time 처음으로 (2) show around 안내하다 (3) look like ~처럼 보이다

04 (1) take a walk 산책하다 (2) have a runny nose 콧물이 흐르다

05 (1) temperature 온도, 기온 (2) smooth 매끄러운

06 not only A but also B A뿐만 아니라 B도

교과서 Conversation

핵심 Check   p.66~67

1 ⑤

2 Could[Can] you recommend a good book for my sister?

교과서 대화문 익히기

Check(√) True or False   p.68

1 F   2 F   3 T   4 T

교과서 확인학습   p.71~73

Listen and Speak 1 Listen 1

they / called / Could, again / made, from

Listen and Speak 1 Listen 2

eating / say / like, food

Listen and Speak 1 Listen 3

that, looks / Sorry, again / popular

Listen and Speak 1 A-1

favorite, What / traditional / say, again / sweet / try

Listen and Speak 1 A-2

tried / could / salad, popular / special / with, only but, healthy

Listen and Speak 1 B

1. Have / Sorry / dessert
2. tried / traditional
3. ever / that / in

Listen and Speak 2 Listen

1. recommend / Try
2. Could, for / touching
3. beginners / about
4. snack / How

시험대비 기본평가 p.74

01 ③   02 made

03 ⓐspecial something → something special

04 Can you recommend something easy to cook?

01 문맥상 (A)에는 상대방에게 했던 말을 다시 말해 달라고 요청하는 표현이 들어가야 적절하다. 따라서 ③ 왜 그걸 다시 말했니?(Why did you say that again?)라는 표현은 빈칸 (A)에 들어가기에 어색하다.

02 수동태가 되어야 하므로 과거분사 made로 고친다.

03 ⓐsomething은 형용사가 수식할 때 항상 뒤에서 수식한다. 따라서 something special이 옳은 표현이다.

04 'Can you recommend ~?'는 상대방에게 추천해 달라고 요청할 때 사용하는 표현이다.

시험대비 실력평가 p.75~76

01 ⑤   02 ②

03 It's tasty and also good for your health.

04 ⑤   05 the Happy Snack House 06 ③

07 traditional 08 Sikhye   09 (A) many (B) visiting

10 local   11 ①

01 (A) '몇 분 후에'의 뜻이므로 a few가 알맞다. (B) be made with ~로 만들어지다 (C) is served 제공된다

02 위 대화의 초반부는 식당에 입장할 때의 상황이므로 M과 B의 관계는 ② '웨이터 - 손님'이 적절하다.

03 위 대화에서 B의 말에 따르면, 비빔밥은 맛도 좋고 건강에 좋다고 한다.

04 위 대화의 think가 포함된 문장에서 think는 주어의 역할을 하기 때문에 동명사 thinking의 형태가 되어야 한다.

05 대명사 it이 가리키는 것은 문맥상 앞서 언급된 식당을 가리킨다.

06 'Can you say that again?'은 '다시 말해 주세요.'라는 뜻으로 상대방에게 했던 말을 반복해달라고 요청할 때 사용하는 표현이다. ③은 '그것에 대해 미안해.'라는 뜻으로 상대방에게 반복을 요청하는 나머지와는 다른 뜻이다.

07 '오랫동안 만들어진 행동 방식이나 믿음에 속하거나 따르는'이라는 뜻을 가진 단어는 traditional(전통적인)이다.

08 대명사 it이 가리키는 것은 대화의 문맥상 앞 문장에서 언급된 식혜이다.

09 (A) places라는 셀 수 있는 명사가 사용되었으므로 many가 오는 것이 적절하다. (B) 동사 recommend는 목적어로 동명사(~ing)를 취한다.

10 '전체 주 또는 국가가 아닌 도시, 마을 또는 작은 구역에 관련된'이라는 뜻이 의미하는 것은 local(지역의)이다.

11 위 글은 시드니의 the Rocks Markets를 소개하면서 글을 읽는 사람에게 추천하고 있다. 따라서 ① 추천하기(to recommend)가 글의 목적으로 가장 적절하다.

서술형 시험대비 p.77

01 (B) – (A) – (C)   02 poke

03 Because it's not only delicious but also very healthy.

04 Could you recommend a cell phone for my grandmother?

05 Can you recommend a good place to have the party?

06 the onion rings

07 Because the food is really good and it'll be large enough.

01 B가 poke를 먹어 봤냐고 묻자 이에 대한 대답으로 (B)에서 상대방은 그게 무엇인지 다시 말해달라고 한다. B가 (A)에서 반복해서 말해 주면서 하와이에서 유명한 샐러드라고 말을 해 주고, (C)에서 상대방이 다시 그것이 그렇게 특별한 이유를 묻는 순서가 되어 마지막에 B가 맛도 좋고 건강하다고 대답하는 것이 가장 자연스럽다.

02 위 대화에서 A가 poke가 특별한 점이 무엇이냐고 물어 보고 B가 poke에 대해 설명하고 있다.

03 위 대화에서 B의 마지막 말에 나와 있듯이, poke는 맛도 좋고 건강에도 좋다고 한다.

04 상대방에게 추천해달라고 요청할 때 사용하는 표현으로는 'Can you recommend ~?', 또는 'Can/Could you give me a recommendation for ~?' 등이 있다.

05 상대방에게 추천해달라고 요청할 때 'Can[Could] you recommend ~?', 또는 'Can/Could you give me a

recommendation for ~?' 등을 사용할 수 있다. have a party 파티를 열다, 파티를 하다

06 대명사 They는 바로 앞 문장에서 언급한 the onion rings를 가리킨다.

07 위 대화에서 G의 말에 따르면 그 식당이 음식도 정말 맛있고 충분히 크다고 생각한다고 말했다.

교과서
Grammar

핵심 Check   p.78~79

1 (1) respect → respects   (2) are → is
2 (1) while   (2) while

시험대비 기본평가   p.80

01 ⑤   **02** ③   **03** ⑤   **04** ⑤

01 상관접속사 not only와 but also 뒤에는 문법적으로 대등한 것이 있어야 한다. 동사이면서 3인칭 단수 현재형인 helps가 적절하다.

02 보기의 두 문장이 서로 대조되는 내용이므로, 대조의 역할을 하는 종속접속사 While이 적절하다.

03 ⑤ 상관접속사 not only와 but also 뒤에는 문법적으로 대등한 것이 들어가야 한다. not only 뒤에 동사 speaks가 오면, but also 뒤에도 동사가 와야 하는데, handsome은 형용사이다.

04 첫 번째 빈칸은 '~하는 동안'이라는 뜻을 가진 접속사가 필요하고, 나머지 두 빈칸은 '~인 반면에'라는 뜻을 가진 접속사가 들어가는 것이 적절하다. 두 가지 의미를 동시에 전달하는 접속사는 while 뿐이다.

시험대비 실력평가   p.81~83

01 ①   **02** ⑤   **03** ④   **04** ⑤
05 ④   **06** ①   **07** ④   **08** ④
09 ②   **10** Not only Sean but also   **11** ⑤
12 ⑤   **13** ①
14 (1) While I was taking a shower
　　　(2) While she prefers to take the subway to work

01 ① not only ~ but also에서는 but also 뒤의 명사에 동사의 수를 일치시킨다. have → has가 적절하다.

02 ① neither ~ nor는 부정문과 함께 사용할 수 없다.(doesn't have → has) ② '그녀는 배가 고팠을 뿐만 아니라 더 이상 걸

어갈 수 없었다.'는 문장이다. not only가 문두에 오면 주어와 동사를 도치시킨다.(she was → was she) ③ both는 복수 주어(is → are) ④ 'not only A but also B'는 B에 수의 일치를 한다.(have → has)

03 ① making → makes ② you want → what you want ③ know → knows ⑤ speak → speaks

04 '대조'의 부사절을 이끄는 접속사 'while'이 적절하게 쓰인 것을 고르는 문제이다. ①, ②는 어법상 문제가 없으나, 우리말과 반대로 '녹두전이 ~인 반면에'로 해석되며, ③, ④는 접속사의 성격이 다르다. *ground: 간, 갈린('갈다' grind의 과거분사)

05 오답들을 해석해 보면, ① '맛이 없지만 영양가가 있다.' ② '맛있을 뿐 아니라 영양가가 좋아진다.' ③ '맛이 있거나 또는 영양가가 좋다.' ⑤ '영양가가 좋을 뿐 아니라 맛있다.'가 되어 적절한 문장은 ④이다.

06 '비가 오고 있는 것'과 농구 연습을 하는 것은 대조적인 상황이므로 '역접'의 접속사가 필요하다.

07 ④ Both A and B는 복수 동사를 써야 한다. watches → watch가 적절하다.

08 (A) 혜진이는 안경을 쓰는 반면에, 유나는 아니다. (B) 그는 비록 늦게 일어났지만, 수업에 늦지 않았다. (C) 소연이는 머리가 길고, 반면에 예지는 머리가 짧다.

09 <보기>는 'Grace뿐만 아니라 Ken도 달리기만 아니라 수영하는 것도 좋아하지 않는다.'라는 문장이다. ① 문법적 오류 ③ '둘 중 하나는 수영도 달리기도 좋아하지 않는다.' ④ '둘 다 수영이 아닌 달리기를 좋아한다.' ⑤ '둘 다 달리기가 아닌 수영을 좋아하는 것은 아니다.'

10 Sean과 그의 학급 친구들이 2주 전에 체육관에서 운동을 시작했으므로, 5개의 빈칸에 알맞게 쓰려면 'not only A but also B'를 활용하는 것이 적절하다.

11 '바이러스가 중국에서 왔다.'는 문장과, '그러나 중국의 몇몇 정치인들은 타국을 비난했다.'는 문장은 대조된다. 그러므로 '대조'의 부사절을 이끄는 접속사 while 또는 Though 등이 적절하다.

12 ① the audience were → were the audience ② sees → see ③ only → not only ④ and also → but also

13 ② nor → or ③ or → and ④ know → knows ⑤ wonder → wonders

14 (1) '~하는 동안'의 의미를 가진 접속사를 추가하여, 단어를 적절하게 배열한다. (2) '~하는 반면에'의 의미를 가진 접속사를 추가한다. (1)과 (2)에 공통으로 들어가는 접속사로서 '~하는 동안'과 '~하는 반면에'의 의미를 모두 갖는 것은 While 뿐이다.

01 (1) not only good for people with colds, but also popular

(2) made with not only eggs but also honey

(3) Not only you but also they were

(4) Both Minju and Yena are responsible for

02 (1) How   (2) and   (3) until   (4) as   (5) while

03 A chicken soup is great for not only a sore throat but also a stuffy nose.

04 Samgyetang not only warms your body but also helps reduce the pain in your throat.

05 The onion milk is a drink that is boiled with not only milk but also chopped onion.

06 While Steve was born into a super rich family, Bob's parents were very poor.

07 While I was doing my homework, Linda left my room to watch TV.

08 While Marco sets the alarm to wake up early in the morning, his wife doesn't use the alarm.

09 While I was taking a walk along the lake park, I could hear so many kinds of birds singing in the woods.

10 (1) Ms. Elena is not only a good teacher but also a great artist.

(2) Jenny can not only sing well but also rap fast in English.

(3) Dahyun is not only pretty but also very smart.

(4) Not only Anna but also her sisters are rich.

11 (1) not only promotes your health but is

(2) while the rest of his family members love chicken

01 (1), (2), (3)은 'not only A but also B'를, (4)는 'both A and B'를 활용하는 문제이다. 의미에 맞게 단어를 배열한다. *people with colds: 감기에 걸린 사람들 *be responsible for: ~에 대해 책임이 있다.

02 의문사 how를 제외하고는 모두 접속사들이다. 문장의 자연스런 연결상 알맞은 단어를 넣도록 한다. (1) 고골모골을 만드는 방법 (2) 그리고, 그것들을 섞으시오. (3) 버터가 녹을 때까지 (4) 부으면서 저으시오. (5) 뜨거울 때 마시세요.

03 닭고기 수프는 부은 목뿐만 아니라 막힌 코에도 좋다.

04 삼계탕은 당신의 몸을 따뜻하게 해줄 뿐만 아니라, 목의 통증을 줄이도록 도와준다.

05 양파 우유는 우유뿐만 아니라 잘게 썬 양파로 만들어지는 음료이다.

06 Steve가 엄청나게 부유한 가정에서 태어난 반면에, Bob의 부모님은 매우 가난했다.

07 내가 숙제를 하는 동안 Linda는 TV를 보기 위해서 내 방을 나

08 Marco가 아침에 일찍 일어나기 위해 알람을 설정하는 반면에, 그의 아내는 알람을 사용하지 않는다.

09 호수 공원을 따라 산책을 하는 동안, 나는 아주 많은 종류의 새들이 숲속에서 노래하는 것을 들을 수 있었다.

10 (1) Ms. Elena는 좋은 선생님일 뿐 아니라 훌륭한 화가이다. (2) Jenny는 노래를 잘할 수 있을 뿐 아니라, 영어로 빠르게 랩을 할 수 있다. (3) 다현이는 예쁠 뿐만 아니라 매우 똑똑하다. (4) Anna뿐만 아니라 그녀의 언니들도 부유하다.

11 (1) 삼계탕은 당신의 건강을 증진시켜 줄 뿐만 아니라, 맛있다. (2) Andy는 피자를 즐기는 반면에, 그의 나머지 가족들은 치킨을 좋아한다.

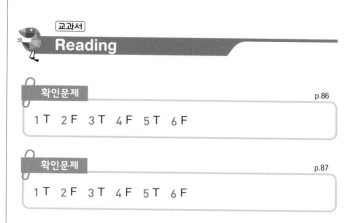

교과서
Reading

확인문제   p.86

1 T   2 F   3 T   4 F   5 T   6 F

확인문제   p.87

1 T   2 F   3 T   4 F   5 T   6 F

교과서 확인학습 A   p.88~89

01 Fight Colds

02 catch a cold

03 stay warm

04 to drink hot tea

05 something, often drink

06 helps reduce the pain

07 What do people drink or eat

08 find out

09 have a special drink

10 a cup of onion milk

11 chopped onion, over low heat

12 is said to be good

13 While, a bowl of chicken soup

14 from one family to another

15 can be added

16 great for a sore throat and a stuffy nose

17 called

18 is made with

19 to make it taste better

20 looks like

21 have a sore throat

22 not only, but also

23 served, at room temperature

24 Why not, about

25 good for

26 How to Make

27 You need

28 mix them

29 Pour

30 Add
31 Warm, melts
32 Pour, into, with
33 Stir as
34 while

1 Foods That Fight Colds

2 What do you do when you catch a cold?

3 Of course, you want to stay warm, so maybe you put on more clothes.

4 Some people like to drink hot tea.

5 Ginger tea is something people in Korea often drink.

6 With its special taste, it warms your body and helps reduce the pain in your throat.

7 What do people drink or eat in other countries when they catch a cold?

8 Let's find out.

9 In Finland, where it is very cold in winter, people have a special drink when they catch a cold.

10 It is a cup of onion milk.

11 They put chopped onion in milk and boil it over low heat for half an hour.

12 This simple drink is said to be good for a cold.

13 While people in Korea and Finland look for drinks when sick, many people in America want a bowl of chicken soup.

14 It is usually made with chicken and vegetables, but the recipe is different from one family to another.

15 Salt and pepper can be added before eating.

16 People in America believe that a bowl of warm chicken soup is great for a sore throt and a suffy nose.

17 In Russia and in Eastern Europe, when people get sick, they eat a dessert called *gogol-mogol*.

18 It is made with eggs and honey.

19 Some people add chocolate, butter, lemon juice, or milk to make it taste better.

20 It looks like thick yogurt.

21 People often drink a cup of warm *gogol-mogol* when they have a sore throat.

22 *Gogol-mogol* is not only good for people with a cold but also popular as a dessert for healthy people.

23 When served as a dessert, it is usually served cold or at rcom temperature.

24 Why not try making one of the foods you have found out about?

25 It will be fun and good for your health.

26 How to make *Gogol-mogol* (Serves one)

27 You need: 1 egg, 1/2 cup of milk, honey (5 g), butter (15 g)

28 1. Put the egg and the honey in a large cup and mix them.

29 2. Pour half a cup of milk in a pan.

30 Add the butter.

31 Warm it until the butter melts.

32 3. Pour the hot milk and butter into the cup with the egg and the honey.

33 Stir as you pour.

34 4. Drink while it is hot.

01 ④   02 warmly → warm   03 ⑤

04 ②, ⑤

05 Many people in America → People in Korea and Finland 또는 look for drinks → want a bowl of chicken soup

06 Salt and pepper can be added.

07 a special drink   08 chopped

09 (A) over   (B) for   (C) for   10 ①

11 ②, ④, ⑤   12 ④   13 ④

14 the recipe is different from one family to another

15 ③   16 ②   17 ④   18 ③

19 ③   20 ④   21 making   22 ②

01 주어진 문장의 its에 주목한다. ④번 앞 문장의 'Ginger tea'를 가리키므로 ④번이 적절하다.

02 stay의 '보어'에 해당하므로, warmly를 '형용사 warm'으로 고치는 것이 적절하다.

03 글의 마지막에서 '다른 나라에서는 사람들이 감기에 걸렸을 때 무엇을 마시거나 먹을까? 함께 알아보자.'라고 했으므로, 뒤에 올 내용으로는 '전 세계 사람들이 감기와 싸우기 위해서 마시고 먹는 것들'이 적절하다.

04 ⓐ와 ②, ⑤: ~인 반면에(대조를 나타내는 접속사), ①과 ④: ~하는 동안, ~하는 사이(접속사), ③ 시간, 일정 기간(명사)

05 '한국 사람들과 핀란드 사람들은' 아플 때 음료를 찾는다. 미국의 많은 사람들은 아플 때 '닭고기 수프를 원한다.'

06 닭고기 수프를 먹기 전에 '소금'과 '후추'를 넣기도 한다.

07 핀란드에서 사람들이 감기에 걸리면 마시는 '특별한 음료'를 가리킨다.

08 '잘게 썬 양파'라고 해야 하므로 'chopped(다져진, 잘게 썰린)'

로 쓰는 것이 적절하다. chop 다지다, 잘게 썰다

09 (A) over low heat: 약한 불에서, (B) 'during+기간을 나타내는 명사, for+숫자'이므로 for가 적절하다. half an hour = thirty minutes, (C) '감기에 좋다'고 해야 하므로 for가 적절하다. be good at: ~을 잘하다, be good for: ~에 좋다

10 주어진 문장의 It에 주목한다. ①번 앞 문장의 gogol-mogol을 받고 있으므로 ①번이 적절하다.

11 not only/just/simply/merely A but (also) B = not only/just/simply/merely A but B as well = B as well as A: A뿐만 아니라 B도

12 '고골모골을 만드는 데 얼마나 오래 걸리는지'는 대답할 수 없다. ① They eat a dessert called *gogol-mogol*. ② It is made with eggs and honey. ③ They add chocolate, butter, lemon juice, or milk. ⑤ No. *Gogol-mogol* is not only good for people with a cold but also popular as a dessert for healthy people.

13 물질명사는 그 물질을 세는 단위나, 물질을 담고 있는 그릇(용기)의 단수, 복수형을 이용해서 수량을 표시한다. '닭고기 수프'는 보통 '그릇'에 담아 먹으므로 'a bowl of chicken soup'로 세는 것이 적절하다.

14 from one family to another: 가정마다

15 '닭고기 수프가 얼마나 오래 끓여져야 하는지'는 대답할 수 없다. ① They look for drinks. ② They want a bowl of chicken soup. ④ It is usually made with chicken and vegetables. ⑤ They believe that a bowl of warm chicken soup is great for a sore throat and a stuffy nose.

16 (B)가 주어진 글에 대한 답을 설명하는 것이므로 제일 먼저 오고 (A)의 'Ginger tea'가 (B)의 'hot tea'의 예에 해당하므로 (B) 다음에 (A)가 이어지고, (A)에서 '한국인이 자주 마시는 것'을 소개한 다음에 (C)에서 '다른 나라 사람들은 감기에 걸렸을 때 무엇을 마시거나 먹을지 알아보자'고 해야 하므로 (A) 다음에 (C)가 와야 한다. 그러므로 (B)-(A)-(C)의 순서가 적절하다.

17 ①, ②, ③, ⑤: '고골모골'

18 이 글은 '러시아와 동유럽에서는 사람들이 아픈 사람들뿐만 아니라 건강한 사람들도 고골모골이라는 후식을 먹는다.'는 내용의 글이므로, 주제로는 ③번 '러시아와 동유럽에서 아플 때나 건강할 때나 인기 있는 후식인 고골모골'이 적절하다. ② relieve: 없애[덜어] 주다, ⑤ therapy: 치료, 요법

19 이 글은 '사람들이 감기에 걸렸을 때 무엇을 마시거나 먹는지'에 관해 알아보려는 글이므로, 제목으로는 ③번 '당신은 감기에 걸렸을 때 무엇을 마시거나 먹는가?'가 적절하다.

20 생강차는 '특별한 맛'을 가지고 있다.

21 try+동명사: ~해 보다, ~을 시도하다

22 이 글은 '고골모골을 만드는 방법'에 관한 글이므로, 제목으로는 ②번 '고골모골을 만드는 방법'이 적절하다.

01 take off → put on

02 Ginger tea is something people in Korea often drink

03 (A) warms   (B) throat   **04** where

05 chopped onion in milk   **06** this simple drink is

07 be added

08 While people in Korea and Finland look for drinks when they are sick

09 They usually make it with chicken and vegetables

10 (1) trying   (2) Why don't you

11 Ingredients

12 the egg and the honey

13 tasting → taste

14 *Gogol-mogol* is popular as a dessert for healthy people as well as good for people with a cold.

01 감기에 걸리면 따뜻함을 유지하려고 아마도 옷을 '더 입을 것'이라고 하는 것이 적절하다. 그러므로 take off(옷을 벗다)를 put on(옷을 입다)으로 바꾸는 것이 적절하다.

02 'something' 다음에 목적격 관계대명사 'that'이 생략되었다.

03 그것은 여러분의 몸을 '따뜻하게 하고' '목' 통증을 완화하는 데 도움을 준다.

04 선행사가 'Finland'이므로, 장소를 나타내는 관계부사 'where'를 쓰는 것이 적절하다.

05 '우유에 넣은 잘게 썬 양파'를 가리킨다.

06 This simple drink를 '종속절의 주어'로 쓰고, to부정사는 시제에 맞춰 '종속절의 동사'로 바꿔 쓰는 것이 적절하다.

07 먹기 전에 소금과 후추가 '넣어지는' 것이므로 수동태로 쓰는 것이 적절하다.

08 when 다음에 'they[people in Korea and Finland]are'가 생략되어 있다. 부사절의 주어가 주절의 주어와 같고 뒤에 be동사가 나오면 '주어+be동사'를 생략할 수 있다.

09 They 대신 Many people in America를 써도 적절하다.

10 Why not 동사원형? = How about ~ing? = Why don't you 동사원형?: '~하는 게 어때?'(제안하는 표현)

11 '필요한 것'은 '요리재료'로 바꿔 쓰는 것이 적절하다. ingredient: (특히 요리 등의) 재료[성분]

12 '달걀과 꿀'을 가리킨다.

13 사역동사 make의 목적격보어로 '원형부정사'를 써야 하므로 tasting을 taste로 고치는 것이 적절하다.

14 not only A but also B = B as well as A: A뿐만 아니라 B도

01 whereas 02 ② 03 ①

04 You need to breathe through the nose, not through the mouth.

05 ②

06 Pardon? / I beg your pardon? / Pardon me?

07 It is from India.

08 ④ 09 ⑤ 10 ② 11 ③

12 ⑤ 13 ③, ⑤ 14 ①, ③ 15 ④

16 ② 17 ② 18 ⑤

19 chicken soup

20 a bowl of chicken soup 21 ① 22 served

23 to make it taste better 24 ③

25 The chopped tomato and some water should be mixed in a pan first.

26 ④

01 blend(섞다)와 compound(혼합하다, 섞어서 만들다)는 유의어 관계에 있는 단어들이다. 따라서 while과 whereas는 모두 '반면에'라는 뜻을 가진 유의어 관계의 단어들이다.

02 ②에서 사용된 desert는 '사막'이라는 뜻이며, '후식'이라는 뜻을 가진 단어는 dessert이다.

03 주어진 문장에서 warm은 '(날씨, 온도가) 따뜻한'이라는 뜻으로 사용되었다. ①에서 역시 같은 의미로 사용되었다. ②,③,⑤는 '따뜻하다, 따뜻하게 하다', ④는 '(색깔이) 따뜻한'이라는 뜻이다.

04 breathe through ~를 통해서 숨쉬다

05 '어떤 것 안에 혹은 위에, 혹은 하나의 용기에서 다른 용기로 흐르다'라는 뜻의 영영풀이는 pour(붓다, 따르다)를 가리킨다.

06 'Could you say that again?'은 '다시 말해 주세요.'라는 뜻으로 상대방에게 했던 말을 반복해달라고 요청할 때 사용하는 표현이다.

07 위 대화의 마지막 부분에 G가 말했듯이, rasmalai는 인도에서 온 전통 음식이다.

08 'Could you say that again?'은 '다시 말해 주세요.'라는 뜻으로 상대방에게 했던 말을 반복해달라고 요청할 때 사용하는 표현이다.

09 문맥상 빈칸에는 상대방에게 전통 음식 추천을 부탁하는 말이 들어가야 한다. 그러나 ⑤ 'Can I make a recommendation for ~?'는 '제가 추천을 해도 되겠습니까?'라는 뜻으로 상대방에게 추천을 제안하는 표현이다.

10 '나는 한국 음식에 대해 잘 알지 못해.'라는 문장은 대화의 문맥상 한국 음식을 추천해달라는 말 앞인 ②에 오는 것이 가장 적절하다.

11 ③ G가 한국 음식을 먹어본 적이 있는가?(Has G ever tried any Korean food before?)라는 질문에 대한 대답은 위 대화

12 G는 매운 음식을 좋아하고 한국 음식을 먹어 보고 싶다고 말했다. 따라서 G의 심정으로 가장 적절한 것은 ⑤ excited (신난, 흥분한)이다.

13 ③ 'not only A but also B'는 등위접속사이므로 not only 뒤에 명사가 오면, but also 뒤에도 명사에 해당하는 단어가 와야 한다. ⑤ not only가 문두에 와서 주어인 Victor가 아닌 동사 was를 강조하고 있으므로, '도치'가 일어나야 한다. 'Not only was Victor good at ~'이 적절하다.

14 ①, ③ 'Both A and B' 또는 'Either A or B'를 쓰는 것이 적절하다. ①은 or를 and로 고치고, ③은 Either를 Both로 고치는 것이 더 좋은데, 그 반대로 either에 맞춰 고쳐 줄 경우에는 동사들도 모두 is[was]로 바꿔야 하기 때문이다.

15 'Sarah는 그 뉴스를 믿었지만, 반면에 그녀의 딸은 그것을 믿지 않았다.'는 문장이다. '대조'의 역할을 하는 접속사 while이 쓰인 ④가 적절하다.

16 'Harrison은 회사에서 해고를 당했던 반면, 다른 사람들은 직장이 있어서, 생계를 꾸려나갈 수 있었다.'는 문장이다. '대조'의 역할을 하는 접속사 while이 쓰인 ②가 적절하며, ⑤의 during은 전치사이기 때문에, 접속사 자리에 쓸 수 없다.

17 ⓐ와 ②: 관계부사, ①, ④, ⑤: [장소·방향·도착점] 어디에[로] (의문부사), ③: 부사절을 이끄는 접속사

18 이 단순한 음료(양파 우유)는 감기에 좋다. too ~ to: so ~ that ... cannot

19 '닭고기 수프'를 가리킨다.

20 한국 사람들과 핀란드 사람들과는 달리, 미국의 많은 사람들은 아플 때 '닭고기 수프'를 찾는다.

21 ⓐ be made with: ~으로 만들어지다, with 다음에는 재료가 온다. be made from: 화학적 변화가 일어날 때 사용, ⓑ as a dessert: 후식으로

22 후식으로 '제공될 때'라고 해야 하므로 When it is served에서 it is를 생략하고 'served'로 쓰는 것이 적절하다.

23 목적을 나타내는 to부정사를 쓰고, '사역동사 make+목적어+동사원형'의 형식으로 쓰는 것이 적절하다. taste+형용사: ~한 맛이 나다

24 '쌀'은 '인도의 토마토 수프'를 만드는 재료에 속하지 않는다.

25 먼저 잘게 썬 토마토'와 '약간의 물'이 팬에서 섞여야 한다.

26 not A but B: A가 아니라 B, not only/just/simply/merely A but (also) B = not only/just/simply/merely A but B as well = B as well as A = Besides A, B: A뿐만 아니라 B도

01 ①

02 (1) a bottle of   (2) is good for   (3) as well as

03 many places people want to visit in Sydney

04 We recommend visiting the Rocks Markets

05 ③

06 I would recommend cooking something for him.

07 It's easy to make and it's delicious.   08 ④

09 ⑤   10 traditional   11 ①   12 ⑤

13 ③   14 ①   15 ⑤   16 ③

17 Ginger tea is something that people in Korea often drink.

18 ginger tea   19 recipe   20 ②   21 ④

22 called   23 (A) to make   (B) thick   (C) healthy

24 it is usually served cold or at room temperature

---

01 '열의 결과로 액체에서 기체로 변하다'라는 영영풀이가 가리키는 것은 ① boil(끓다, 끓이다)이다.

02 (1) a bottle of ~ 한 병 (2) be good for ~에 좋다 (3) A as well as B B뿐만 아니라 A도

03 대명사 them은 앞서 언급한 복수 명사를 가리킨다. 이 대화에서는 화자가 말한 시드니에 있는 '당신이 방문하고 싶어 할 많은 장소'(many places you will want to visit)를 가리킨다.

04 recommend는 목적어로 동명사를 취한다. 따라서 recommend to visit이 아니라 recommend visiting이라고 써야 한다.

05 위 글의 중반에 화자는 the Rocks Markets에서 예술 작품, 옷, 책 그리고 많은 다른 것을 살 수 있다고 했으며 그곳에서 지역 음식 역시 먹을 수 있다고 언급했다.

06 'How about ~?'는 상대방에게 추천해 줄 때 쓸 수 있는 표현으로, 'What about ~?', 'I recommend ~.', 'I'd recommend ~.', 'Try ~.' 등으로 대체할 수 있다.

07 easy to make 만들기 쉬운

08 ④ 'B의 아빠가 가장 좋아하는 음식은 무엇인가?'에 대한 대답은 위 대화에서 언급 되지 않았다.

09 (A) tried는 '~ 해 보다, 먹어 보다, 시도해 보다'라는 의미로 사용되었다. ⑤ '자기 전에 아기를 너무 흥분시키지 않도록 해라.'라는 문장에서 try는 '노력하다, 애쓰다'라는 의미로 사용되었다.

10 tradition의 형용사형이 알맞다.

11 'Could you recommend ~?'는 '~를 추천해 주시겠어요?'라는 뜻으로 상대방에게 추천해달라고 요청할 때 사용하는 표현이다.

12 but also 뒤에 형용사 generous가 있으므로, 부사 truly(진심으로, 진정으로)는 적절하지 않다. 나머지는 모두 형용사들이다.

13 not only 뒤에 형용사가 나왔으므로, 형용사 역할이 아닌 것을

찾는다. ③ acts는 동사이다.

14 (A) '수미는 오래 걸었기 때문에, 너무 피곤했다.' (B) '그 쇼를 보고 있던 중에, 나는 무대 뒤에서 무엇인가가 우는 소리를 들을 수 있었다.' (C) '그는 낚시하러 가는 것을 좋아했던 반면에, 그의 아내는 낚시를 몹시 싫어했다.' 등에 적합한 부사절 접속사를 찾는다.

15 접속사 while은 '~하는 동안', '~하는 반면에' 등으로 쓰인다. ①~④ 모두 '~하는 동안'의 의미로 사용되었고, ⑤는 어떤 의미로도 어색하다. If 또는 When으로 고칠 경우, '조금이라도 필요한 것이 있다면, 어느 때든 전화하시오.'라는 의미가 된다.

16 catch/get/have/take a cold = come down with a cold: 감기에 걸리다, catch/get/take/ cold처럼 a를 생략할 수도 있다. ③ have a cough: 기침이 나다

17 'something' 다음에 목적격 관계대명사 'that'이 생략되었다.

18 '생강차'를 가리킨다.

19 recipe: 요리법, 조리법, 재료의 목록과 어떤 것을 요리하는 법을 말해주는 일련의 지시

20 이 글은 '미국의 많은 사람들은 따뜻한 닭고기 수프 한 그릇이 부은 목과 막힌 코에 좋다고 믿으면서 아플 때 닭고기 수프를 원한다'는 내용의 글이므로, 제목으로는 ②번 '미국 사람들은 아플 때 무엇을 원하는가?'가 적절하다.

21 요리 도중에 소금과 후추를 넣는 것이 아니라, 소금과 후추는 '먹기 전'에 넣기도 한다.

22 '고골모골이라는 후식'이라고 해야 하므로, 과거분사 called로 쓰는 것이 적절하다.

23 (A) '그것을 더 맛있게 하기 위해'라고 해야 하므로 to make가 적절하다. (B) '진한' 요구르트라고 해야 하므로 thick이 적절하다. thick: (액체가) 진한, 걸쭉한, huge: (크기·양·정도가) 막대한, 거대한, (C) '건강한' 사람들이라고 해야 하므로 healthy가 적절하다. healthy: 건강한, 건강에 좋은, healthful: 건강에 좋은

24 빈도부사는 be동사, 조동사 뒤, 일반동사 앞에 위치하는 것이 보편적이다. at room temperature: 실온으로

01 G's favorite Korean traditional drink is Maesil-tea.

02 He describes that his favorite drink is cool and sweet.

03 who → that[which]

04 (A) not only[just, simply, merely] (B) but also

05 (1) believe → believes   (2) is → are

   (3) have → has   (4) excited → exciting

   (5) is → are

21

06 (1) While he talks a lot, he acts little.
   (2) While Paula was cooking, her uncle visited her house.
07 (A) clothes   (B) With   (C) other
08 to reduce
09 (A) hot tea   (B) reduce the pain
10 looks → looks like
11 serve
12 They often drink a cup of warm *gogol-mogol*.

01 대화 시작에서 G는 자신이 가장 좋아하는 한국 전통 음료가 매실차라고 밝히고 있다.
02 B에 따르면 그가 좋아하는 한국 전통 음료인 식혜가 시원하고 달콤하다고 언급했다.
03 위 대화에서 B의 말에서 poke가 하와이에서 인기 있는 샐러드라고 말한다. 이때 관계대명사 who가 쓰였는데, 이는 선행사가 사람일 때만 쓰일 수 있다. 따라서 관계대명사 that[which]으로 고쳐야 한다.
04 빈칸이 포함된 문장은 '그것은 맛도 좋고 매우 건강하다'라는 뜻의 문장이다. not only[just, simply, merely] A but also B A뿐만 아니라 B도
05 (1), (5) but also 뒤의 주어에 일치시킨다. (1)은 Julie가 (5)는 the stores가 주어이다. (2) 'both A and B'가 주어일 때는 항상 복수 동사가 온다. (3) 'either A or B'는 동사와 가까운 주어에 수를 일치시킨다. (4) 노래가 사람의 흥미를 유발하는 것이므로 excited가 아니라 현재분사형의 형용사 exciting을 쓰는 것이 적절하다.
06 (1) 3인칭 단수 현재시제임을 유의한다. (2) 과거진행시제와 과거시제에 유의한다.
07 (A) '옷'을 더 입을 것이라고 해야 하므로 clothes가 적절하다. clothes: 옷, 의복, cloths: 옷감들, 직물의 종류를 나타낼 때의 복수 형태, (B) 특별한 맛과 '함께'라고 해야 하므로 With가 적절하다. (C) 'another' 뒤에는 단수 명사를 써야 하므로 other가 적절하다.
08 help+원형부정사 = help+to부정사
09 사람들이 감기에 걸릴 때 그들 중 몇몇은 생강차와 같은 '따뜻한 차'를 마시는 것을 좋아한다. 그것은 특별한 맛을 가지고 있고 몸을 따뜻하게 해주면서 목 '통증을 완화하는 데' 도움을 준다.
10 'looks' 뒤에 '명사인 yogurt'가 나오기 때문에, 'looks'를 'looks like'로 고치는 것이 적절하다. looks+형용사, looks like+명사: ~처럼 보이다
11 people[they]을 주어로 하여 능동태로 고치는 것이 적절하다.
12 러시아와 동유럽에서, 사람들은 목이 아플 때 종종 '따뜻한 고골모골 한 잔'을 마신다.

[모범답안]
01 (1) While Hana wears glasses, Duna does not.
   (2) Hana likes singing while Duna likes dancing.
   (3) While Hana got an A in math, Duna got a C.
02 (A) chop   (B) pour some water
   (C) for ten minutes   (D) to cool down
   (E) blend it   (F) some black pepper and salt

01 표의 단어들을 적절히 조합하여 어법에 맞게 영작한 답이면 된다.

01 ③   02 ①
03 (1) added   (2) held   (3) mix   04 ⑤
05 They're sweet and made with rice cake powder.
06 Could you recommend something?
07 It's made with lots of vegetables, beef and anegg over rice.
08 ②, ⑤   09 (C) – (B) – (A)   10 ⑤
11 ②   12 ④   13 ①   14 ③
15 ④   16 ④
17 (1) broke the speed limit, but alsomade an illegal
   (2) a guitar, while I wasinterested in
18 Onion milk 19 ⑤   20 ②
21 They can add salt and pepper before eating.
22 ①   23 ⑤   24 ④   25 ③

01 '표준 척도를 기준으로 한 물체의 온기 측정'은 ③ temperature(온도, 기온)를 가리킨다.
02 '우리가 집을 비운 사이에 도둑이 들었다.'라는 문장에서 들어갈 것으로 가장 적절한 것은 ① while(~하는 동안, 반면에)이다.
03 (1) add 더하다, 첨가하다 (2) hold 열다, 개최하다 (3) mix 섞다
04 'Could you say that again?'은 '다시 말해 주세요.'라는 뜻으로 상대방에게 했던 말을 반복해달라고 요청할 때 사용하는 표현이다. 따라서 ⑤ 'G에게 했던 말을 반복해달라고 요청하기 위해'이다.
05 be made with ~로 만들어지다 / rice cake powder 쌀가루
06 상대방에게 추천해달라고 요청할 때 '~를 추천해 주시겠어요?'라는 뜻을 가진 'Could you recommend ~?'를 사용할 수 있다.
07 be made with ~로 만들어지다 / lots of ~ 많은 ~
08 ② G가 B에게 한국 음식을 먹어 보라고 하는 것은 옳지 않다. ⑤ G는 매운 음식을 좋아한다고 말한다.
09 (C)가 rasmalai를 먹어 본 적이 있는지 물어보자 (B)에서 상

대방이 다시 말해 달라고 요청하며 (A)에서 다시 반복하여 말해 주면서 덧붙여 설명해 주는 순서로 이어지는 것이 가장 자연스럽다.

10 주어진 문장의 대명사 They가 무엇을 가리키는지 아는 것이 중요하다. 이때 복수형 대명사 they가 fantastic하다고 말했으므로, 문맥상 the onion rings를 가리킨다.

11 ② '누가 파티에 초대될 것인가?'라는 질문에 대한 대답은 위 대화에서 언급되어 있지 않다.

12 ④ '제 여동생을 위한 책을 추천해 주시겠어요?'(Could you recommend a good book for my sister?)라는 질문에 B가 '다시 말해 주시겠어요? 이 이야기는 감동적이에요.'(Pardon me? The story is touching.)라는 대답은 문맥상 어색하다.

13 'not only ~ but also' 구문의 영작이다. delicious와 too much가 병렬이 된 ①이 정답이다. ④는 Not only를 문두로 보내 ①을 도치한 문장인데, too much 뒤의 is가 없다면, 옳은 문장이 될 수 있다.

14 not only와 but also 뒤의 동사가 병렬이 되므로, 조동사 can이 동시에 동사를 받는다. ①에서 solves의 s를 빼면 정답이 될 수 있다. ①을 도치시킨 문장이 ③이다. 동사를 받는 Not only가 문두로 나오면, 주어와 동사는 '도치'된다. 원형동사 solve가 바르게 나왔다. ⑤는 but also 뒤에 he를 다시 썼기 때문에, 앞의 can을 받을 수 없으므로 부적절하다.

15 접속사 while은 '~하는 동안', '~하는 반면에' 등으로 쓰인다. ①, ②, ③, ⑤ 모두 '~하는 반면에'의 의미로 사용되었고, ④는 '~하는 동안'이다.

16 ①, ②, ③, ⑤ 모두 '~하는 동안'의 의미로 사용되었고, ④는 '~하는 반면에'이다. 'Walter의 여자친구 Celine은 한국사를 매우 좋아하는 반면, Walter는 그렇지 않다.'

17 (1) 그 차는 속도 제한을 위반했을 뿐 아니라, 불법 차선 변경도 했다. (2) 그녀는 나에게 기타를 팔려고 했는데, 반면 나는 다른 악기들에 관심이 있었다.

18 '양파 우유'를 가리킨다.

19 '왜 양파 우유가 감기에 좋은지'는 알 수 없다. ① It is very cold. ② They drink a cup of onion milk. ③ I need onion and milk. ④ It is to put chopped onion in milk and boil it over low heat for half an hour.

20 ⓐ: 대조를 나타내는 접속사, '~인 반면에', ③ 그렇지 않으면, ④ ~이 아닌 한, 만약 ~이 아니면, ⑤ ~하는 한

21 막연한 사람을 나타내는 They를 주어로 하여 능동태로 고치는 것이 적절하다.

22 ⓐ와 ①: 부사적 용법, ②, ④, ⑤: 명사적 용법, ③: 형용사적 용법

23 고골모골은 감기에 걸린 사람들에게 좋을 뿐만 아니라 '건강한 사람들의 후식으로도 인기가 있다.'

24 ⓐ 음식들에 '대해' 알아본 것이므로 about이 적절하다. ⓑ pour A into B: A를 B에 붓다

25 (A)와 ③: (음식의 양이) 돌아가다, ③ 이 한 접시면 배고픈 사람 네 명에게 돌아간다[4인분이 된다]. ① (특히 다른 것을 구할 수 없을 때 특정한 용도로) 쓰일 수 있다[적합하다], ② ~에 봉사하다, ~을 섬기다, ④ ~에 근무[복무]하다, ⑤ (상점에서) 손님을 접대하다, serve behind a counter: 점원으로 일하다

23

A Christmas Miracle

교과서
Reading

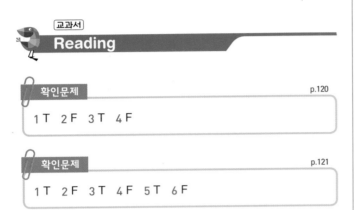

1 T   2 F   3 T   4 F

1 T   2 F   3 T   4 F   5 T   6 F

교과서 확인학습 A   p.122~123

01 Miracle	02 the first year
03 were facing, had done	04 cold and wet
05 all the more so	06 was heard coming
07 carol	08 going on
09 might be a trick	10 boldly looked out of
11 One by one	12 What
13 lit with lanterns	
14 one Christmas song after another	
15 by also singing	16 made them forget
17 came out from	
18 whose aim, exchange greetings	
19 in several months	20 It truly was
21 came	22 on both sides
23 in the no man's land	24 such as
25 sang carols	26 exchanged addresses
27 unbelievable, about	28 between the two lines
29 had bike races	30 were at war
31 Here we were	
32 like us, waiting to welcome	

교과서 확인학습 B   p.124~125

1 A Christmas Miracle

2 It was Christmas Eve in 1914, the first year of World War I.

3 English soldiers were facing German soldiers from their trenches as they had done for the last few months.

4 The trenches were cold and wet.

5 The soldiers were tired and missed their home, all the more so because it was Christmas.

6 Suddenly, a familiar song was heard coming from the German trenches.

7 It was a Christmas carol!

8 What's going on?

9 It might be a trick to make them come out of the trenches.

10 A few English soldiers boldly looked out of their trenches.

11 One by one, other soldiers followed their example.

12 What they saw was a sight they never expected.

13 Along the German trenches, Christmas trees were standing lit with lanterns!

14 The German soldiers sang one Christmas song after another.

15 The English soldiers began to answer by also singing Christmas songs.

16 The warm lights and the Christmas carols made them forget they were on the front line.

17 Then a shout came out from the German side: "Happy Christmas! You no shoot, we no shoot!"

18 Soon, soldiers whose aim had been to kill each other just a few hours before began to exchange greetings.

19 For the first time in several months, the soldiers were able to spend a night in peace.

20 It truly was a silent night.

21 Christmas morning came.

22 Soldiers on both sides put down their weapons and came out of their trenches.

23 They met in the no man's land between their trenches and shook hands.

24 They exchanged small gifts such as wine and cake.

25 They sang carols together.

26 Some even exchanged addresses and played football.

27 This unbelievable Christmas Day was written about in letters English soldiers sent home.

28 One soldier wrote, "On Christmas Day, English and German soldiers met between the two lines

and had talks."

29 We also had bike races."

30 Another wrote, "We didn't think that we were at war.

31 Here we were, enemy talking to enemy.

32 They were like us, with mothers, with friends, with wives who were waiting to welcome their men home again."

서술형 실전문제
p.126~127

01 unfamiliar 02 for the first time

03 (1) come out (2) one by one (3) have a talk

04 (1) They had to think of a trick to get past the teacher.

(2) The early morning street was silent.

(3) Lana shares a house with three other students.

05 (1) They fell in love with each other.

(2) You have to follow the example of great scientists.

(3) The marathon runners arrived at the finish line one after another.

06 World War One 또는 the First World War

07 had done 08 Because it was Christmas.

09 forgetting → forget 10 whose

11 (A) singing Christmas songs (B) peacefully

01 begin(시작하다)와 end(끝나다)는 반의어 관계에 있는 단어들이다. 따라서 familiar(익숙한, 친숙한)과 반의어 관계에 있는 단어는 unfamiliar(익숙지 못한)이다.

02 for the first time 처음으로

03 (1) come out 나오다 (2) one by one 차례로 (3) have a talk 이야기하다

04 (1) trick 속임수 (2) silent 고요한 (3) share 공유하다, 나누다

05 (1) each other 서로 (2) follow one's example ~의 사례를 따르다, 모범으로 삼다 (3) one after another 잇따라서

06 제일차 세계 대전은 World War부터 읽으면 'I'을 'One'으로 읽고, 'I'을 먼저 읽으면 'I'을 'the First'로 읽는 것이 적절하다.

07 과거에 일어났던 일보다 더 앞서 일어난 일에 대해 언급하는 것이므로, 과거완료 'had done'으로 쓰는 것이 적절하다.

08 글의 마지막 문장에서 그 이유를 설명하고 있다.

09 '사역동사 make+목적어+목적격 보어' 구문에서 목적격 보어에는 '동사원형'을 쓰는 것이 적절하다.

10 소유격 관계대명사 'whose'가 적절하다.

11 독일 군인들이 크리스마스 캐럴을 연이어 불렀을 때. 영국 군인들도 '크리스마스 캐럴을 부르며' 화답하기 시작했다. 몇 달 만에 처음으로, 군인들은 '평화롭게' 밤을 지낼 수 있었다. in peace = peacefully

단원별 예상문제
p.128~131

01 quiet 02 ③

03 Although it is small, the kitchen is well designed.

04 ② 05 such as 06 ⑤

07 English soldiers 08 ②, ④

09 They were facing the German soldiers.

10 ② 11 ③ 12 ③

13 soldiers whose aim had been to kill each other just a few hours before began to exchange greetings

14 ⑤ 15 changed → exchanged

16 ⑤ 17 ②

18 (A) unbelievable (B) between (C) like 19 ④

20 English soldiers heard a familiar song coming from the German trenches

21 English soldiers

22 looked out of their trenches

01 entire(전체의)와 whole(전체의, 모든)은 유사한 뜻을 가진 단어들이다. 따라서 silent(고요한)와 유사한 뜻을 가진 quiet(조용한)이다.

02 ③ aim은 '목표'라는 뜻이 아니라 '~를 겨냥하다'라는 뜻으로 사용되었다.

03 although 비록 ~이긴 하지만

04 주어진 문장에서 light는 '불을 붙이다'라는 뜻으로 사용되었다. ①, ③ 빛, ④, ⑤ 가벼운

05 such as ~와 같은

06 '보이는 어떤 사물이나 볼 가치가 있는 것'이라는 뜻을 가진 영영풀이가 가리키는 것은 ⑤ sight(광경)이다.

07 '영국 군인들'을 가리킨다.

08 ⓑ와 ②, ④: 계속 용법, ①, ⑤: 경험 용법, ③ 완료 용법

09 1914년의 크리스마스 이브에 영국 군인들이 그들의 참호에서 대치하고 있었던 것은 '독일 군인들'이었다.

10 (B)에서 그들이 무인 지대에서 만났다고 한 다음에 (A)에서 그들이 작은 선물도 교환했다고 해야 하므로 (B) 다음에 (A)가 이어지고 (C)의 'even exchanged addresses'는 (A)의 'exchanged small gifts'에 이어 '심지어 주소를 교환하기도

했다'는 것이므로 (A) 다음에 (C)가 와야 한다. 그러므로 (B)-
(A)-(C)의 순서가 적절하다.

11 'what'은 선행사를 포함하고 있는 관계대명사로 'The thing
which[that]'로 풀어 쓸 수 있다.

12 주어진 문장의 also singing Christmas songs에 주목한다.
③번 앞 문장에서 '독일 군인들이 크리스마스 캐럴을 연이어 부
른 것'에 '영국 군인들이 크리스마스 캐럴을 부르며 화답한 것'이
므로 ③번이 적절하다.

13 'whose'는 소유격 관계대명사로, 사람 또는 사물을 선행사로
취하며 생략할 수 없다.

14 '몇 달 동안'이 아니라, '몇 달 만에 처음으로', 군인들은 평화롭
게 밤을 지낼 수 있었다

15 몇몇은 심지어 주소를 '교환하기도' 했다고 해야 하므로,
changed를 exchanged로 고치는 것이 적절하다. change: 바
꾸다, exchange: 교환하다

16 '영국 군인들과 독일 군인들이 얼마나 오래 축구를 했는지'는 대
답할 수 없다. ① They met on Christmas morning. ②
They put down their weapons and came out of their
trenches. ③ They met in the no man's land. ④ They
exchanged small gifts such as wine and cake, and
some even exchanged addresses.

17 ⓐ 날짜 앞에는 'on'을 쓰는 것이 적절하다. On Christmas
Day: 크리스마스에, ⓑ be at war: 전쟁[교전] 중이다

18 (A) 이 '믿을 수 없는' 크리스마스라고 해야 하므로
unbelievable이 적절하다. unbelievable: 믿을 수 없는,
(B) '두 경계선 사이에서' 만났으므로 between이 적절하다.
among: (셋이상이 관련된 분배·선택 시) ~ 간에, ~ 중에서,
between: (둘) 사이에, (C) 뒤에 'us'가 나오므로 like가 적절
하다. alike: 비슷한(뒤에 목적어를 가질 수 없고, 서술적 용법
으로만 쓰임), like는 전치사로서 뒤에 목적어를 가진다.

19 '크리스마스 후에 영국 군인들과 독일 군인들이 다시 싸웠을
때 그들이 어떻게 느꼈는지'는 알 수 없다. ① It was written
about in letters English soldiers sent home. ② They
met between the two lines. ③ They had talks and bike
races. ⑤ They thought the German soldiers were like
them, with mothers, with friends, with wives.

20 문장의 주어인 a familiar song을 목적어로 바꾸고, 주격보어
coming from the German trenches를 목적격보어로 바꿔
서 고치는 것이 적절하다.

21 '영국 군인들'을 가리킨다.

22 '차례차례 다른 군인들도 앞사람을 따랐다'는 것은 '다른 군인들
도 용감하게 자신들의 참호 밖을 내다보았다'는 뜻이다. one by
one = one after another: 연달아, 차례로

교과서 파헤치기

Lesson 7

단어 TEST Step 1   p.02

01 주의 깊은, 조심스러운, 세심한	02 판유리
03 놀랍게도	04 바삭한	05 아마, 어쩌면
06 삼키다	07 결과	08 돌리다, 비틀다
09 막다	10 환상적인	11 수리하다
12 압력	13 알아채다, 의식하다	
14 수증기, 김	15 끓기; 끓이다	
16 주의 깊게, 조심스럽게	17 죽음
18 비상사태	19 양, 총계	20 지붕
21 균형; 균형을 잡다	22 호흡, 숨	23 특히
24 소파, 긴 의자	25 필수적인	26 최근에
27 ~ 모양의	28 숨기다, 숨다	29 뚜껑
30 안개; 수증기가 서리다	31 회사, 동료
32 ~을 야기하다; 원인	33 생산물, 상품
34 유용한, 도움이 되는	35 점점 커지다
36 A가 ~하는 것을 방지하다	37 끓어 넘치다
38 안개로 흐려지다, 김이 서리다	39 내보내다
40 주위를 둘러보다	41 ~로 구성되다	42 ~의 결과
43 거쳐 지나가다, 통과하다	

단어 TEST Step 2   p.03

01 surprisingly	02 twist	03 hide
04 crispy	05 notice	06 pane
07 hidden	08 breathing	09 swallow
10 couch	11 helpful	12 repair
13 death	14 recently	15 shaped
16 product	17 emergency	18 amount
19 pressure	20 lid	21 carefully
22 boil	23 especially	24 prevent
25 balance	26 fog	27 careful
28 necessary	29 result	30 perhaps
31 cause	32 company	33 roof
34 steam	35 boil over	36 let out
37 the result of ~	38 look out	39 pass through
40 look around	41 keep A from -ing	
42 be made up of	43 in an emergency	

단어 TEST Step 3   p.04

1 recently, 최근에   2 swallow, 삼키다

3 helpful, 유용한, 도움이 되는   4 notice, 알아채다, 의식하다

5 normally, 보통, 보통 때는   6 emergency, 비상사태

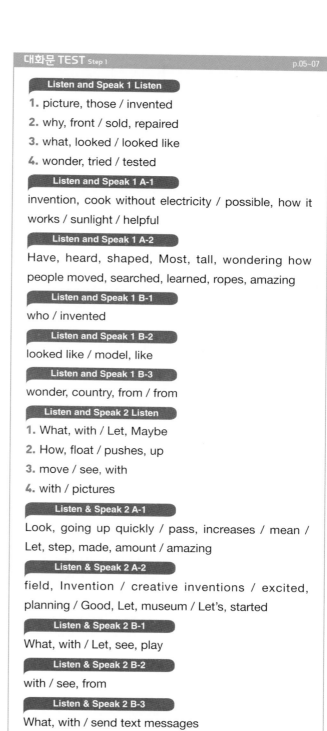

7 necessary, 필수적인   8 couch, 소파, 긴 의자

9 repair, 수리하다   10 roof, 지붕   11 breathing, 호흡, 숨

12 especially, 특히, 특별히   13 prevent, 막다

14 amount, 양, 총계   15 product, 생산물, 상품

16 balance, 균형을 잡다

대화문 TEST Step 1   p.05~07

Listen and Speak 1 Listen

1. picture, those / invented
2. why, front / sold, repaired
3. what, looked / looked like
4. wonder, tried / tested

Listen and Speak 1 A-1

invention, cook without electricity / possible, how it works / sunlight / helpful

Listen and Speak 1 A-2

Have, heard, shaped, Most, tall, wondering how people moved, searched, learned, ropes, amazing

Listen and Speak 1 B-1

who / invented

Listen and Speak 1 B-2

looked like / model, like

Listen and Speak 1 B-3

wonder, country, from / from

Listen and Speak 2 Listen

1. What, with / Let, Maybe
2. How, float / pushes, up
3. move / see, with
4. with / pictures

Listen & Speak 2 A-1

Look, going up quickly / pass, increases / mean / Let, step, made, amount / amazing

Listen & Speak 2 A-2

field, Invention / creative inventions / excited, planning / Good, Let, museum / Let's, started

Listen & Speak 2 B-1

What, with / Let, see, play

Listen & Speak 2 B-2

with / see, from

Listen & Speak 2 B-3

What, with / send text messages

Real-Life Zone

these / why, little holes / think, maybe, make, look tastier / possible, must, reasons / look, what / says during, through, thin / make, crispy / why

27

what, going / sounds, that, Saturdays, what they are / advertisement, Here / say / says / both, fantastic / call, what

invention competition / sounds / enter, ideas / when, competition is / from / wonder, have / talk, science

---

대화문 TEST Step 2   p.08~10

Listen and Speak 1 Listen

1. G: Look at this picture. I wonder who those men are.
   B: They're the Wright brothers. They invented the airplane.
2. G: I wonder why they are standing in front of the bicycle shop.
   B: They had a bicycle shop. They sold and repaired bicycles.
3. G: I wonder what the first plane looked like.
   B: Look! There is a model. It looked like a big bird.
4. G: I wonder where they first tried to fly their airplane.
   B: They tested their airplane on a hill in North Carolina.

Listen and Speak 1 A-1

B: Look at this invention. It can help us cook without electricity.
G: Is that possible? I wonder how it works.
B: It uses sunlight to cook food.
G: Wow. That would be really helpful when you go camping.

Listen and Speak 1 A-2

B: Hi, class. Have you ever heard about the Moai? They are tall, human-shaped stones in Chile. Most of the stones are four meters tall, but the tallest one is 20 meters tall. I was wondering how people moved them long ago. So I searched the Internet and learned that they used ropes. Isn't that amazing?

Listen and Speak 1 B-1

A: I wonder who those men are.
B: They're the Wright brothers. They invented the airplane.

Listen and Speak 1 B-2

A: I wonder what the first plane looked like.
B: Look! There is a model. It looked like a big bird.

Listen and Speak 1 B-3

A: I wonder what country they're from.
B: They're from the U.S.

Listen and Speak 2 Listen

1. G: What can we do with these VR glasses?
   B: Let me see.... Maybe we can play soccer.
2. B: How does the ball float in the air?
   G: Let me see.... I think air pushes the ball up.
3. G: How does this train start to move?
   B: Let me see.... I think you can move it with a smartphone app.
4. B: What can we do with this drone?
   G: Well, let me see.... Maybe we can take pictures from the sky.

Listen & Speak 2 A-1

G: Look at the number. It's going up quickly.
B: When people pass by, the number increases.
G: Oh, you're right. What does the number mean?
B: Let me see.... Oh, when people step on the floor, energy is made. It shows the amount of energy that is made.
G: Wow, that's amazing!

Listen & Speak 2 A-2

G: We're going on a field trip tomorrow to the Invention Museum.
B: I've heard that it has a lot of creative inventions.
G: That's why I'm so excited. How about planning the tour before we go?
B: Good idea. Let me see.... I have the school letter and a map of the museum.
G: Perfect. Let's get started.

Listen & Speak 2 B-1

A: What can we do with this VR glasses?
B: Let me see… We can play soccer.

Listen & Speak 2 B-2

A: What can we do with this drone?
B: Let me see… We can take pictures from the sky.

Listen & Speak 2 B-3

A: What can we do with the smart watch?
B: Let me see… We can send text messages.

Real-Life Zone

G: I like these crackers. They're really good.
B: Yeah, me, too. I wonder why crackers have these little holes in them.
G: I don't know. Let me think.... Um ... well ... maybe it's because the holes make the crackers look tastier.
B: That's possible, but there must be some other

reasons.

G: Let's look up crackers on the Internet and see what it says.

B: Okay. Oh, look at this.

G: It says during baking, steam comes out through the holes and that makes the crackers thin.

B: It also says that the holes make the crackers crispy.

G: Wow! So that's why they have holes!

Wrap Up 1-2

B: Hi, Kate. Today's Saturday, so what about going to the Einstein Science Park today?

G: That sounds like a good idea. I heard that they have special programs on Saturdays. I wonder what they are.

B: Let me see.... I saw an advertisement in the newspaper. Here it is.

G: What does it say?

B: It says that today they have two shows: the Smart Design Show and the International Drone Show in Einstein Hall 101.

G: They both sound fantastic.

B: I'll call them and ask what time they start.

Wrap Up 3~4

G: John, look. The school is having an invention competition.

B: Really? That sounds interesting.

G: Yeah. You should enter that. You always have great ideas.

B: Does it say when the competition is?

G: Let me see.... It says it's November 11. That's two weeks from today.

B: I wonder what I have to do to enter the competition.

G: It says here you should talk to Mr. Harrison, the science teacher.

본문 TEST Step 1   p.11~12

01 Hidden Holes

02 Think, hole, seen recently

03 Was, good, or, bad   04 If, hole, sock, bad

05 hole, for, button, good

06 There, holes everywhere   07 so, may, even notice

08 hidden, make, life safe   09 Take, pen

10 Look at, carefully   11 small hole, cap

12 why it is there   13 hole, help save lives

14 especially, put, like, in

15 Sometimes, even swallow

16 stop, breathing, cause death

17 famous, company, putting, hole

18 lets, pass through, lives

19 look around, helpful role

20 with, lid, perhaps, noticed 21 hole, too, safety

22 cooking, pressure, builds up

23 inside, boil over, hole

24 out, keeps, from coming   25 Have, ever been on

26 Wasn't it exciting, below

27 Surprisingly, there was, in

28 are made up of   29 in the middle pane

30 balances, air pressure

31 Without, little, break, emergency

32 prevents, from fogging up

33 more products, hidden holes

34 why it is there

35 result, careful, life safer

본문 TEST Step 2   p.13~14

01 Hidden   02 have seen recently

03 good, bad   04 in your sock

05 for a button   06 There, everywhere

07 so small, notice

08 well hidden, make your life safe

09 Take   10 Look at, carefully

11 a small hole   12 why it is there

13 help save lives   14 put, like, in

15 Sometimes, swallow them

16 stop their breathing, cause death

17 putting a small hole

18 lets, pass through, saved lives

19 look around, play a helpful role

20 with a lid, noticed, lid   21 for safety

22 When cooking, pressure, builds up

23 boil over

24 steam out, keeps, from coming

25 Have, been

26 Wasn't it exciting, look out

27 Surprisingly

28 are made up of   29 in the middle pane

30 balances, air pressure

31 Without, little hole, in an emergency

32 prevents, from fogging up, fantastic view

33 that have, hidden holes   34 why it is there

본문 TEST Step 3 p.15~16

1 숨겨진 구멍들

2 여러분이 최근에 본 구멍에 대해 생각해 보라.

3 그것은 좋은 구멍이었는가, 아니면 나쁜 구멍이었는가?

4 만약 그것이 여러분의 양말에 있는 구멍이었다면, 그것은 좋지 않은 것이었다.

5 만약 그것이 단추를 위해 셔츠에 있는 구멍이었다면, 그것은 좋은 것이었다.

6 구멍은 어디에나 있다.

7 어떤 것들은 너무 작아서 인지하지 못할 수도 있다.

8 그것들은 잘 숨겨져 있지만, 이 작은 구멍들 중 많은 것들이 매우 중요하고 여러분의 삶을 안전하게 해 준다.

9 펜을 꺼내라.

10 그것을 자세히 관찰해 보라.

11 뚜껑에 작은 구멍이 보이는가?

12 여러분은 왜 거기에 구멍이 있는지 아는가?

13 펜 뚜껑에 있는 구멍이 생명을 구하는 데 도움을 줄 수 있기 때문이다.

14 사람들, 특히 아이들은 종종 펜 뚜껑 같은 작은 것들을 그들의 입에 넣는다.

15 때때로 그들은 심지어 그것들을 삼키기도 한다.

16 이것은 그들의 호흡을 막고 죽음을 초래할 수도 있다.

17 유명한 펜 회사가 자사의 펜 뚜껑에 작은 구멍을 넣기 시작했다.

18 뚜껑에 있는 그 구멍은 공기를 통하게 해 주고 생명들을 구했다.

19 여러분이 주위를 둘러본다면, 여러분의 생활에 도움을 주는 다른 구멍들을 보게 될 것이다.

20 만약 여러분이 뚜껑 있는 냄비에 어떤 것을 요리해 본 적이 있다면, 아마도 여러분은 뚜껑에 작은 구멍이 있다는 것을 알아챘을 수도 있다.

21 이 구멍 역시 안전을 위해 존재한다.

22 뚜껑이 있는 냄비에 무언가를 요리할 때, 냄비 안쪽의 압력이 상승한다.

23 만약 뚜껑에 그 구멍이 없다면, 그 안의 물은 금방 끓어 넘칠 것이다.

24 그 구멍이 수증기를 나가게 해 주고 물이 밖으로 넘치는 것을 막아 준다.

25 비행기를 타 본 적이 있는가?

26 창밖을 내다보고 아래에 있는 세상을 보는 것이 신나지 않았는가?

27 놀랍게도, 여러분의 창문에는 작은 구멍이 하나 있었다.

28 비행기 창문은 세 개의 유리판으로 구성되어 있다.

29 그 중간 유리판에 구멍이 있다.

30 그것은 기압의 균형을 맞춰 준다.

31 이 작은 구멍이 없다면, 비행기 창문은 비상시에 깨질 수 있다.

32 그 구멍은 또한, 멋진 경치를 즐길 수 있도록 창문에 김이 서리는 것을 막아 준다.

33 숨겨진 작은 구멍들이 있는 더 많은 제품들이 있다.

34 앞으로, 여러분이 어떤 물건에서 작은 구멍을 본다면, 왜 그것이 거기에 있는지 자신에게 물어보라.

35 아마도 그것은 여러분의 삶을 더 안전하게 만들려는 사려 깊은 디자인의 결과일 것이다.

본문 TEST Step 4-Step 5 p.17~20

1 Hidden Holes

2 Think about a hole that you have seen recently.

3 Was it a good hole or a bad hole?

4 If it was a hole in your sock, it was bad.

5 If it was a hole in your shirt for a button, it was good.

6 There are holes everywhere.

7 Some are so small you may not even notice them.

8 They are well hidden, but many of these small holes are very important and make your life safe.

9 Take a pen.

10 Look at it carefully.

11 Do you see a small hole in the cap?

12 Do you know why it is there?

13 The hole in a pen cap can help save lives.

14 People, especially children, often put small things like pen caps in their mouths.

15 Sometimes they even swallow them.

16 This can stop their breathing and cause death.

17 A famous pen company started putting a small hole in their pen caps.

18 The hole in the cap lets air pass through and has saved lives.

19 If you look around, you will see other holes that play a helpful role in your life.

20 If you have ever cooked anything in a pot with a lid, perhaps you noticed a small hole in the lid.

21 This hole, too, is there for safety.

22 When cooking something in a pot with a lid, the pressure inside the pot builds up.

23 The water inside would quickly boil over if the lid did not have that hole.

24 The hole lets steam out and keeps the water from coming out.

25 Have you ever been on an airplane?

26 Wasn't it exciting to look out the window and see the world below?

27 Surprisingly, there was a small hole in your window.

28 Airplane windows are made up of three panes.

29 There is a hole in the middle pane.

30 It balances the air pressure.

31 Without this little hole, airplane windows might break in an emergency.

32 The hole also prevents the window from fogging up so that you can enjoy that fantastic view.

33 There are many more products that have small hidden holes.

34 In the future, when you see a little hole in something, ask yourself why it is there.

35 Maybe it is the result of a careful design to make your life safer.

구석구석지문 TEST Step 1
p.21

After You Read B

1. lets the air pass through, swallow
2. balances the air pressures
3. lets steam out, prevents, from boiling over

Work Together

1. Sweet Dream
2. helps people dream sweet dreams
3. have a sweet dream every night
4. select the type of dream, so that, while you are sleeping

Writing Workshop

1. Refrigerator
2. Can, imagine without
3. so that, keep food cool, fresh
4. invented, form of the refrigerator
5. developed through, has become a necessary part of modern life
6. If, did not have, would not be able to enjoy

구석구석지문 TEST Step 2
p.22

After You Read B

1. It lets the air pass through even when people swallow the pen cap.
2. It balances the air pressures.
3. It lets steam out and prevents the water in the pot from boiling over.

Work Together

1. Sweet Dream Helmet
2. This invention helps people dream sweet dreams.
3. If you use the Sweet Dream Helmet, you will have a sweet dream every night.
4. You can even select the type of dream you want to dream so that you can have different experiences while you are sleeping.

Writing Workshop

1. A Refrigerator
2. Can you imagine without a refrigerator?
3. We use it every day so that we can keep food cool and fresh.
4. In 1755, William Cullen invented the first form of the refrigerator.
5. After that, it developed through the years and has become a necessary part of modern life.
6. If we did not have refrigerators in today's world, we would not be able to enjoy ice cream on hot summer days.

단어 TEST Step 1 p.23

01 끓다, 끓이다 02 감동적인

03 따뜻하게 하다, 따뜻한 04 잘게 썰다

05 반면에, ~하는 동안에 06 제공하다

07 더하다, 첨가하다 08 섞다 09 생강

10 식히다 11 보물 12 맛

13 아픔, 통증 14 고루 잘 섞인, 매끄러운

15 열다, 개최하다 16 목구멍, 목 17 후추, 고추

18 온도, 기온 19 줄이다 20 녹다

21 지역의, 현지의 22 코가 막힌, 답답한 23 두꺼운, 걸쭉한

24 낮은 25 그대로 있다 26 약

27 해산물 28 추천하다 29 휘젓다

30 혼합물 31 아픈, 따가운 32 붓다, 따르다

33 섞다 34 요리법 35 A와 같은

36 ~로 만들어지다 37 알아내다, 발견하다

38 ~ 한 그릇 39 ~에 더하여, 게다가

40 ~와 다르다 41 A에게 B를 둘러보도록 안내하다

42 ~에 좋다 43 A뿐만 아니라 B도

단어 TEST Step 2 p.24

01 pour 02 recipe 03 cool

04 hold 05 add 06 blend

07 recommend 08 chop 09 boil

10 medicine 11 smooth 12 eastern

13 ginger 14 mixture 15 serve

16 stuffy 17 taste 18 while

19 pain 20 melt 21 pepper

22 temperature 23 thick 24 throat

25 stir 26 reduce 27 touching

28 treasure 29 seafood 30 local

31 mix 32 lamb 33 stay

34 sore 35 be different from

36 a plate of 37 as well as 38 find out

39 put on 40 for the first time

41 such as A 42 not only A but also B

43 be made with

단어 TEST Step 3 p.25

1 pain, 아픔, 통증 2 touching, 감동적인

3 chop, 잘게 썰다 4 treasure, 보물

5 thick, 두꺼운, 걸쭉한 6 reduce, 줄이다

7 boil, 줄이다 8 mixture, 혼합물

9 recommend, 추천하다 10 pour, 붓다, 따르다

11 stay, 그대로 있다 12 stir, 휘젓다

13 temperature, 온도, 기온 14 melt, 녹다

15 local, 지역의, 현지의 16 ginger, 생강

대화문 TEST Step 1 p.26~28

Listen and Speak 1 Listen 1

they called / called / Could, again / made with, from

Listen and Speak 1 Listen 2

eating / say, again / like, traditional food

Listen and Speak 1 Listen 3

that, eating, looks like / Sorry, again / tasty, popular

Listen and Speak 1 A-1

favorite, What / traditional drink / say, again / sweet / try

Listen and Speak 1 A-2

tried / could / salad, popular / special / with rice, fish, only, but, healthy

Listen and Speak 1 B

1. Have, tried / Sorry / traditional dessert

2. tried / traditional

3. ever tried / that / in

Listen and Speak 2 Listen

1. recommend, traditional / Try

2. Could, for / touching

3. beginners / about

4. snack / How

Listen & Speak 2 A-1

something special / How, cooking, would / recommend, easy / about, easy, delicious / idea

Listen & Speak 2 B-2

Welcome, many, visit, There, clothing, other, tasty local, recommend visiting, enjoying

Real-Life Zone

for / Here, back, take / much, recommend / recommend / Could / made, over, good, health / try / served, spicy, pepper, okay / problem

Wrap Up 1-2

Are, have / Can, place / recommend, enough / would, recommend / fantastic / thinking, makes, water

Listen and Speak 1 Listen 1

B: Hi, Grace. Those are pretty. What are they called?

G: They're called *dango*.

B: I'm sorry. Could you say that again?

G: *Dan-go*. They're sweet and made with rice cake powder. They're from Japan.

Listen and Speak 1 Listen 2

B: Alice, what's that you're eating?

G: It's *rasmalai*.

B: Ra…. Could you say that again?

G: *Ras-ma-lai*. It's like a cheesecake in a sweet cream. It's a traditional food in India.

Listen and Speak 1 Listen 3

G: What's that you're eating, David? It looks like a chocolate ball.

B: It's *brigadeiro*.

G: Sorry? Could you say that again?

B: *Bri-ga-dei-ro*. It's sweet and tasty. It's popular in Brazil.

Listen and Speak 1 A-1

G: My favorite Korean traditional drink is Maesil-tea. What about you, Jinsu?

B: Well, my favorite traditional drink is Sikhye.

G: Sik…. Can you say that again?

B: Sik-hye. It's sweet and cool.

G: I want to try it.

Listen and Speak 1 A-2

B: Have you ever tried *poke*?

G: Sorry, could you say that again, please?

B: *Po-ke*. It's a salad that is popular in Hawaii.

G: What's so special about it?

B: It's made with rice and fish. It's not only delicious but also very healthy.

Listen and Speak 1 B

1. A: Have you ever tried *rasmalai*?

   B: Sorry, could you say that again?

   A: *Rasmalai*. It's a traditional dessert in India.

2. A: Have you ever tried *brigadeiro*?

   B: Sorry, could you say that again?

   A: *Brigadeiro*. It's a traditional dessert in Brazil.

3. A: Have you ever tried *macaron*?

   B: Sorry, could you say that again?

   A: *Macaron*. It's a traditional dessert in France.

Listen and Speak 2 Listen

1. B: Could you recommend a good traditional dish?

   W: Try Samgyetang. It'll give you energy.

2. G: Could you recommend a good book for my little sister?

   M: I recommend this one. The story is touching.

3. B: Could you recommend a guitar for beginners?

   W: How about this one? Many beginners play it.

4. G: Could you recommend a snack for my dog?

   M: Sure. How about this? Dogs really like it.

Listen & Speak 2 A-1

B: Tomorrow is my dad's birthday. I'd like to do something special for him.

G: How about cooking something for him? He would really like that.

B: That sounds great. Can you recommend something easy to cook?

G: Umm. How about Gimchijeon? It's easy to make and it's delicious.

B: Oh, that's a good idea. He'll love it.

Listen & Speak 2 B-2

M: Welcome to the Sydney Information Center. Sydney has many places you will want to visit. The Rocks Markets is one of them. There you can buy art, clothing, books and many other things. You can also eat fresh, tasty local food. We recommend visiting the Rocks Markets and enjoying the food and the fun there.

Real-Life Zone

M: Good afternoon. A table for two?

B: Yes.

M: This way please. Here is the menu. I'll be back in a few minutes and take your order.

B: Okay. Thank you.

G: I don't know much about Korean food. Could you recommend something?

B: Well, I'd recommend the Bibimbap.

G: I'm sorry. Could you say that again, please?

B: This one. Bi-bim-bap. It's made with lots of vegetables, beef and an egg over rice. It's tasty and it's also good for your health.

G: That sounds great. I'll try it.

B: It's served with a spicy red pepper sauce. Is that okay?

G: No problem. I like spicy food.

Wrap Up 1-2

B: Tomorrow is my birthday.

G: I know. Are you going to have a birthday party, Alex?

B: Yes. Can you recommend a good place to have the party?

G: I'd recommend the Happy Snack House. The

33

food is really good and it'll be large enough.

B: What dish would you recommend?

G: I'd recommend the onion rings. They're fantastic!

B: Oh, just thinking about them makes my mouth water.

01 Foods, Fight Colds
02 when, catch, cold
03 stay warm, put, clothes
04 Some, drink hot tea
05 something people, often drink
06 taste, warms, reduce, pain
07 What, other countries, cold
08 Let's find out
09 have, special drink, catch
10 cup, onion milk
11 chopped, over low, half
12 simple, said, be good
13 While, drinks, sick, bowl
14 recipe, one, to another
15 can be added, eating
16 sore throat, suffy nose
17 Eastern, get sick, called
18 is made with
19 to make, taste better
20 looks like thick
21 warm, have, sore throat
22 only, but, popular, healthy
23 served, usually, cold, temperature
24 Why not, found, about
25 fun, good for, health
26 How to Make
27 You need, honey
28 Put, in, mix them
29 Pour half, in, pan
30 Add, butter
31 Warm, until, melts
32 Pour, hot, into, with
33 Stir as, pour
34 Drink while, hot

01 Fight Colds
02 catch a cold
03 stay warm, put on
04 to drink hot tea
05 something, often drink
06 helps reduce the pain, throat
07 What do people drink or eat
08 find out
09 have a special drink
10 a cup of onion milk
11 chopped onion, over low heat, half an hour
12 is said to be good
13 While, look for, a bowl of chicken soup
14 from one family to another

15 can be added, eating
16 great for a sore throat and a stuffy nose
17 called
18 is made with
19 add, to make it taste better
20 looks like thick
21 have a sore throat
22 not only, but also, healthy
23 served, served, at room temperature
24 Why not, found out about
25 good for
26 How to Make
27 You need
28 Put, in, mix them
29 Pour
30 Add
31 Warm, until, melts
32 Pour, into, with
33 Stir as, pour
34 while

1 감기와 싸우는 음식들
2 여러분은 감기에 걸리면 어떻게 하는가?
3 당연히, 따뜻함을 유지하고자 할 것이고, 아마도 옷을 더 입을 것이다.
4 몇몇 사람들은 따뜻한 차를 마시는 것을 좋아한다.
5 생강차는 한국인들이 자주 마시는 것이다.
6 특별한 맛과 함께, 그것은 여러분의 몸을 따뜻하게 하고 목 통증을 완화하는 데 도움을 준다.
7 다른 나라에서는 사람들이 감기에 걸렸을 때 무엇을 마시거나 먹을까?
8 함께 알아보자.
9 겨울이 매우 추운 핀란드에서는 사람들이 감기에 걸리면 특별한 음료를 마신다.
10 그것은 양파 우유이다.
11 그들은 우유에 잘게 썬 양파를 넣고 30분 동안 약한 불에서 끓인다.
12 이 단순한 음료는 감기에 좋다고 한다.
13 한국 사람들과 핀란드 사람들이 아플 때 음료를 찾는 반면, 미국의 많은 사람들은 닭고기 수프를 원한다.
14 그것은 보통 닭고기와 야채로 만들어지는데, 요리법은 가정마다 다르다.
15 소금과 후추를 먹기 전에 넣기도 한다.
16 미국인들은 따뜻한 닭고기 수프 한 그릇이 부은 목과 막힌 코에 좋다고 믿는다.
17 러시아와 동유럽에서는 사람들이 아플 때, 고골모골이라는 후식을 먹는다.
18 그것은 달걀과 꿀로 만든다.
19 어떤 사람들은 그것을 더 맛있게 하기 위해 초콜릿, 버터, 레몬주스, 또는 우유를 첨가한다.
20 그것은 진한 요구르트처럼 보인다.
21 사람들은 목이 아플 때 종종 따뜻한 고골모골 한 잔을 마신다.

22 고골모골은 감기에 걸린 사람들에게 좋을 뿐만 아니라 건강한 사람들의 후식으로도 인기가 있다.

23 후식으로 제공될 때에는 보통 차갑게 또는 실온으로 제공된다.

24 여러분이 알아본 음식들 중 하나를 만들어 보는 것은 어떨까?

25 그것은 재미있고 여러분의 건강에 좋을 것이다.

26 고골모골 만드는 방법 (1인분)

27 필요한 것: 달걀 1개, 우유 1/2컵, 꿀 5g, 버터 15g

28 1. 달걀과 꿀을 큰 컵에 넣고 섞는다.

29 2. 우유 반 컵을 팬에 붓는다.

30 버터를 추가한다.

31 버터가 녹을 때까지 데운다.

32 3. 뜨거운 우유와 버터를 달걀과 꿀이 있는 컵에 붓는다.

33 부으면서 젓는다.

34 4. 뜨거울 때 마신다.

1 Foods That Fight Colds

2 What do you do when you catch a cold?

3 Of course, you want to stay warm, so maybe you put on more clothes.

4 Some people like to drink hot tea.

5 Ginger tea is something people in Korea often drink.

6 With its special taste, it warms your body and helps reduce the pain in your throat.

7 What do people drink or eat in other countries when they catch a cold?

8 Let's find out.

9 In Finland, where it is very cold in winter, people have a special drink when they catch a cold.

10 It is a cup of onion milk.

11 They put chopped onion in milk and boil it over low heat for half an hour.

12 This simple drink is said to be good for a cold.

13 While people in Korea and Finland look for drinks when sick, many people in America want a bowl of chicken soup.

14 It is usually made with chicken and vegetables, but the recipe is different from one family to another.

15 Salt and pepper can be added before eating.

16 People in America believe that a bowl of warm chicken soup is great for a sore throt and a suffy nose.

17 In Russia and in Eastern Europe, when people get sick, they eat a dessert called *gogol-mogol*.

18 It is made with eggs and honey.

19 Some people add chocolate, butter, lemon juice, or milk to make it taste better.

20 It looks like thick yogurt.

21 People often drink a cup of warm *gogol-mogol* when they have a sore throat.

22 *Gogol-mogol* is not only good for people with a cold but also popular as a dessert for healthy people.

23 When served as a dessert, it is usually served cold or at room temperature.

24 Why not try making one of the foods you have found out about?

25 It will be fun and good for your health.

26 How to make *Gogol-mogol* (Serves one)

27 You need: 1 egg, 1/2 cup of milk, honey (5 g), butter (15 g)

28 1. Put the egg and the honey in a large cup and mix them.

29 2. Pour half a cup of milk in a pan.

30 Add the butter.

31 Warm it until the butter melts.

32 3. Pour the hot milk and butter into the cup with the egg and the honey.

33 Stir as you pour.

34 4. Drink while it is hot.

After You Read B

1. I've made

2. What is

3. that, in Eastern Europe, when, are sick

4. looks delicious, made with

5. made with eggs

6. put on top of it

7. to make, taste better

8. when they're not sick

9. popular dessert. When served, usually served, at room temperature

Writing Workshop

1. While, when they are sick, many people in India

2. how to make

3. You need, black pepper, salt

4. chop, put, chopped, in, pour, over

5. boil the mixture, turn off, leave, to cool down

6. blend, until, is, add, black pepper, salt

7. can enjoy

8. not only healthy but also delicious

구석구석지문 TEST Step 2 p.43

After You Read B

1. Look! I've made *gogol-mogol*.

2. Happy07: What is *gogol-mogol*?

3. Bora: It's a dessert that people in Russia and in Eastern Europe eat when they are sick.

4. Yumyum: It looks delicious. What is it made with?

5. Bora: It's made with eggs and honey.

6. Yumyum: What's that you put on top of it?

7. Bora: I put chocolate on top to make it taste better.

8. Happy07: Do people also eat it when they're not sick?

9. Bora: Sure. It's a popular dessert. When served as a dessert, it's usually served cold or at room temperature.

Writing Workshop

1. While many Koreans eat Samgyetang when they are sick, many people in India eat tomato soup.

2. Here is how to make it.

3. You need: 1 tomato, some water, black pepper, salt

4. First, chop one fresh tomato. Then put the chopped tomato in a pan and pour some water over it.

5. Next, boil the mixture for ten minutes. Then turn off the heat and leave it to cool down.

6. Next, blend it until it is smooth. Finally, add some black pepper and salt.

7. Now you can enjoy the tomato soup.

8. This tomato soup is not only healthy but also delicious.

단어 TEST Step 1 p.44

01 목표	02 무기	03 ~를 따라
04 갑자기	05 일어나다	06 마주하다
07 인간, 사람	08 놀라게 하다	09 기적
10 참호	11 전체의	12 광경
13 비록 ~이긴 하지만		14 젖은
15 ~일지도 모른다	16 따라가다	17 사실은
18 믿기 힘든	19 군인, 병사	20 주소
21 최전선, 최전방	22 인사, 안부의 말	23 그리워하다
24 정말로, 진심으로	25 대담하게	26 교환하다
27 외침, 고함	28 ~도, ~ 또한	29 적군, 적
30 속임수	31 익숙한, 친숙한	32 공유하다, 나누다
33 몇의, 수개의	34 유지하다, 계속 있다	
35 ~ 밖을 내다보다	36 더욱 더	
37 서로	38 평화 속에서	39 전쟁 중인
40 사망하다	41 ~와 같은	42 내려놓다
43 잇따라서		

단어 TEST Step 2 p.45

01 several	02 entire	03 trick
04 actually	05 miss	06 along
07 shout	08 aim	09 face
10 light	11 address	12 truly
13 weapon	14 soldier	15 familiar
16 unbelievable	17 miracle	18 boldly
19 sight	20 wet	21 suddenly
22 enemy	23 exchange	24 surprise
25 trench	26 greeting	27 human
28 expect	29 lantern	30 although
31 happen	32 share	33 either
34 follow	35 one after another	
36 at war	37 one by one	38 put down
39 shake hands	40 such as	
41 on the front line		42 pass away
43 look out of		

단어 TEST Step 3 p.46

1 carol, 캐럴 2 shout, 외침, 고함

3 greeting, 인사, 안부의 말 4 share, 공유하다, 나누다

5 sight, 광경 6 trick, 속임수 7 aim, 목표

8 exchange, 교환하다 9 peace, 평화

10 race, 경주, 시합　11 shoot, 쏘다　12 boldly, 대담하게

13 address, 주소　14 weapon, 무기

15 soldier, 군인, 병사　16 surprise, 놀라게 하다

본문 TEST Step 1　p.47~48

01 Christmas Miracle　02 It, in, first year

03 facing, had done, few　04 trenches, cold, wet

05 tired, missed, more so

06 Suddenly, familiar, heard coming

07 It, Christmas carol　08 going on

09 might be, trick, out　10 boldly looked out of

11 by, other, followed, example

12 What, sight, never expected

13 Along, standing lit with

14 one, song after another

15 answer by also singing

16 lights, made, forget, front

17 came out from, shoot

18 whose aim, exchange greetings

19 several, able, in peace　20 truly, silent night

21 morning came　22 on both sides, down

23 man's land between, and

24 exchanged, gifts such as

25 sang carols together

26 Some even exchanged addresses

27 unbelievable, written, letters, soldiers

28 wrote, between, lines, talks

29 also had, races　30 Another, think, at war

31 Here, were, talking, enemy

32 like, wives, waiting, welcome

본문 TEST Step 2　p.49~50

01 Miracle　02 the first year

03 were facing, had done, few months

04 cold and wet

05 missed, all the more so because

06 Suddenly, was heard coming

07 carol　08 going on

09 might be a trick, trenches

10 boldly looked out of　11 One by one, followed

12 What, sight, expected　13 lit with lanterns

14 one Christmas song after another

15 by also singing

16 made them forget, front line

---

17 came out from, shoot

18 whose aim, each other, exchange greetings

19 in several months, in peace

20 It truly was　21 came

22 on both sides, came out of

23 in the no man's land, shook hands

24 such as　25 sang carols

26 exchanged addresses

27 unbelievable, about, sent

28 between the two lines

29 had bike races　30 were at war

31 Here we were, enemy

32 like us, waiting to welcome

본문 TEST Step 3　p.51~52

1 크리스마스의 기적

2 제일차 세계 대전의 첫해였던 1914년의 크리스마스이브였습니다.

3 영국 군인들은 지난 몇 달 동안 그래왔듯이 그들의 참호에서 독일 군인들과 대치하고 있었어요.

4 참호는 춥고 축축했습니다.

5 군인들은 지쳤고 자신들의 집을 그리워했는데, 크리스마스라는 이유로 더욱 더 그랬습니다.

6 갑자기 익숙한 노래가 독일 군인들의 참호로부터 들려왔습니다.

7 그것은 크리스마스 캐럴이었어요!

8 무슨 일이 벌어지고 있는 걸까요?

9 어쩌면 그들을 참호 밖으로 유인하고자 하는 속임수일지도 모릅니다.

10 몇몇 영국 군인들이 용감하게 자신들의 참호 밖을 내다보았어요.

11 차례차례 다른 군인들도 앞사람을 따랐습니다.

12 영국 군인들이 본 것은 그들이 절대 예상하지 못한 광경이었어요.

13 독일 군인들의 참호를 따라, 크리스마스트리들이 랜턴으로 밝혀진 채 있었습니다!

14 독일 군인들은 크리스마스 캐럴을 연이어 불렀어요.

15 영국 군인들도 크리스마스 캐럴을 부르며 화답하기 시작했습니다.

16 따뜻한 불빛과 크리스마스 캐럴은 그들이 최전선에 있다는 것을 잊게 만들었어요.

17 그리고 독일 군인들 쪽에서 고함이 터져 나왔습니다. "행복한 크리스마스예요! 당신들이 쏘지 않는다면, 우리도 쏘지 않을게요!"

18 곧, 단지 몇 시간 전까지만 해도 서로를 죽이는 것이 목적이었던 군인들은 인사를 나누기 시작했습니다.

19 몇 달 만에 처음으로, 군인들은 평화롭게 밤을 지낼 수 있었어요.

20 그날은 정말로 조용한 밤이었습니다.

21 크리스마스 아침이 밝았습니다.

22 양편의 군인들은 자신들의 무기를 내려놓고 참호 밖으로 나왔어요.

23 그들은 무인 지대에서 만났고 악수를 했습니다.

24 그들은 와인과 케이크 같은 작은 선물도 교환했어요.

25 그들은 캐럴을 함께 불렀습니다.

26 몇몇은 심지어 주소를 교환하기도 했고 함께 축구를 했습니다.

27 이 믿을 수 없는 크리스마스는 영국 군인들이 집으로 보낸 편지에 적혀 있었습니다.

28 한 군인은 "크리스마스에 영국 군인들과 독일 군인들은 두 경계선 사이에서 만났고 대화를 나눴어.

29 우리는 자전거 시합도 했어."라고 적었어요.

30 다른 군인은 "우리는 전쟁 중이라는 생각이 들지 않았어.

31 여기서 우리는 적대 관계인 서로와 대화를 나누고 있는 상황이었어.

32 그들은 우리와 마찬가지로, 그들의 남자들이 집으로 다시 돌아오기를 고대하는 어머니와, 친구들, 부인이 있는 사람들이었어."라고 썼습니다.

본문 TEST Step 4–Step 5

p.56~56

1 A Christmas Miracle

2 It was Christmas Eve in 1914, the first year of World War I.

3 English soldiers were facing German soldiers from their trenches as they had done for the last few months.

4 The trenches were cold and wet.

5 The soldiers were tired and missed their home, all the more so because it was Christmas.

6 Suddenly, a familiar song was heard coming from the German trenches.

7 It was a Christmas carol!

8 What's going on?

9 It might be a trick to make them come out of the trenches.

10 A few English soldiers boldly looked out of their trenches.

11 One by one, other soldiers followed their example.

12 What they saw was a sight they never expected.

13 Along the German trenches, Christmas trees were standing lit with lanterns!

14 The German soldiers sang one Christmas song after another.

15 The English soldiers began to answer by also singing Christmas songs.

16 The warm lights and the Christmas carols made them forget they were on the front line.

17 Then a shout came out from the German side: "Happy Christmas! You no shoot, we no shoot!"

18 Soon, soldiers whose aim had been to kill each other just a few hours before began to exchange greetings.

19 For the first time in several months, the soldiers were able to spend a night in peace.

20 It truly was a silent night.

21 Christmas morning came.

22 Soldiers on both sides put down their weapons and came out of their trenches.

23 They met in the no man's land between their trenches and shook hands.

24 They exchanged small gifts such as wine and cake.

25 They sang carols together.

26 Some even exchanged addresses and played football.

27 This unbelievable Christmas Day was written about in letters English soldiers sent home.

28 One soldier wrote, "On Christmas Day, English and German soldiers met between the two lines and had talks.

29 We also had bike races."

30 Another wrote, "We didn't think that we were at war.

31 Here we were, enemy talking to enemy.

32 They were like us, with mothers, with friends, with wives who were waiting to welcome their men home again."

MEMO

MEMO

적중 100

영어 기출 문제집

정답 및 해설

시사 | 송미정